Living Economics

Canadian Perspectives on the Social Economy,
Co-operatives, and Community Economic Development

Edited by J.J. McMurty, York University

2010
Emond Montgomery Publications Limited
Toronto, Canada

Emond Montgomery Publications Limited
60 Shaftesbury Avenue
Toronto ON M4T 1A3
http://www.emp.ca/university

Printed in Canada on 100 percent recycled paper.

We acknowledge the financial support of the Government of Canada through the Book Publishing Industry Development Program (BPIDP) for our publishing activities.

Acquisitions and developmental editor: Mike Thompson
Marketing manager: Christine Davidson
Sales manager, higher education: Dave Stokaluk
Supervising editor: Jim Lyons
Copy editor: Stephan Dobson
Proofreader and indexer: Paula Pike
Text designer and typesetter: Shani Sohn
Cover designers: Stephen Cribbin & Simon Evers
Cover image: "Social Spirograph" courtesy of Michael Ingrassia
   (www.michaelingrassia.com)

Library and Archives Canada Cataloguing in Publication

   Living economics : Canadian perspectives on the social economy, co-operatives, and community economic development / [edited by] J.J. McMurty.

Includes bibliographical references and index.
ISBN 978-1-55239-282-9

   1. Social economy—Canada—Textbooks.   I. McMurty, J. J.

HC115.L628 2009   361.7'630971   C2009-901487-4

Brief Contents

Contents

CHAPTER THREE
The Social Economy in Quebec and Canada:
Configurations Past and Present   *Yves Vaillancourt*

CHAPTER FOUR
Building the Social Economy Using the Innovative Potential of Place
Doug Lionais and Harvey Johnstone

CHAPTER FIVE
Educating for the Social Economy   *Jorge Sousa*

CHAPTER SIX
Social Accounting for Sustainability in the Social Economy
Laurie Mook and Jennifer Sumner

CHAPTER SEVEN
Aboriginal Perspectives on the Social Economy   *Wanda Wuttunee*

CHAPTER EIGHT
Building Bridges with Government: The Social Economy in Practice
Denyse Guy and Jen Heneberry

Preface

The origins of this book date back to 2005. In that year, the first disbursement of the Social Economy Research Fund was allocated through the Social Sciences and Humanities Research Council (SSHRC) to the National Social Economy Hub at the University of Victoria, BC. Six regional "nodes" were established as subsets of this hub, and, as a result of this funding, various actors across Canada began to coalesce around a wide range of research projects relating to the social economy. In 2007 the First International CIRIEC (International Center of Research and Information on the Public, Social and Cooperative Economy) Research Conference on the Social Economy was held in Victoria. For the first time, researchers and practitioners involved in the hub and the nodes, as well as from around the world, came together to discuss the social economy as an emerging and independent field of research. It was in this exciting and unique context that the framework of this collection was conceived.

What was clear from the CIRIEC meeting was that the field of social economy research had not yet solidified, but rather was emerging cautiously in Canada from a variety of perspectives, often with long histories and established research agendas. In English Canada, the fields of co-operative studies, community economic development, and non-profit research had been constructed largely in academic and practitioner silos, rarely if ever meaningfully engaging with each other. In French Canada, more work had been done to establish a unified framework of activity under the conceptual framework of a "solidaristic" as well as a "social" economy, but this had been largely wrapped up in a unique cultural history difficult to translate for the rest of Canada. For First Nations, the experience of colonialism had understandably coloured the issue of economic development, a fact that had not been adequately addressed in the social economy literature or practice. Finally, the separation between the various theories that inform the social economy and the experience of practitioners had not been breached, leading to animosities and underdevelopment of the social economy in government policy, in academic courses and literature, and in practice.

Given this reality, rather than force an artificially unified view on these diverse perspectives, this book was constructed to give voice to them in order to move the conversation forward toward a more unified future. Specifically, the chapters in this book have been selected to enable a discussion of the *values* of the social economy as shared. These values can be seen to underlie the social economy's diverse practice as a central and unifying component of Canadian history and experience—a history and experience that point toward the possibility for a uniquely sustainable and just world future.

Each of the eight chapters in this book reflects a component of the variety of perspectives on the social economy. In Chapter 1, I outline the definitional issues that have bedevilled the concept of social economy in Canada since its emergence into public discourse. I use the literatures of economics, history, and sociology as well as the social economy to work through these issues and arrive at a conception of the social economy that unites the various perspectives by identifying the underlying values that guide them. In Chapters 2 and 3, Ian MacPherson and Yves Vaillancourt, founding figures of social economy research in Canada, discuss the unique histories and issues of the social economy in English and French Canada, respectively. Both authors attempt to uncover the guiding issues, traditions, and values that have shaped these histories and look forward to the possibilities available in the future for social economy research and practice. For MacPherson, the role of co-operatives in English Canada is decisive; for Vaillancourt, the unique cultural context of Quebec is of particular relevance. In Chapter 4, Doug Lionais and Harvey Johnstone challenge the theory of the social economy from the perspective of place. The authors ground the theory of the social economy in the very real issue of globalization as well as the value of community. In Chapter 5, Jorge Sousa examines the relationship between education and the social economy through the lens of community service learning. Sousa is particularly interested in how universities, as social economy institutions, facilitate critical education about, define practices for, and develop the values of the social economy. In Chapter 6, Laurie Mook and Jennifer Sumner engage the key issues of sustainability and accounting from the perspective of the social economy. Without a clear accounting of the social and environmental practices of the social economy, they argue, there can be no understanding on a policy or practice level of the values central to the social economy, nor can there be a believable claim to adherence to the value of sustainability within these organizations if the practices that constitute it are not clearly understood and measured. In Chapter 7, Wanda Wuttunee examines the social economy from the perspective of the First Peoples. Wuttunee argues that self-managed development is a value that is crucial to addressing the oppressive colonial history of First Peoples in Canada—a value that the social economy has the potential to realize. In Chapter 8, Denyse Guy and Jen Heneberry look at the development of the social economy research and policy agenda in Ontario from the perspective of practitioners. They outline the various roadblocks and possibilities for unifying the community economic development, non-profit and co-operative movements through a social economy movement in Ontario similar to that which has occurred in Quebec. Such a movement, they argue, must be built on shared vision and values.

Edited books are the result of enormous effort and support from a variety of actors, most of whom never get the acknowledgment they deserve. First and foremost, the authors have donated significant time and effort to providing cutting-edge, insightful, experience-based observations on the social economy in Canada that have never before been found in one book. I am extremely grateful for the time and effort that they have put into their chapters, and hope that the final result proves worthy of their efforts. Mike Thompson of Emond Montgomery Publications merits special praise. His patience and encouragement have been central to this book. The fact that he initiated it shows great vision and self-confidence, signs that augur well for both Emond Montgomery and the Canadian publishing industry as a whole. Stephan Dobson, who did all that a copy editor could do and more, also deserves recognition for his keen observations and steady encouragement. Ian MacPherson, Yves Vaillancourt, and Jack Quarter have offered their support and guidance from the beginning of this project. The value of their assistance to a young academic working in an emerging field cannot be overestimated. Finally, Lisa Schincariol has been a pillar of emotional and academic support throughout this project, from conception to publication. Her patient talking through of every hurdle, endless encouragement, and insightful analysis of drafts and concepts as they emerged have made this book possible. In the end, I finally understand the oft-repeated claim in introductions that the errors of this volume are ultimately mine, but its strengths belong to those mentioned above (and any I may have missed) who made it possible.

I would be remiss if I did not also thank three institutional structures that have made this book possible. In Canada we too often forget the role that these structures play in making our work lives possible and fulfilling. SSHRC deserves thanks for providing the funding for the research nodes mentioned above, which in turn provided funding for my research of which this book is a part. My home academic program of Business and Society at York University, and the larger Department of Social Science, also deserve thanks for providing an academically challenging, interdisciplinary, and supportive environment within which research on the social economy can occur. The opportunity to teach the only first-year course in Canada focused solely on the social economy, and to engage in fruitful discussions with the students and teaching assistants in this environment, has been foundational to my work. Finally, the Canadian Social Economy Hub in Victoria and the Southern Ontario Research Node at the Ontario Institute for Studies in Education (OISE) have been central in creating a research climate and networks in which work on the social economy in Canada can be undertaken. Without these institutional supports, this book would not have been possible.

J.J. McMurtry, 2009

About the Authors

DENYSE GUY
Executive Director of the Ontario Co-operative Association

JEN HENEBERRY
Co-op Development Manager with the Ontario Co-operative Association

HARVEY JOHNSTONE
Dean of Research at Cape Breton University

DOUG LIONAIS
Assistant Professor in the Shannon School of Business, Cape Breton University

IAN MacPHERSON
Emeritus Professor of History at the University of Victoria and Co-Director,
National Hub of the Canadian Social Economy Research Partnerships

J.J. McMURTY
Assistant Professor in the Business and Society Department at York University

LAURIE MOOK
Director of the Social Economy Centre at OISE/University of Toronto

JORGE SOUSA
Assistant Professor in the Department of Educational Policy Studies at the
University of Alberta

JENNIFER SUMNER
Assistant Professor in the Adult Education and Community Development
Program, OISE/University of Toronto

YVES VAILLANCOURT
Associate Professor in the School of Social Work at the Université du Québec à
Montréal

WANDA WUTTUNEE
Professor and Head of the Department of Native Studies at the University of
Manitoba

CHAPTER ONE

Introducing
the Social Economy
in Theory and Practice

J.J. McMURTRY

Introduction

In Canada, the social economy is not a concept that is broadly understood by academics, students, policy-makers, activists, or the public at large. An example of the newness of this concept can be found on the website of Human Resources and Skills Development Canada (HRSDC 2009), which states that "The Government of Canada is just beginning to understand the power and potential of social economy enterprises and organizations" and that "we need to map out the social economy across Canada." While it could be argued that government ignorance of particular social and economic realities is nothing new, what makes this lack of understanding remarkable is the fact that social economy activity has been estimated to be annually in the tens of billion dollars and to affect millions of Canadians' lives both directly and indirectly (Laville, Levesque, and Mandell 2007, 168).[1] Further-more, while the federal government constructed a Social Economy Secretariat to study and map this economic sector only in 2004, the concept of social economy itself has been featured in Canadian literature since at least 1992, signalling public policy's sluggishness in responding to theoreti-cal and practical realities (Laville, Levesque, and Mandell 2007, 164; and, for example, Quarter 1992). In Europe, comparatively speaking, variations on the concept of social economy have been in use for at least 150 years and have driven government social services policy in recent decades, most famously through the "third way" policies of the United Kingdom (Ailenei and Moulaert 2005, 2037). However, it is not just at the level of public policy in Canada that the emergence of the social economy has been overlooked. The academy has also been behind the times, with little work being done to identify the social economy as an important area of study—a fact demonstrated by the absence of degree programs in Canada dedicated to its study and few journals or books addressing its concerns. Even the vaunted "anti-globalization" movement of the past 15 years—while demanding "another world"—has not seized upon the already existing alternatives of the social economy. One is left wondering how an area of economic and social activity so important to the Canadian, and indeed the global, experience could have been virtually ignored for so long by so many segments of society.

The problem of understanding the social economy is not found just on the national level. The issues outlined above are rendered much more complex by the three founding nations of Canada as a result of the fact that each has developed, experienced, and understood the social economy in unique ways. For example, the HRSDC website (2009) not only recognizes the federal government's late awareness of the social economy, but also indicates that this sector has developed unevenly across the country, with Quebec in the lead: "more is known about the size of the social economy in Quebec ... [which constitutes] an estimated 6,200 social economy enterprises that together employ 65,000 people and generate annual sales in excess of $4 billion." This difference is largely the result of a long history of struggle in that province for an economy that is reflective of a culturally and socially "distinct society," a fact that has resulted in the provincial government recognizing the social economy as a valid, and indeed important, economic sector (see Vaillancourt, in this volume). This developmental difference makes it difficult to map, compare, or replicate the Quebec experience in other areas or cultures in this country, or to make claims about a *Canadian* social economy. Furthermore, while it is true that Quebec, following the European model, is notably advanced in the practice and policy of the social economy, even in that province there remains ambiguity about the exact definition of this economic activity and, consequently, questions about its validity as a concept, as opposed to alternative concepts such as "solidaristic economy" (for example, Laville 1994; Laville, Levesque, and Mandell 2007). The unique and advanced development of the debates around the social economy in Quebec makes a discussion of the Canadian social economy difficult, and as a result any discussion of the term is seemingly beset by ambiguity.

In English Canada, the lack of clarity around the definition of social economy has been compounded by the fact that any economic activity other than that based on for-profit market transactions has largely been anathema in public discourse. Even the social economy's most developed sphere of activity, the co-operative sector—which has been estimated by the Canadian Co-operative Association (CCA) to hold almost Cdn$500 billion in assets and can claim at least one in four Canadians as members— struggles in English Canada to be recognized, within academic, activist, and policy circles, as well as among the public at large, as distinct economic activity (CCA 2009). To complicate matters, when "socially focused" economic activity has been recognized in English Canada, it has traditionally been understood as community economic development (CED). The choice to use CED instead of social economy as an organizing concept, however, has not been successful in highlighting the distinct nature of socially focused economic activity because the CED model is caught up in both the often-problematic discourse of development and its own definitional and theoretical ambiguities (Laville, Levesque, and Mandell 2007, 166; Loxley 2007, 1). In other words, while the *practice* of the social economy has been as active in English Canada, the *conceptualization* of this sector is underdeveloped, and this underdevelopment is compounded by the fact that there is no policy framework supporting its development. Furthermore, in the absence of a culturally unifying conception of a "distinct society" and the dominance of a market economic view, the perception of the need for a social economy as a culturally distinct, alternative economic movement is almost non-existent at the national level. Finally, as in the Quebec experience with the concept of a "solidaristic economy," the social economy in English Canada is further confounded by the competing discourse of CED. In short, the "two solitudes" created by the different histories and practices of English and French Canada make a discussion of a "Canadian" social economy seemingly very difficult.

For the First Peoples, violently squeezed for centuries by the colonial economic attitudes of the other two founding cultures, the idea of a social economy is even more complex. On the one hand, the articulation of both the practice and concept of an economy that serves First Peoples' specific histories and contemporary social needs has been a life and death struggle for generations. In fact, one could see this history developed over the years as forming various articulations of an indigenous social economy(ies). However, far too often these traditional and adapted forms of economic production for social well-being have been destroyed in a variety of ways and have been replaced by an economy of destitution, dislocation, and reliance on government. Consequently, the experience of "economics" in these communities has often been one of imposition from outside rather than development from within. However much self-started creative and socially focused economic practices continue to develop in these communities in response to conditions of need (such as the cases with co-operatives and mutual aid organizations), their very isolation from mainstream economic activity and their insecurity in the face of government interference (and even support) has created an atmosphere of suspicion toward non-native social actors and concepts. Not surprisingly, the social economy, with its conceptual roots in continental Europe, has not been embraced as a concept or as a practice by First Peoples because it lacks a clear connection to their various economic traditions. This lack of affinity is further amplified by the fact that the social economy as a policy solution, when advocated or imposed by the state, is often viewed by First Peoples as a continuation of colonialism (see Wuttunee, in this volume). In short, conceptualizing the social economy within the context of First Peoples' experience, and as with the other two founding nations, is a complex and often contradictory task. When the three are considered in combination, it is hard to see how one could talk of a "Canadian" social economy.

Indeed, the social economy *as a concept* has had remarkably little support or traction among various economic actors and cultural traditions in Canada, a pattern that is generally true around the world. Why then discuss the social economy at all? We do so because against this backdrop of contradictory tendencies and interpretations there lies another, perhaps more remarkable, reality, one alluded to above. Despite the fact that there is no widespread acceptance of the concept of social economy, there *is* a persistent engagement in economic activity that falls under its most general definition—*economic activity neither controlled directly by the state nor by the profit logic of the market, activity that prioritizes the social well-being of communities and marginalized individuals over partisan political directives or individual gain.* Organizations such as co-operatives, non-profits (including hospitals and most universities in Canada), mutual aid organizations, and volunteer-run endeavours are most often cited as examples of the social economy. In other words, at the broadest level of understanding the *practice* of the social economy, despite the disagreement around definition (more on this below), it is practised everywhere throughout Canada and around the globe by an incredibly diverse population of social actors. In fact, it is in no way an exaggeration to claim that there is neither a rural or urban community nor a cultural group that does not actively have a great number of social economy activities thriving within its boundaries. Thus one might argue, as this chapter does, that the defining feature of the Canadian economic experience and of each culture within it (including those not identified as founding cultures)

BOX 1.1   Life Stories: Pitseolak

First Nations' experiences and understandings of the social economy are unique. Particularly important are the ways in which First Nations have responded to the culturally devastating effects of government policies and capitalist pressures with social economy activity. The following example of the importance of co-operatives to Inuk artist Pitseolak, from the British Columbia Institute for Co-operative Studies website (http://www.bcics.coop/node/3250), gives a sense of this difference. The full story can be found on the website.

> Pitseolak was born sometime during the first few years of the twentieth century on Nottingham Island in Hudson's Bay. She grew up on the Fox Peninsula, travelled by sealskin boat and hunted with her family. The construction of government buildings in Cape Dorset attracted Inuit [in search of employment and shelter]. This is exactly what Pitseolak did. She moved with her family into a house provided by the government and subsisted on family allowance, welfare and what country food could be obtained.
>
> In 1957, James Houston [a government employee tasked with developing the arts and crafts industry in Dorset] recalled, "The concept of printmaking as a method was new to Inuit, but the images and ideas they created were firmly based on centuries of their ancient traditions, myths and skill of hand." In 1959, the Inuit [took control of their economic future and] formed the West Baffin Eskimo Co-operative to market their arts and crafts. Printmaking took off. The co-op used the profits to order canoes, nets, parka material and tent canvas for the members to buy and the artists and craftspeople to use. A bakery, run by two Inuit women, was established as well as a women's sewing project; eventually a co-op store was built. Pitseolak's art became recognised; she and the co-operative became famous. Pitseolak says of the co-op,
>
>> Since the co-op began I have earned a lot of money with my drawing. I get clothes from the drawings and I earn a living from paper. Because Ashoona, my husband is dead I have to look after myself, and I am grateful for these papers—papers we tear so easily. Whenever I am out of everything, I do some drawings and I take them to Terry at the co-op and he gives me money, which I can buy clothes and tea and food for the family with. He is paying well. I am happy to have the money and I am glad we have a Co-op.
>
> By selling her art to the co-operative, Pitseolak was more than able to support her family and she contributed to the fame of her community.

is not the market activity that is so often lionized, but the fundamental role played by social economy forms in their wide variety. What is at issue then is not the fact that social economy activity exists, but rather that while it forms the essential economic life-blood of Canada (and the world), there is no recognition of, let alone agreement on, what this is *conceptually*. The concept of social economy thus presents the reader and researcher with a paradox: Why has the conceptual understanding of the social economy lagged so far behind its practice? Why have there been so few developed analyses of this remarkable economic story?

This chapter aims to go some distance toward explaining this paradox by examining both the conceptual makeup of the social economy and some of the theories most often employed to understand it. By so doing, this chapter will provide a framework for understanding the social economy in a more conscious and rigorous way, highlighting and harmonizing both its social and economic content. To achieve this goal, it will proceed in three parts. First, and most important, there will be an analysis of how the two concepts "social" and "economy" that make up the term social economy can be conceived of not as conflicting interests or even as constituting an oxymoron, but rather as indicating a need for a different kind of economic theory—one that is built on premises that differ from neoclassical economics. Second, contemporary debates concerning social economy theory will be outlined and engaged, the latter especially by addressing how the various and broad definitions usually employed limit the possibilities—and even contradict the central purpose—of the concept. Third, a modified conception of the social economy based on the general definition outlined above will be articulated to fill this gap. The chapter will conclude by briefly discussing how this modified conception of social economy might be employed in practice and, by doing so, create a social economy movement based on a unique understanding of the imperative for ethical economic practice.

Social Economy as a Theoretical Concept

To begin to understand the social economy as a theoretical concept, one needs to start, perhaps counterintuitively, with the fact that, in its broadest sense, its *practice* is everywhere engaged in and, in important ways, has always been with us. For example, Jean-Marc Fontan and Eric Shragge (2000, 3) argue that the social economy "has been with us as long as humans have worked communally and shared in the results of their labour." We start with this counterintuitive reality because it creates a tension with the conceptual definition of the social economy given above, "an activity neither controlled directly by the state nor by the profit logic of the market." This tension is created by the negative conception of the social economy employed in the latter definition, which relies on the idea and practice of the state and the capitalist market, ideas, and practices that have not always been with humanity.[2] While there are reasons to define the social economy in this way (some of which are discussed below), if one starts an investigation by limiting the social economy to this "modern" definition, one would have to accept that most of humanity's economic activity, as neither state nor market, has been part of a social economy and we have no clear idea of what this activity consists of except that it is neither state nor market. We have no positive sense of what the social economy is or why it developed and what its significance is in a modern context. To develop a positive definition, one must first turn to the deceptively simple question of what the terms "social" and "economic" mean. We must examine these concepts individually as well as in the particular ways that they play a role in defining the social economy as a distinct activity that has both "been with us as long as humans have worked collectively" and is neither directly controlled by the state nor by market or for-profit goals.

The Economy

In common understanding, "economy" has broadly come to mean market activity—the production, distribution, and consumption of goods to meet human need or desire through for-profit monetary exchange. Thus, an iPod is produced in China and consumed in North America to satisfy a desire of a consumer who expresses this desire through her purchase of this object with money, with Apple Inc. facilitating this exchange for its profit. While this simple example is recognizable as an economic activity, the conception that *all economics consists of this kind of activity* is too narrow to capture most historical and even most contemporary economic activity. The claim that for-profit economic activity is too narrow a definition for economics seems on the surface to contradict our most basic assumptions. However, the limits of this definition come into focus when we think of the many societies *not* based on monetary exchange for profit that clearly have accomplished enormous social works through functioning economies. For example, one can consider the vast pool of slave labour that built the Mayan and Egyptian pyramids for the glory of the kings, or the slavery basis of ancient Greece and Rome.[3] Even today, very large amounts of work—from the raising of children to the staffing of food banks, from the millions of hours of volunteer labour each year to the provision of education and health care in Canada—are not conducted on the basis of a for-profit model, and yet these activities are clearly economic in that they require societal and individual resources to meet human need. The social economy, even in its most general sense as it is defined above, has been consciously constructed as a concept to refer to this kind of economic activity, activity that is *not focused* on profit or even monetary-based. Given all of the obvious limitations of the common understanding of "economics," a more useful and inclusive definition is needed: *the efficient production, distribution, and consumption of goods otherwise in short supply.*[4] This definition is more useful and inclusive because it can apply to all human economic activity throughout history *regardless of the particular goals of that activity* and regardless of the ways in which economics has been practised in each community or society across time.

To clarify this term "economics" further, we can turn to an example. When medieval peasants produced food, clothing, shelter, and furniture for themselves and their lord, they did not perform that activity on a for-profit basis or even necessarily use money. Using the common understanding of economics, this kind of activity would be invisible. Yet if we apply the concept of economy as the production, distribution, and consumption of goods otherwise in short supply, we can clearly see the peasant's activity as economic. In other words, by not imposing an idea of what economic activity is, the peasant's economic activity can be understood on its own terms, which is to say in the way that it meets human need—which in this case might be loosely understood as feudal production (see Box 1.2). In fact, by applying this definition to all of human history, we can see that "as long as humans have worked communally and shared in the results of their labour," they have been participating in an economic activity. To borrow a concept from the economic historian Robert Heilbroner (Heilbroner and Milberg 2008), no matter what the society, the "economic problem" of meeting people's needs must be solved.

So far, this explanation has been fairly straightforward; however, there is more to the definition of economics above than just the production, distribution, and consumption of goods otherwise in short supply. The broader conception of economics allows the observer the tool with which to *evaluate* the economic activity in terms of *efficiency* (meaning the least wasteful) and, therefore, to compare contemporary and historical economic systems. With such a tool we can ask: Was the peasant economy of medieval Europe an efficient way to produce, distribute, or consume goods otherwise in short supply? In other words, are people's needs being met and are the environmental conditions upon which humans rely being sustainably managed? Significantly, this question does not assume an answer concerning what economic form "should" be in place, but allows an answer to develop through an examination of the conditions of production in place. And significantly, for this chapter, this definition of economics allows us to identify positive content within the definition of social economy prior to the introduction

BOX 1.2 Feudalism

One historical example of a socially embedded economy is feudalism, a so-cial and economic system that was dominant in medieval Europe, from about the 9th century until the 14th century. The dates for feudalism are in-exact because there is much debate about its nature and practice. Generally, the term refers to a political, legal, social, military, and economic hierarchy featuring a monarch at the top and peasants and/or serfs (agricultural slaves) at the bottom. Tying the system together was a framework of social and economic obligations, which, it is important to note, were mutual. Thus, while lords owed their monarch political loyalty, social servitude, military service, and taxes, the monarch in return was obligated to protect the lords, maintain their social status, share the spoils of war, and provide services such as a legal system. This system of mutual obligation also extended to serfs in relation to their lords. The difficulty in defining the feudal period lies in the fact that the social systems, cultures, and practices within which feudalism was located varied widely. The "great transformation" to capitalism over time replaced this patchwork of cultural and social diversity with a singular focus on profit without social obligation (see, for example, Wood 1996).

of the state or market into human economic activity. For once we under-stand the economic system on its own terms, we can examine its social content and be clear about the basic ways in which it functions.

Uncovering an economic system on its own terms is, however, not as easy as it might seem on the surface. While most economists agree that the definition of economics must be broadly constructed, there is strong dis-agreement about *how* economics has actually been practised—how the "economic problem" has been answered—and, more important, how it *should* be practised within various societies. These questions are important because the answers to them direct our current understanding of economic possibilities and practices as well as our recognition of unique forms of practice such as the social economy. To return to the peasant example above, if one argues that the peasants' well-being and the economy's effi-ciency were limited by the fact that they were largely denied the opportunity to participate in a for-profit market based on monetary transactions, we would have one answer to both the "how" and the "should" of an economy. This argument can be found today in the work of contemporary market theorists such as Jeffery Sachs (2005), who argue that the economic prob-lems of "poorer" continents such as Africa are based on their minimal par-ticipation in markets. On the other hand, if one argues that the peasants' well-being as well as the economy's efficiency were enhanced by access to the commons (that is, common land to feed themselves and their animals, collective labour and resource sharing) and through participation in hundreds of holidays or feasts per year, one's answer to the "how" and "should" of the economy would be different. This kind of argument around the economic importance of the commons applied to the contemporary context can be found in the various writings of the World Social Forum (see Box 1.3). Thus, depending on one's understanding of the "how" and the "should" of economic activity, one tends to evaluate the actual activities and possibilities of their own economic situation. In other words, economics is a contested and debated concept; these debates concerning, and evaluations of, economic activity are significantly influenced by our beliefs (as is the common neoclassical understanding of economics), which significantly rest on what we understand of what has happened before and on what we believe is possible for the future.

BOX 1.3 World Social Forum

The World Social Forum (WSF) defines itself as "an open meeting place where social movements, networks, NGOs and other civil society organizations opposed to neo-liberalism and a world dominated by capital or any other form of imperialism come together to pursue their thinking, to debate ideas democratically, ... and network for effective action." The first meeting of the World Social Forum was in January 2001, in the Brazilian city of Porto Alegre, and has been held almost every year since. The WSF is an important global space where the actors themselves articulate social and economic alternatives, famously claiming, "another world is possible." One can see the World Social Forum meetings as an important articulation of social economy activity. More information can be found on the WSF website at http://www.forumsocialmundial.org.br.

This debate over the "how" and the "should" of economics has gripped thinking on the economic problem since at least the work of Adam Smith. Unfortunately for the study of the social economy, this debate has been focused on singular and dominant forms of economic practice in a particular society or time period—like the market or feudalism—which are assumed to be *universal*. This obscures the fact that while one form of economic practice may be *dominant* within a given culture or a community, a variety of economic forms and combinations can be practised simultaneously. Our peasant, for example, if living in the 11th century, may have never seen money in her lifetime, being focused only on providing for herself and her community's needs, yet a merchant in the same period may have relied extensively on market interactions for his personal livelihood and felt little connection to any community at all. Two types of economic activity, in the sense of the definition above, are occurring within a cultural and historical space at the same time. The general fact that multiple economic practices are overlooked by economic theory is specifically relevant to practice, especially in the contemporary context, where such practice operates within the dominant economic system of market capitalism within most of the world. The results of such an oversight are at the root of the definitional ambiguity outlined in the introduction and in the fact that the social economy is not yet widely considered to be an economic practice.

Examples of this problem can be found in most of the central economic texts of the last 50 years. For example, Robert Heilbroner, in his classic *The Making of Economic Society* (Heilbroner and Milberg 2008), classifies three wide-lens definitions of economic forms—traditional, command, and market—that have existed throughout history. However, by casting economic practice in this way, he limits understanding of both the variety of economic activity that has occurred as well as the choice of economic responses to contemporary "economic problems." Thus, an economic problem, such as the recession experienced in 2009, has three possible policy responses based on these forms, or a combination of them. First, there is state ownership or command to a greater or lesser degree of the economic entities of society that are central to citizen well-being—banks, manufacturing, resources, education, and health care, to name a few. Second, there is market-directed economic activity that leaves most or all economic ownership and decision making up to private for-profit entities. Third, there is the possibility of a return to traditional (pre-capitalist) forms of economic activity that stress local and status-based economic activity. Yet we know from our focus on the social economy that there are activities that do not fit easily into these basic types—for example, how would a non-profit, democratically run co-operative selling outdoor equipment fit into any of these models? Further, many people have argued that it is these types of social economy forms that emerge in times of crisis because these organizations respond to people's needs, for example, for food and job banks. Yet it is precisely these from-the-ground-up organizations that are ignored by conventional economic theory. Furthermore, there is little understanding of why particular economic choices have been made in particular historical circumstances—the "how" of economic theory—partially because of the idealized nature of these three economic forms. Finally, without a more nuanced understanding of economic activity, one cannot develop a sense of the "should" within particular circumstances such as the 2009 recession.

There are theories that understand the "economic problem" differently and are more helpful for understanding the specificity of the social economy as well as for developing conceptions of the "how" and the "should" of economic activity. Perhaps the most important of these "heterodox" economists is the Austro-Hungarian Karl Polanyi, who is considered a pioneer in identifying the social foundations of economics throughout history (see Box 1.4). Polanyi's argument in his most famous book *The Great Transformation* (1957) is similar to Fontan and Shragge's position (see above) that for most of history "man's economy, as a rule, is submerged in his social relationships" (46). This means that rather than displaying a for-profit orientation, the "economic problem" was solved within the context and for the benefit of social relationships. For example, the peasant mentioned above would produce goods for her lord not for profit, but rather in exchange for the lord's protection, his maintenance of a community storehouse of food in case of famine, enforcement of law, the hosting of feasts, and maintenance of the common land (such as forests or streams) upon which everyone relied. Such "economic" rights were protected socially, both by the monarch and in national law, such as the English Magna Carta and the Charter of the Forests, as well as through common law or practice, or both (Linebaugh 2008). The "great transformation" to which the title of Polanyi's book refers is therefore the transformation of the economy from one that is socially focused to one that is based on the separation of the economy from social goals. This separation is seen when economic activity happens *without* or *despite* concern for social consequences. For an example, one need only think of supermarkets throwing out food while many go hungry, housing that is vacant while there are people without homes, or the denial of education to students because of their inability to pay.

It is important to note, however, that for Polanyi the "social" content of the economy was not necessarily "good"; such content could and often did support tyranny or was based on human misery such as slavery. The pharaohs of ancient Egypt in this sense developed a "social" economy wherein a small aristocracy controlled all economic activity, had a massive system of slavery, and, as noted in the Bible, was responsible for feeding the people in times of famine. What drives the economic activity in this case is not profit, but *social power*. What Polanyi is trying to point out is that however one evaluates the efficiency of these kinds of social organization, the economic activity that they participated in is markedly different from the economic activity undertaken in the market system—*social issues drive the*

BOX 1.4   Three Economic Theorists and the Social Economy

Three economic theorists—Adam Smith, Karl Marx, and Karl Polanyi—are central to the economic theory of the social economy. Their work has, in different ways, defined both what the social economy is not and the ways in which the social economy can be thought of as an economic practice distinct from capitalism.

For Adam Smith (1723–1790), economic activity is understood as individual, rational, and self-interested. Smith's views comprise the basis of neoclassical economics, the dominant economic theory today. The social economy challenges neoclassical economics implicitly by searching for a socially sensitive economy.

For Karl Marx (1818–1883), economic activity, even capitalism, can only be understood as a social activity based on social decisions. Crucially for him, therefore, human history is reflective of the economic structures of production. For the social economy, Marx is important because he sees the economic structures of any society as changeable and fundamentally social.

For Karl Polanyi (1886–1964), economic activity throughout history before capitalism was marked by its social nature. While the forms of activity are infinitely variant in practice, they reflect the social structures of society. According to Polanyi, what distinguishes capitalism as an economic system is the fact that it appears to separate the social concerns of society from its economic functioning. Polanyi is therefore important to the economic theory of the social economy because he highlights the importance of this separation as historically unique and problematic.

economy, rather than economic concerns drive society. To a greater extent than in Heilbroner's work, then, Polanyi gives some direction to understanding how one might consider the social economy as having existed throughout history, although the *normative* distinction between types of social economy according to what social need they serve is not developed by him. This problem will be addressed below.

Having discussed both a "traditional" understanding as well as a more "heterodox" view of economic theory and the social economy, we need to briefly turn toward two other key figures that have profoundly influenced this debate. The first of these is Adam Smith, the central figure in classical economic theory of the market and, consequently, a key participant in the "great transformation" of economic society outlined by Polanyi. Smith forms a bridge between the social economy of the pre-capitalist economic period and the capitalist market that still influences our conceptions of economics today. He does so because, as Polanyi makes clear, while Smith's economic theory has "humanistic foundations," including the idea that wealth was "merely an aspect of the life of the community," he also lays the groundwork for the conceptualization of economics as a sphere of activity separate from society (1957, 115 and 111, respectively). Perhaps most important to this latter conceptual development was Smith's conception of the individual—rather than social status or community need—as the fundamental unit of economic activity. For not only were individuals the core unit of economic activity, they were also, according to Smith, naturally and always in search of the opportunity to participate in market exchange for their own selfish benefit. In Smith's words, humanity had a "propensity to truck, barter and exchange," not for social good but for individual gain (1976, 17). Like the division of labour he found so compelling, wherein individuals specialized in a particular task for productive efficiency, economics, and the societies that relied upon it, needed to be broken down into and understood in terms of their constituent parts—individuals.

Importantly for Smith, collective good and community needs did not disappear from view through this focus on the individual, but rather were left to the almost magical "invisible hand" of the market, an automatic mechanism that ensured that private greed turned into social benefit. Thus, Smith argued: "it is not from the benevolence of the butcher, the brewer, or the baker, that we expect our dinner, but from their regard to their own interest" (1976, 18). For Smith, this propensity of humanity to act as self-interested market agents was an eternal reality; it had existed from the beginning of time in all cultures. In the language of this chapter, the "economic problem" really only had one solution, according to Smith, which was the freeing of this compulsion of humanity to participate in economic activity as self-maximizing, profit-seeking individuals. This has relevance to the social economy because by implication (since the concept was not in use in Smith's time) its focus on social concern rather than individual self-interest could lead to limits on market activity and therefore, in Smith's opinion, on economic freedom and development. Smith is crucial for an understanding of economic theory and the social economy because his economic (as opposed to his moral) views are dominant today. In this sense, Smith has done more than any other thinker to create the problem outlined in the introduction; that is, to obscure the functioning and the concept of the social economy as economic activity.

The second classical economic figure to be examined, of central relevance to the social economy, is Karl Marx. Marx is relevant because he is the first historical figure to construct a systematic economic critique of capitalist market economics while at the same time developing a conception of the *social* nature of economic production. Central to Marx's theoretical and political project was the idea that economic systems are at the heart of human history. For Marx, economic systems formed the "base" of any society on which a "superstructure" of ideas (that is, philosophy) and social practices (such as laws or systems of government) was erected. This does not mean, as is often argued, that economic practice "determines" ideas in the manner of a mathematical formula. While Marx did argue that "out from the material production of life itself" come "forms of consciousness, religion, philosophy, ethics, etc.," he meant literally out of *the production of all of life* (Tucker 1978, 164). Material production had for Marx therefore at least two, equally important, components: the economic material or "forces of production," like a plough or a factory, and the social organization of human labour or the "relations of production," such as wage labour, agricultural and domestic slave labour, or feudal peasant labour. The social and the economic, in other words, are intertwined at the core of Marx's theory, even in the capitalist or market economic system where they *appear* to be separated.

In important ways, then, economics for Marx is always social, but in different ways during different historical periods. This does not mean that humanity can choose how and what it produces, because for Marx the forces of production always form a limit to the economic choices available to humanity, because they are relatively stable. As Marx argues, people "are not free to choose their productive forces—which are the basis for all their history—for every productive force is an acquired force" based upon available technology (Tucker 1978, 137). However, and crucially, there is always a chance to alter the social relations of production under which human labour is organized to work within these forces of production. In other words, humanity cannot create technological change at will, but social groups can decide how to organize themselves socially using available forces of production. Our peasant does not have to accept being a slave, even if the most advanced technology is a cattle-drawn plough, but a given peasant cannot choose to be a computer programmer if computers do not exist. Marx's conception of both the material limits (forces of production) to and the possibility of change (the social relations of production) within economics is an important framework for the social economy because it allows for the analysis of a variety of economic activities within a particular historical period based on the forces of production. Furthermore, since it is within the social relationships of economics where change occurs, this is the area of activity for most social economy activity. A co-operative that produces food uses the same forces of production as does a corporation that does the same, but the former organizes itself differently, *socially*. In short, for Marx, and in opposition to Smith, economics is not a realm of eternal relationships, but a subject of debate and analysis. How this debate is resolved is in important ways what drives change throughout history.

Having considered some theories that engage the "how" and the "should" of economic activity, we can now return to the theory and practice of the social economy with a better understanding of what is at stake. If we can conceive of the economy—the efficient production, distribution, and consumption of goods otherwise in short supply—as an activity that occurs throughout human history, we have the ability to begin to conceive of some if not all economic activity as social. It is social because, even within capitalism as Marx pointed out, and certainly beforehand, humans are organized socially in the economy to meet human needs. Furthermore, we can also recognize, as Polanyi has outlined, that the economy has been, at least *conceptually*, separated from this social base, as a result of the work that Adam Smith began and generations of economists following his lead continued. Thus, the concept of social economy has been generally avoided in Canada and around the world because it does not fit easily into the now dominant conception of economics. Finally, we know that if there is a social choice in the economy we have to confront the question, mentioned above, that economists have been wrestling with for generations—what *should* the economy look like in an ideal world. In this sense, the social economy is an idea which requires us to confront the economy not as a choice already made for us, but one which we are making all the time.

The Social

With this choice in mind, we need to turn from our focus on the economy to the second key concept of the social economy—the social. Given that Smith, Marx, and Polanyi all disagree about the role of the social within economics, a debate (outlined below) that continues within conceptions of the social economy, we need to understand this term. First, we need to develop clarity concerning the kinds of social activities that were prioritized in pre-market societies in order to move us beyond Polanyi's rather broad idea of what the social focus *means*, as well as to give us some clarity on what it *means within* capitalist economies. Second, we need to understand what the positive meaning of the social is that guides the contemporary practice of the social economy in Canada, and indeed around the globe.

The basis of all human "communal" activity, which Fontan and Shragge identify as the starting point of the social economy, is social relationships. In its most basic sense, the social refers to *the collective activities of a number of individuals*. While this may seem to be an obvious starting point, it is important to remember that this type of activity is clearly distinct from Smith's employment of the individual as the focal point of economic analysis. Just as Smith's view does not eliminate collective well-being from the economic equation (the "invisible hand" takes care of that), this social view does not eliminate the individual but rather places the focus on the social contexts within which individuals gain their identity, well-being, and understanding of themselves as part of a larger whole (such as a culture or nation). C. Wright Mills, in *The Sociological Imagination*, captures the interaction between the social and the individual well: "The sociological imagination enables us to grasp history [the social] and biography [the individual] and the relations between the two within society" (1999, 349). For Mills, the important question is what makes a particular social problem not simply an individual "trouble," but rather a social "issue" (1999, 350). One can think this distinction through with an example. When a problem (and indeed its solution) such as poverty can no longer be attributed to the specific biography of an individual, because so many individuals in so many societies experience it, Mills argues that it should then be attributed to the ways in which individuals have organized themselves socially. When we take this broader social view, we are able to observe different levels of poverty as a result of particular policies, for example, the availability of government support of some kind (such as welfare or unemployment insurance), that are themselves the result of social choices. Collective problems require collective solutions. The question for the social economy in light of this general definition of the social is what kind of economic problems could be considered as social issues within its framework? Further, what kind of solutions does the social economy offer to solve these problems? We now turn to understanding the *social* nature of the "economic problem" to answer these questions.

The "social" has been identified by many divergent groups and individuals as being under threat for well over a century. We can think of issues such as the decline in family values, increases in crime rates, or the reduction in civil mindedness (helping others or volunteering) as recent examples of this concern reflected in popular media. However, this concern is not limited to the popular media; it also has a long history in sociological writing, the most famous instance perhaps being in Ferdinand Tönnies's book *Community and Civil Society* (1887), in which he introduced his concepts of *Gemeinschaft* and *Gesellschaft*. For Tönnies, there is a positive human relationship of *Gemeinschaft* (community) that is challenged and even broken apart by the individuated and impersonal *Gesellschaft* (social relations based on the division of labour—individualism) of emerging capitalism:

> The [social] relationship itself, and the social bond that stems from it, may be conceived either as having real organic life, and that is the essence of *Community* [*Gemeinschaft*]; or else as a purely mechanical construction, existing in the mind, and that is what we think of as *Society* [*Gesellschaft*]. (Tönnies 2001, 17)

While the terms seem contradictory on the surface—how is society different from social relationships?—Tönnies is making an argument about the breakdown of social relationships in the face of a society constructed on the twin ideas (advocated by Adam Smith) of the individual and an economy based on the division of labour. In this sense, Tönnies is making an argument similar to the one put forward by Marx—that is, the close relationship between economic and social practice. Tönnies's framework reveals two distinct points about the social that are relevant to the discussion here. First, when one talks about the social, one is talking about *communal* engagement above and beyond the individual. In community there is a sense of belonging to a whole that is greater than the sum of its parts. Second, in Tönnies's understanding the social is not permanent, but rather something created and recreated through participation (and importantly for the social economy, therefore open to democratic intervention). These two senses of the social inform the meaning the social economy. Most important, it is this sense of the social in *Gemeinschaft* as reflective of community concerns that is appealed to by the negative definition of the social economy as economic activity directly controlled neither by the state nor by principles of a for-profit market. Rather, the concept of the social for the social economy is meant to indicate an area of economic activity where social or community issues are of central concern.

The difficulty with the conception of society as *Gesellschaft*, especially in the contemporary context, is that the economy is seen to be by definition an area of activity separate and indeed immune from social concern. Economic efficiency is often cast as relying on making "hard choices" that harm societies and communities (for example, massive layoffs) in order for the "economy" (in this case, corporations) to continue to thrive. Thus, while there are many examples of a widespread belief about the breakdown of society on a social level as a result of individualism (the breakdown of the family or reduction of civic-mindedness mentioned above), this argument of breakdown rarely extends to the economy where Adam Smith's first principles of individualism, self-interest, and division of labour generally continue to be conceived as positive developments. But, as is the case with the social economy as a whole, while this separation of society and economy holds sway on a conceptual level around most of the globe, it is not complemented on the ground by actual economic practice. Thus, when we look at historical pre-capitalist market economic activity, we find that Polanyi's observation that "man's economy, as a rule, is submerged in his social relationships" (1957, 46) remains true. This is important for at least two reasons. First, not only is Smith's self-interested economic individual not an issue for these societies, but, more important, there is instead a strong sense (practically lived) of belonging to a community, a sense that is crucial to the ways in which these various societies address the economic problem. While for much of human history this "social" production is often performed by a local group (as can be seen in the remaining "tribal" societies around the globe), the economic activity of these social groups is often "quite complex" (when viewed on its own terms) while at the same time being bound by community obligation (Earl 2002, 15). One need only think of how gathering and hunting societies have built in obligations to share work and divide economic production (that is, the hunt or gathering) among members. This type of social division of economic production is not limited to pre-state societies, however. As John Craig (1993, 24) argues in the context of co-operatives and cooperation, which form crucial components of the social economy in the modern context, all co-operation before the emergence of the market economy was "traditional" and not subject to conscious reflection but was, rather, an embedded part of social norms. Simply put, the idea of economic activity separate from social concerns is not one that is comprehendible to pre-market societies. In this way, one can say that most pre-capitalist economic activity can be conceived of as belonging to the social economy (and again, this point is made by Fontan and Shragge 2000). However, this conception conceals more than it reveals, because the economic activity taking place is widely variant and does not help us to uncover what is distinct about these societies.

What is useful in the application of this general concept of the social to this period of pre-capitalist market activity is that it gives the observer an idea of what is being replaced as capitalism emerges. While the process of transition is not simple or unidirectional in any way, the defining feature of capitalism is its constant de-linking of the economic from the social. This de-linking occurs as a result of, first, a conceptual focus on the individual, second, an active encouragement of self-interested economic activity, and third, a focus on profit as itself a good. None of these can be seen as social in their aims. By de-linking the social nature of the economy, the social nature of pre-capitalist market activity comes into focus as an issue and becomes for the observer an object of study as their assumed nature is removed. If we take our peasant again as the example, the emergence of market capitalism (which generally occurred over lifetimes, not just one) based on a focus on individual, self-interested and for-profit activity would be experienced at a number of levels. The common land on which she and her community relied would be increasingly "enclosed," privatized, and fenced off. If our peasant was lucky enough to have land, it would in all likelihood be too small to produce enough to feed her or her family and she would have to look for extra work (for example, spinning wool for clothing) to supplement her income. If the family did not maintain access to land, they would be forced to either work as agricultural wage-labourers or move to the city to look for waged work. In all of the above scenarios, the economic life of the peasants would be turned increasingly into wage labour and market relations in order that they could secure what they needed to survive. This would include, for the first time, the purchase of food, clothing, and housing as opposed to growing, sewing, or building these for themselves. In the course of these upheavals, the family would be separated from the social forms that had previously supported them, and would enter an economic world where each member was considered to be an individual in search of his or her own self-interest (notwithstanding the patriarchal, economic, and racial limitations to these interests). This process is evident in any representation of the industrial revolution in Europe.

However, what is absent from most explanations of the industrial revolution is the fact that the social and economic relationships that sustained our peasant previously did not disappear, although they were under threat. Rather the role of such relationships in sustaining communities and individuals transformed, over generations, *from their status as assumed activities into conscious practices*, as a result of the "great transformation" to capitalism. In other words, it was not until rights, such as the right to the commons, were under threat that the value of these institutions became visible as unique *social* activities as opposed to assumed practices (see, for example, Linebaugh 2008, 68). To be clear, what is being described here is not that the social economy as a *concept* was accepted by communities to describe their social practices. This is still not the case today as the introduction to this chapter outlines. Rather, what is highlighted here is *the persistence of the practice of an economy that is focused on social goals wherever the market capitalist system emerged.* We gain some insight into this pattern from the groundbreaking work of E.P. Thompson on the "moral economy," insofar as he exposes the shared moral belief in 18th-century England that economic price should follow social tradition (for example, the price of grain) rather than market practice. Thompson argues that there was "a consistent traditional view of social norms and obligations, or the proper economic functions of several parties within the community, which taken together, can be said to constitute the moral economy of the poor" (Thompson 1991, 188). Even in the face of widespread capitalist market activity, the view that economics should reflect other, social, realities stubbornly persisted. What Thompson also highlights is that it is only as capitalism develops that the moral economy can be recognized as a distinct social claim. If we extend Thompson's observations to other societies and practices, we can discover that the social forms of economic practice that appeared to communities as natural prior to the emergence of market capitalism become visible for those communities only after capitalism developed. The wide variety of economic practices that persist or are sites of struggle within dominant market capitalist practice, both historically and at present, are examples of forms of economic activity determined by social concern. The social economy forms that continue today are, in other words, an indicator of what forms of social economic practice existed prior to market capitalism.

It is important to emphasize that forms of the social economy are not stagnant or necessarily conservative, but rather develop to meet the new conditions of the "society," in Tönnies's sense, of capitalism. Again, we can turn to Karl Polanyi for an explanation of this reality. Polanyi argues that as the market economy developed, so too did the movement to protect the institutions that delivered social need; this is the "double movement" of the great transformation. Polanyi (1957, 132) describes the two sides of this process in the following manner:

> The one was the principle of economic liberalism aiming at the establishment of a self-regulating market, relying on the support of the trading classes, and using largely laissez-faire and free trade as its methods; the other was the principle of social protection aiming at the conservation of man and nature as well as productive organization, relying on the varying support of those most immediately affected by the deleterious action of the market—primarily, but not exclusively, the working and the landed classes—and using protective legislation, restrictive associations, and other instruments of intervention as its methods.

The "principle of social protection" emerges primarily to protect the *social* rights of those marginalized by the market, using law and collective organization as its methods. This "principle" has not disappeared in recent years, and some economics research has come to the conclusion that, contrary to Smith's concentration on the self-interested individual as the dominant form of economic behaviour in modern society, "Self-seeking behavior appears to be a special case, rather than the rule followed by individuals" (Borzaga and Tortia 2007, 42). From this perspective, the social economy does not represent marginal economic activity in Canada or the world, but is in fact at the core of all economic activity.

We then come to an understanding of what the "social" in social economy means in the contemporary context. As market capitalism develops and challenges community (*Gemeinschaft*) through its promotion of increasing individualism (*Gesellschaft*) in society and especially in the economy, there is an increasing awareness of the need for a counterbalance to this process on both a policy and community level. This counterbalance is located in the memory and experience of the very community spaces that have been threatened by market capitalism. This role of counterbalance would be just as true of experiences under oppressive state-centred social and economic regimes that have plagued, and continue to plague, so many communities throughout history. The social for the social economy in the contemporary context, therefore, is *the space of community where the individualism of the market and the alienation of state bureaucracy are replaced with community voice and economic activity responding to community need.* The increasing interest in the social economy, in Canada and the world, is a result of the fact that it is bringing to light a broad-based yet divergent social response, with an embedded economic aspect, to the limitations of the market.

The historical and conceptual examination of the economic and the social provided above informs how the concept of the social economy can be usefully employed to understand the diverse range of practices within each founding Canadian culture and indeed within the nation as a whole. Through this examination, the social economy has been shown to mean economic activity (the efficient production, distribution, and consumption of goods otherwise in short supply) focused on protecting and developing the social (the practices that enable community voice and economic activity in response to community need marginalized by the market). When we acknowledge that the social economy reflects the variety of social and economic practices of pre-capitalist economic forms in the face of the dominant economic practice of the market, the diversity of practice within it becomes a sign of its strength and not of its definitional weakness. The confusion around the concept of the social economy in the Canadian context (that is, involving three distinct cultures) is resolved through an understanding that each community can develop distinct responses based on their distinct history and experiences. Basic human needs, such as for clean water, employment, housing, education, and food, can all be met through a variety of forms according to this broader understanding of the social economy. Thus, Quebec social movements can develop their own non-profit, the *Chantier de l'économie sociale*, for example, to help develop the social economy as a provincial movement reflective of their historical experience, while local First Nations can develop Neechi Foods, a co-operative store in downtown Winnipeg, as a response to community needs, and both can be conceived of as the social economy (Mendell 2003, 7; Loxley 2007, 39). The combination of the concepts of the social and the economic allow for this wide variety of activities. Yet if this conception of the social economy is sufficient to explain the different institutions and organizations of Canada and indeed around the globe, why has it not been accepted by more actors, policy-makers, and academics, and also by the public at large? It is to this question that this chapter now turns.

Theories of the Social Economy

The social economy is still a contested term. That is, despite the variety of practices that could be conceived to be part of it, various agents involved in and observers of the social economy do not agree upon what this concept means. This issue requires further investigation in two areas. First, the definitional debate needs to be examined in light of the observations above around the nature of the economic and the social, looking at how the definition of the social economy can be refined to move past this debate. Second, the debate over definition itself needs to be placed within the context of the "how" and "should" of the economy, as discussed above. That is, definitions of the social economy too often have been coloured by the ideological beliefs of the actors and observers involved in the discussion. In the end, the definitional debates within the social economy are based on the broader debate over economics (again, as outlined above). Therefore, the conclusions that one draws about these definitional debates have implications for the economic and social possibilities that can emerge within the social economy and within economics more generally, an issue that will be examined in the final section of this chapter.

The definition of the social economy is perhaps more contested in Canada than anywhere else in the world, partially as a result of the differing perceptions of this concept within the founding nations, as outlined in the introduction. There are innumerable positions and modifications of the definition of the social economy depending on the political position as well as the cultural and geographical location of the observer. The essence of this debate can be found on the website of the Canadian Social Economy Hub. The purpose of this organization, which was founded in 2005, is "coordinating research to build the social economy" (CSEHub 2009). The website provides three "definitions" for the social economy, one for Canadian practitioners, one for the Canadian government, and one that applies internationally. For Canadian practitioners, the "definition" is as follows:

> The social economy consists of association-based economic initiatives founded on values of: Service to members of community rather than generating profits; Autonomous management (not government or market controlled); Democratic decision-making; Primacy of persons and work over capital; Based on principles of participation, empowerment ... The social economy is a continuum that goes from the one end of totally voluntary organizations to the other end where the economic activity (social enterprise) blurs the line with the private sector. (CSEHub 2009)

While this definition is broad and inclusive in scope, it contains a strong tension within it. On the one hand, it clearly outlines a series of values on which the social economy might be based, including the prioritizing of community over profit and autonomy from the state and the market. On the other hand, it is inclusive of private sector-like (capitalist-like) social enterprise activity that, given the preceding argument about the self-interested foundation of capitalism, seems to be in contradiction with an emphasis on the values of "community" over "generating profits" and on the "primacy of persons and work over capital." There is within the definition itself an encoding of a debate around the economic and social goals of the social economy and a tension between the market economics of Adam Smith and social economics based in a broader definition of economics and the social. This creates the confusion around what exactly the social economy is—in other words, this definition "blurs the lines" rather than making the issue clearer.

This internal debate concerning the concept of social economy is further demonstrated by the next "definition," the one proposed to represent the Canadian government's perspective:

> Separate from the private sector and government, the social economy
> includes co-operatives, foundations, credit unions, non-profit organizations,
> the voluntary sector, charities and social economy enterprises. Social econ-
> omy enterprises are a component of the social economy that are run like
> businesses, producing goods and services for the market economy, but man-
> age their operations and redirect their surpluses in pursuit of social and
> environmental goals. (CSEHub 2009)

Here the focus is on separation from the state and the market and pursuit
of social goals, with a clear list of organizations that could easily be included
in the definition of social economy. However, on close examination one
realizes that special emphasis is given to "social enterprises" as distinct from
other social economy forms, again with the emphasis on the fact that they
operate "like businesses" within the market economy. The only difference
from "normal" (read "capitalist") for-profit behaviour in this definition is
that the surplus is directed toward social goals. Thus, under this definition
any corporation that directs some of its surplus to a social goal could be
considered to be a participant in the social economy—McDonald's, for
example, which largely funds Ronald McDonald House, a separate non-
profit corporation that is effectively part of the corporate "family" of
McDonald's, can blur the line between corporate for-profit activity and the
social economy. The social and economic distinction between these organizations is again equivocated because there is no value distinction made
in it.

The tension between these two understandings of the social and the
economic becomes even more evident in the international definition provided by the Social Economy Hub:

> Private companies created to meet their members' needs through the market
> by producing goods and providing services, insurance and finance, where
> profit distribution and decision-making are not directly linked to the capital
> contributed by each member, each of whom has one vote. The social econ-
> omy also includes non-profit organisations that are private non-market pro-
> ducers, not controlled by government, produce not-for-sale services for
> specific groups of households and whose main resources come from volun-
> tary contributions by the households as consumers, payments from the gov-
> ernment and income from property. (CSEHub 2009)

Market activities are here again central, but even more so, placed at the
forefront of the social economy. Again, while there is a distinction between
the social economy and "regular" market activity through the proviso that
the profit created by this market activity is not directly linked to capital

invested, and additionally that there is some form of democracy practised through the principle of "one member, one vote," the unique economic nature of the social economy is obscured since this definition broadens further the ability of market activity to count as social economy activity since only "direct" linkage between investment and control is deemed problematic. Thus, an investor could own 95 percent of an organization, but if he only maintains 80 percent control, this organization would still be labelled social economy under this definition. Member needs could even be equated to profit. In other words, a more exacting distinction must be made between market capitalist forms and social economic activity. Within all three of these definitions there is a tension created by constructing an inclusive continuum from *values*, as the defining feature of the social economy on the one hand, to *market activity*, as a legitimate form of social service, on the other. This tension must either be explained or corrected.

Social Economy as a Movement for Ethical Economics

In some ways, the attempt to outline a continuum from social values to market is understandable as an attempt to be as inclusive as possible of the widely variant activity of the social economy. This indeed has been highlighted above as a strength of the social economy sector rather than a weakness. However, there is a fundamentally important difference between recognizing social economy practices as being diverse as a *result of the socially and historically unique conditions of their development*, and the claim that social economy practice is inclusive of the *dominant economic practice that creates the need for the social economy in the first place*. To insist on the inclusion of this latter form is to impose an economic "should" onto the practice of the social economy rather than to allow its unique form to be understood on its own terms. How is it possible to discern the unique form of the social economy when dominant economic practice is everywhere engaged and the economic theory of the social economy is underdeveloped? It is to this question that this chapter now briefly turns.

Many authors have pointed out that there have been two types of definitions applied to the social economy, one that relies on taxonomy, a list of the legal and institutional forms that the broad definition might include, and another on normative analysis, which outlines the values or principles on which the organizations are based. There are also definitions that are combinations of both (as is the government-oriented definition above) (Clarence and Noya 2007, 10; Westland 2003, 1194). However, this distinction fails to acknowledge that the taxonomy approach *relies on an idea of the normative* that is contested. Consequently, it is crucial to examine the normative debate around the concept of social economy to get at the essence of the concept. In the case of social economy, the contestation is not just in comparison to other economic theories, but also within its own tradition. In other words, not only do most definitions of the social economy argue for a continuum of organizations that should be considered within the term, there is also a continuum of *normative* positions within the social economy itself. The polarities of this continuum range from the "pragmatic/reformist" tradition, which sees the social economy as a functional part of market capitalism, to the "utopian/social change" tradition, which sees the social economy as a part of the revolutionary socialist tradition (Fontan and Shragge 2000, 3). Normatively, these positions outline a continuum between the ethical nature of individual self-interested activity on one hand and, on the other, positions adhering to the social belief of community well-being as requiring the reform or outright removal of capitalist economic and social relations. The academic literature is full of examples of these positions. For example, there are commentators who believe that the social economy should be a term that is used to describe a socialist and anti-capitalist state-centred alternative (for example, Hill 2002), and others who believe that the social economy refers to a practice and a normative ethic of "conservative capitalism" (for example, Reisman 1999). Others argue that the term is interchangeable with "political economy," revealing power relations within society (for example, Bruyn 1977), while others see it as a theory of the development of capitalism (for example, Everling 1997). In short, there appears normatively to be "no single unifying definition of the social economy," since the range of positions that co-exist under its umbrella are what in fact marks this theory of economic activity as unique (Uluorta 2009, 11).

This perception of a lack of normative agreement itself is in need of examination. The above framework, while useful for understanding the motivation of various actors within the social economy both presently and historically, does not identify the social economy as a field of study separate from other economic theories or social and political ideologies. Rather than see the practice on its own terms, other terms and concepts (in a way similar to Heilbroner's economic forms) are imposed on social economic activity in order to explain it. This chapter, however, has argued that the social economy is—as a policy choice, an activity in which social actors are interested, or as a subject of academic study—*intriguing for its unique contribution to economic and social practice.* If this area of activity simply consists of *either* the replication of existing market activity or state socialist strategy, while not in itself uninteresting, this activity would not be unique. Clearly, observers and practitioners of the social economy are experiencing something different. In the Canadian context for example, what observers are generally interested in is how the social economy indicates "an alternative arena for economic activity and progressive social change" (Biewener 2006, 126). This understanding, while itself contested, does indicate a different set of value premises on which the idea of the social economy, as directly controlled neither by the state nor by the for-profit logic of the market, rests. However, it is also clear from the definitional debate above and, especially in the Canadian context, from the practice of social economy organizations on the ground that this activity is not entirely separate from the influence of state and market. For example, both the state, through health-care or education funding, and the for-profit logic of the market, for example, in social enterprise activities, are deeply invested in the social economy. How, then, is one to make social economy activity as a unique economic and social activity explanatory on a normative level when its practice is so complex? It seems that we have returned to the problem posed in the introduction, only at another level.

The answer to this question is perhaps deceptively simple—what distinguishes social economics on the normative level *is precisely the fact that it is normative.* What makes the social economy unique as an economic activity is that it is economic activity that is focused on normative behaviour as its goal, rather than the apparently law-like and eternal economics of Adam Smith and neoclassical economics. To put it simply, "social economics must be normative," while market economics must ignore normative issues in an apparently norm-free pursuit of profit (Hunt 2005, 429). This necessity is a result of two key realities. First, the social economy, as outlined above, is developed to create an alternative economic and social space for those excluded from the necessities of life by the functioning of market capitalism. The very reason to articulate its presence is to highlight the fact that all is not working well within the dominant system. Social economy forms, from co-operatives to non-profits, emerge as alternatives to existing forms *precisely because they are seen to be more ethical* in the view of academics, practitioners, students, and policy-makers alike. Second, the social economy itself is not just a recent phenomenon but is based on historical practices that have developed, often over centuries, to respond to human needs. In this sense, the social economy is like an economic and social museum where the historical struggles of various societies answering their specific "economic problems" are available for all to see. Its forms are reflective of the normative answers that these societies developed in response to their specific conditions. The social economy is fundamentally a normative concept, then, and its practice should be defined as such, not by applying taxonomic definitions to it. While the normative character of social economy agents has priority in any comprehensive and consistent understanding of the social economy, organizational forms are not irrelevant, and must indeed reflect in their structure and core mandate the normative content of the movement. Hence, the problematic of attributing "corporate social responsibility" endeavours to the social economy. As a result of this discovery, we can conclude that in fact it is not the market or state-funded practices of an organization that are of critical concern to the observer of the social economy, but rather how well it serves its normative aims.

This leaves the final question of how to evaluate the social economy in its particular practice from this normative perspective. We know that not all normative practices fit easily within the social economy definition, a fact that is made more complex by the fact that the efficiency of the economic practice undertaken in its name must also be examined. While these are complex issues, there are ways in which they can be understood. Most basically, we must remember that the social economy exists to meet the human needs of those excluded from the dominant system of market capitalism. The meeting of needs has two fundamental normative aspects to it. The first is that human needs can be understood within the framework of life-needs required for life-capacity development (John McMurtry 2002, 218). This is not simply an observation or a list of basic human requirements, like Maslow's hierarchy of needs, but a normative claim that to deny or limit access to these life-needs is ethically wrong. The efficiency of an economy, therefore, can be judged by how well it provides these life-needs. Second, for the social economy to be effective in realizing this normative claim around life-needs means that it is also compelled to articulate itself not as isolated activities plugging the gaps of the existing economic system, but rather as a movement toward economic and social change: "By opening up this alternative theoretical frame of life, we can start to liberate our practice and theory from the no-alternative dogma of the 'free market' with its 'iron laws' and productivist demands to the actually experienced life-needs of a membership or society at large" (J.J. McMurtry 2004, 876). Only by creating a movement can the social economy meet the demands posed by its definition by becoming more than the sum of individual organizations in order to realize its social character. In short, the defining feature of the social economy is the ability to realize its normative claims in both the practical actions of meeting life-needs and in articulating these needs beyond the confines of particular organizations, as a movement for ethical economic practice.

Conclusion

This chapter has argued that the defining feature of the Canadian economic experience, inclusive of each culture within it (and we should now include those not identified as founding cultures), is not market capitalist activity, but rather the fundamental role that social economy forms, in their wide variety, have played in developing this experience. However, the problem with this view is the fact that the conceptual definition of the social economy has not been developed to match the practice of the social economy in Canada or in the world. By developing an understanding of the economy (that is, the efficient production, distribution, and consumption of goods otherwise in short supply) and the social (that is, the space of community where the individualism of the market and the alienation of the state bureaucracy are replaced with community voice and economic activity responding to community need), the social economy (that is, economic activity neither controlled directly by the state nor by the profit logic of the market, prioritizing the social well-being of communities and marginalized individuals over partisan political directives or individual gain) as a concept and practice was explained. Furthermore, it was argued that, in order for the definition of the social economy to develop as a useful tool for observers and practitioners, we must move away from a taxonomy approach, an approach that is fixated on the institutional form of the practice, and instead move toward a normative understanding focused on the life-needs of the actors within it. In this sense the most important aspect of the definition provided above is its second section: *prioritizing the social well-being of communities and marginalized individuals over partisan political directives or individual gain.* This is, after all, why people participate in the social economy—not to be non-profit or non-state per se, but to actually make a difference in their own lives and in the lives of others, to build community of one sort or another. They do so because they feel that the existing options available in the capitalist market are not sufficient to their needs or to their community's needs, however minor or major their understanding of this insufficiency. In order to achieve the normative goals of meeting life-needs and changing the social conditions within which they find themselves, social economy actors must begin to conceptualize themselves not as individual agents, but rather as constituting a part of a movement of national and international proportions. What makes the social economy innovative in practice and in theory is the fact the organizations within it are focused on these normative goals rather than on the single-minded and inward-looking activities of for-profit or political power and control.

Glossary

Economy   The efficient production, distribution, and consumption of goods otherwise in short supply.

Neo-classical economics   A school of economic thought holding that all economic decisions are based on individual (personal, firm, or government), rational self-interest in order maximize utility or "profit" for that individual. Recognized as the dominant and orthodox school of economics.

Normative   The belief that economic, philosophical, or social norms (standards or rules of behaviour or practice, whether conscious or unconscious) *should* exist. To argue that a particular idea or behaviour is normative is to argue that it is good or proper—that one *ought* to behave in particular way.

Social economy   Economic activity neither controlled directly by the state nor by the profit logic of the market; activity that prioritizes the social well-being of communities and marginalized individuals over partisan political directives or individual gain.

Notes

1. Further demonstrating the limited interest of the government in the social economy, this section of the website has not been updated since late 2005—not coincidentally, just months before former prime minister and social economy advocate Paul Martin was voted out of government. One might argue that at the federal level in Canada, the social economy has been on the policy radar for less than two years in total.
2. It is often forgotten that the state form is a human development rather than an ahistorical, *a priori* political form or a universal human experience. Morton Fried (1967) provides a classic outline of the possibilities of other human forms of "political society" outside of the state form, even though he argues that the state form "could not be avoided" (226) once it had been invented.
3. One can look to the groundbreaking work of Ellen Meiksins Wood for a detailed account of this claim, particularly *Peasant-Citizen and Slave: The Foundations of Athenian Democracy* (1989).
4. This definition is a slight alteration of the standard definition of economics. For example, the *Oxford Dictionary of Economics* defines economics as "A

social science that studies individual and group decisions on how to use scarce resources to satisfy their wants and needs" (Black, Hashimzade, and Myles 2009, 131). Perhaps more usefully, Samuelson (Samuelson and Nordhaus 2005) in his famous text defines economics as "the study of how societies use scarce resources to produce valuable commodities and distribute them among different people" (4).

Discussion Questions

1. Outline three features of the social economy as defined in this chapter.
2. Are you involved in any activities that are about "the efficient production, distribution, and consumption of goods otherwise in short supply" and yet are not achieved through "normal" economic activity? Does it help to think of this as social economy activity?
3. Why has the concept of the social economy been difficult to articulate when its practice has been central to the Canadian history?

Suggested Further Readings

Heilbroner, R.L. and W. Milberg. 2008. *The making of economic society*. 12th ed. New Jersey: Pearson.

Linebaugh, P. 2008. *The Magna Carta manifesto: Liberties and commons for all*. Berkeley and Los Angeles: University of California Press.

McMurtry, John. 2002. *Value wars: The global market versus the life economy*. London: Pluto.

McMurtry, J.J. 2004. Social economy as political practice. *International Journal of Social Economics* 31 (9): 868–878.

Polanyi, K. (1957 [1944]). *The great transformation: The political and economic origins of our time*. Boston: Beacon.

References

Ailenei, O., and F. Moulaert. 2005. Social economy, third sector and solidarity relations: A conceptual synthesis from history to present. *Urban Studies* 42 (11): 2037–2053.

Biewener, C. 2006. France and Québec: The progressive visions embodied in different social economy traditions. In *Ethics and the market: Insights from social economics*, ed. B.J. Clary, W. Dolfsma, and D.M. Figart, 126–139. New York: Routledge.

Black, J., N. Hashimzade, and G. Myles. 2009. *Oxford dictionary of economics*. 3rd ed. Oxford: Oxford University Press.

Borzaga, C., and E. Tortia. 2007. Social economy organizations in the theory of the firm. In *The social economy: Building inclusive economies*, ed. E. Clarence and A. Noya. Paris: Organisation for Economic Co-operation and Development.

Bruyn, S.T. 1977. *The social economy: People transforming modern business.* Toronto: John Wiley.

Canadian Co-operative Association (CCA). 2009. The power of co-operation: Co-operatives and credit unions in Canada—Facts and figures. http://www.coopscanada.coop/assets/firefly/files/files/pdfs/ Power_of_cooperation_08_E_web.pdf.

Clarence, E. and A. Noya. 2007. Executive summary. In *The social economy: Building inclusive economies*, ed. E. Clarence and A. Noya. Paris: Organisation for Economic Co-operation and Development.

Canadian Social Economy Hub (CSEHub). 2009. What is the social economy? http://www.socialeconomyhub.ca/hub/index.php?page_id=9.

Craig, J.G. 1993. *The nature of co-operation.* Montreal: Black Rose.

Earle, T. 2002. *Bronze age economics: The beginnings of political economies.* Boulder, CO: Westview.

Everling, C. 1997. *Social economy: The logic of capitalist development.* London: Routledge.

Fontan, J.-M., and E. Shragge. 2000. Tendencies, tensions and visions in the social economy. In *Social economy: International debates and perspectives*, ed. E. Shragge and J.M. Fontan, 1–15. Montreal: Black Rose.

Freid, M. 1967. *The evolution of political society: An essay in political anthropology.* Toronto: McGraw-Hill.

Heilbroner, R.L., and W. Milberg. 2008. *The making of economic society.* 12th ed. New Jersey: Pearson.

Hill, C. 2002. *Anti-capitalism: The social economy alternative.* London: Spokesman.

Human Resources and Skills Development Canada (HRSDC). 2009. Social economy: Questions and answers. http://www.hrsdc.gc.ca/eng/cs/comm/sd/ social_economy.shtml.

Hunt, E.K. 2005. The normative foundations of social theory: An essay on the criteria defining social economics. *Review of Social Economy* 63 (3): 423–445.

Laville, J.L. (ed.). 1994. *L'économie solidaire, une perspective internationale.* Paris: Desclee de Brouwer.

Laville, J.-L., B. Levesque, and M. Mendell. 2007. The social economy: Diverse approaches and practices in Europe and Canada. In *The social economy: Building inclusive economies*, ed. E. Clarence and A. Noya. Paris: Organisation for Economic Co-operation and Development.

Linebaugh, P. 2008. *The Magna Carta manifesto: Liberties and commons for all.* Berkeley and Los Angeles: University of California Press.

Loxley, J., ed. 2007. *Transforming or reforming capitalism: Towards a theory of community economic development.* Halifax: Fernwood.

McMurtry, John. 2002. *Value wars: The global market versus the life economy.* London: Pluto.

McMurtry, J.J. 2004. Social economy as political practice. *International Journal of Social Economics* 31 (9): 868–878.

Mendell, M. 2003. The social economy in Quebec. VIII Congreso Internacional del CLAD sobre la Reforma del Estado y de la Administración Pública, Panama City. October 28–31. http://www.envision.ca/pdf/SocialEconomy/ SocialEconomyinQuebecMendell.pdf.

Mills, C.W. 1999. *The sociological imagination.* In *Social theory: The multicultural and classic readings,* 2nd ed., ed. C. Lemert, 348–352. Boulder, CO: Westview Press.

Polanyi, K. 1957. *The great transformation: The political and economic origins of our time.* Boston: Beacon. (Originally published 1944.)

Reisman, D. 1999. *Conservative capitalism: The social economy.* New York: St. Martin's.

Sachs, J.D. 2005. *The end of poverty: Economic possibilities for our time.* Toronto: Penguin.

Samuelson, P., and W. Nordhaus. 2005. *Economics.* 18th ed. New Delhi: Tata McGraw-Hill.

Smith, A. 1976. *The wealth of nations,* ed. C. Cannon. Chicago: University of Chicago Press.

Thompson, E.P. 1991. *Customs in common.* New York: New Press.

Tönnies, F. 2001. *Community and civil society,* ed. Jose Harris, trans. J. Harris and M. Hollis. Cambridge: Cambridge University Press. (Originally published 1887.)

Tucker, R.C., ed. 1978. *The Marx-Engels reader.* New York: W.W. Norton.

Quarter, J. 1992. *Canada's social economy: Co-operatives, non-profits, and other community enterprises.* Toronto: James Lorimar.

Uluorta, H.M. 2009. *The social economy: Working alternatives in a globalizing era.* New York: Routledge.

Westland, H. 2003. Form or contents? On the concept of the social economy. *International Journal of Social Economics* 30 (11): 1192–1206.

Wood, E.M. 1989. *Peasant-citizen and slave: The foundations of Athenian democracy.* London: Verso.

Wood, E.M. 1996. *Democracy against capitalism.* New York: Cambridge University Press.

CHAPTER TWO

Co-operatives and the Social Economy in English Canada: Circles of Influence and Experience

IAN MacPHERSON

Introduction

By any measurement, it is significant. On an institutional level, as of 2004 (the last year for which national statistics are available), there were over 4,000 credit unions and other kinds of co-operatives in Canada outside of the province of Quebec (Co-operatives Secretariat 2007, 1 for non-financial co-operatives; the data are for 2004). These had over 5,000,000 members, only marginally fewer than the movement in Quebec. The total assets of the English-Canadian movement amounted to over $175,000,000,000 (Co-operatives Secretariat 2007, 1, 22). It is a movement with a history that stretches back at least to the 1860s and arguably earlier,[1] and it has been an important part of the history of all Canadian regions for much of the 20th century. It is a movement with remarkable diversity, but it can be divided generally into two groupings: one consisting of older, well-established kinds of co-operatives, such as consumer co-operatives, agricultural marketing co-ops, and credit unions; the other made up largely of new types of co-ops (new at least for Canada) generally serving social needs that became more evident and pressing in the last two decades of the 20th century.

The largest segment of co-operatives, by far, is the credit union movement. Today, it alone has more than $110,600,000,000 in assets (Credit

Union Central of Canada 2009). The next largest is the consumer co-operative movement located, for the most part, in Western Canada, Atlantic Canada, and the North; for a number of very complex reasons, there are very few in Ontario. It has over 3,800,000 members, more than $4,200,000,000 in assets, and in excess of $9,000,000,000 in annual sales (Co-operatives Secretariat 2007). Agricultural marketing co-operatives, long a mainstay of the national movement, can be found in a large number of rural areas serving farm people who produce fruit, vegetables, poultry, livestock, and organic foods. With some 115,000 members, housing co-operatives can be found in most urban areas of English Canada, most of them the product of a special federal program that flourished from the early 1970s through the later 1980s (Co-operatives Secretariat 2008; Cole 2008). Collectively, Canadian co-operatives have developed a number of major businesses, including The Co-operators, one of Canada's largest insurance companies, Concentra Financial, a national trust company, and, within the western co-operative retail system, Canadian Co-operative Refineries, a significant player in the western petroleum industry (Fairbairn 1989, esp. 66–76).

The second cluster of co-ops, those that have been developed largely in the last 30 years, are the result of increasing economic and social pressures caused by globalization, uncertain employment, the growing energy crisis, and community change. They include co-operatives providing health and social services, others providing energy through wind power and ethanol, some providing low-cost and reliable transportation through car co-ops or bicycle co-ops, a few developed by young entrepreneurs in the technology sector, a small but growing band of worker co-ops in a number of kinds of businesses, and some co-operatively managed bookstores.[2] In fact, one can say that the movement is enjoying a renaissance, exploring new areas, and attracting growing numbers of young people (see Smith, Puga, and MacPherson 2006). The list of kinds of new co-operatives is long and growing, as it is in many countries around the world (see International Co-operative Alliance 2009a).

Descriptions such as the kind just provided above, that think of co-operatives in terms of organizational type, numbers of members, and assets, are useful up to a point. They follow common international practice and are based on the assumption that a movement really achieves significance only when it has created institutions that have legal existence and economic clout, thereby giving concrete evidence of ongoing commitment by its proponents. It is, however, the kind of understanding that is akin to caricatures or cartooning: it is suggestive of the most obvious features, but it does not capture the colours and nuances one finds in a well-executed landscape painting.

It ignores, for example, informal but important associations, such as those with other co-operative movements, most notably with francophone Canadians, with whom there have frequently been very productive associations, especially in more recent years (see Vaillancourt in this volume). It does not suggest important ties with American co-operative organizations, for example, in the credit union movement, historically occurring through co-operative insurance programs in both countries and, in recent years, in Ontario through GROWMARK, a major co-operative operating in both countries, the first of its kind. It does not capture the important roles the English-Canadian movement has played in many parts of the world through its international development activities and through the International Co-operative Alliance (ICA) in Geneva. The Canadian Co-operative Association (CCA), beginning with its forerunner, the Co-operative Union of Canada (CUC), has been a member of that organization since 1912, and it has played a very significant role globally since the 1970s. Today, the English-Canadian movement, in productive association with its partner from francophone Canada, *Conseil canadien de la coopération* (CCC), is a much-respected force in the international movement, a reputation built as much on "character" as on asset size.

There are, of course, other ways in which a simple listing of registered institutional strengths undervalues what a movement means for the people involved in it. There are intellectual dimensions, matters of belief and understanding. Over the years, the co-operative movement has embodied a range of ideas about how society can be organized, not only to provide cheaper and more reliable goods and services, but also to be more responsive and responsible to people and their communities—their present needs and their future requirements. Over the years, there have been many schools of thought within the English-Canadian movement as to why it exists, what it can do, and how it should be developed (see MacPherson 1979; MacPherson 2007). These are not captured in member and asset statistics, but they are among the creative tensions of the movement, the ways in which co-operatives are tied to their members and their communities.

Similarly, the statistics do not reflect the social roles that co-operatives play and have played: for example, in the communities of the Canadian Arctic, the co-operative housing organizations of Toronto, Calgary, and Vancouver, the credit unions of Cape Breton or rural Alberta, the consumer co-ops of small rural communities and the city of Calgary, and the organic food producers on Vancouver Island (see Tunnicliffe 2008). They do not suggest the social roles they have played historically among ethnic communities—for example, the Mennonites of southern Manitoba, the Ukrainians in the Prairie Parklands, the Finns of Malcolm Island (see Wilson 2005; Emmanuel 2007), the Francophones of Caraquet, and the Inuit of Pond Inlet.[3] They do not indicate how communities have come together in rather remarkable displays of community activism and empowerment to meet pressing social needs amid diversity: to allow farmers to compete in the marketplace, to amass community financial resources for common purpose and individual or familial benefit, and to empower women or young people. They do not capture how people have found out about the movement or built human and social capital as they have learned how to operate co-operative enterprises. They do not show how people have transferred what they have learned through co-operatives to other economic activities or community-based activities—how they have created private enterprises, strengthened family farms, and helped build community organizations for the common good. In short, they do not reveal the social values and dimensions of the English-Canadian co-operative experience; consequently they do not suggest how co-operatives can be seen as important parts of the social economy.

Perspectives on Co-operatives: "The Big Picture"

To some extent, conceiving of co-operatives as part of a *social* economy is foreign to the mainstream of the inherited English-Canadian co-operative movement. But one way to conceive in this way is to think about how deeply embedded co-operatives have been—and are—within Canadian society. There are many sources—both social and economic—for the development of the English-Canadian movement, but three are arguably particularly important. These are: the pursuit of group and individual economic advantage; the transition from rural to urban Canada; and the inherited mainstream understandings of the nature of the movement. It is important to understand that each of these sources has significant social dimensions that need to be remembered within the co-operative perspective. It is also important to realize that historically none of these strands has easily provided a direct and sustained link to the thought of the social economy. Until now, the connections with the social economy have always been indirect, shadows of what they could have been—or could be.

Obviously, the pursuit of economic advantage by definition instinctively seems to minimize the importance of social dimensions, but it would be misleading to reduce co-operative exchanges to merely ways of achieving individual benefit (see McMurtry in this volume for further development of this point). First, the structures through which co-operative-based exchanges take place have been developed through group or socially constructed entities that are governed by leaders elected democratically by the members who are the primary benefactor of the services that a given co-operative provides. There is a "structural difference" of some consequence, one that invariably raises social dimensions. Second, the surpluses or profits a given co-operative earns are distributed on the basis of patronage or use, not on the basis of investment, with a proportion being employed for general community or social purpose. In fact, many co-operatives have been created largely to build local economies by providing employment and by keeping economic benefits close to home. Third, most local co-operatives are associated with other like-minded co-ops in federations or alliances in order to advance the interests that are important to them, including such issues as community sustainability, environmental degradation, youth involvement, and gender parity (and see Mook and Sumner in this volume for further development of the theme of sustainability).

These concerns are not just matters of business trends or passing emphases related to individual leaders, a perspective one might apply to current interests among investor-driven firms. They emanate (or should emanate) from the values and principles on which co-operatives are based—they are structural in origin. A co-operative must engage social issues and meet social needs as well as more narrow economic motives if it is to be true to what distinguishes it from other kinds of enterprise. Being a member of a co-operative is—or should be—in a distinctive way a social act, in most instances combining economic activities with significant, distinctive social consequences. Being a co-op leader means—or should mean—assessing seriously the organization's and the movement's social impact.[4]

The transition spanning the later 19th through the 20th centuries from a largely rural to an urban nation was one of the great changes in Canada. It was a social and economic revolution that profoundly affected the countryside as well as the growing cities and towns. Many co-operatives within the first wave of co-operative development were rooted in the rural side of this great transition. Most obviously, they grew out of the desire of rural families to stabilize rural economies through reliable marketing relationships and through purchasing "inputs" (seeds, fertilizer, and equipment) at fair prices. They also were characterized first, by significant efforts to empower rural women both economically and politically; second, by increased political lobbying in the interests of rural people and rural society generally; and third, by the creation of other kinds of co-ops (most obviously credit unions, but also consumer co-ops, insurance programs, and even, in a few instances, health co-ops). They can also be seen as manifestations of political change in the countryside, an affirmation of the search for a more complete democratic society, one that tries to embrace responsive, regularized, and accountable practice into daily activities as well as in the usually infrequent bouts of activism associated with the political process. Co-operatives have been—and in many communities still are—embedded in rural culture. They reflect social and political change as well as economic transition (see MacPherson 1972, 207–226; MacPherson 1979).

The roles of co-operatives within urban developments are less pervasive. In part, this is because of the continuous population shifts that weaken community bonds in many urban places and because the more heterogeneous populations have fewer cultural associations. There are, however, several urban neighbourhoods across Canada—such as "Commercial Drive" in Vancouver (Emmanuel 2007, 105–118), the Kensington Market area in Toronto, Main Street in Winnipeg, Fourth Avenue in Saskatoon—where that generalization does not apply or where countervailing forces have been more important. Moreover, the contributions of credit unions to the development of suburbs through more favourable lending and personal loan policies have been substantial: they were a significant contributor to the "growing middle class" that was such an obvious feature of Canadian life from 1945 to 1990. Though typically unobtrusive, credit unions, based on local control, a strong service ethic, and community responsibility, have been important players in many urban places and small towns for over two generations.[5]

Co-operative housing has been an even more obvious contributor to Canadian urban society. Especially as originally conceived by activists within the Canadian Labour Congress (CLC) and the then Co-operative Union of Canada (CUC) in the 1970s, they were intended as integrated communities comprising admixtures of social and economic classes, an intention that was a defiant reaction to the ghettos of poverty and race all too commonly seen in American society and increasingly evident in Canada. They were profoundly "social" in that they were predicated on the belief that human beings could intentionally and systematically create communities in an urban context; they were developed in the belief that co-operative structures could provide the framework through which people could build healthy communities. In this they were supported by co-operative organizations, particularly the Co-operative Union of Canada and its successor the Canadian Co-operative Association (CCA), local credit unions, Co-operative Trust (now Concentra Financial), and The Co-operators, an example of how the co-operative movement can create social capital across institutional barriers. Collectively they were supported by—and they supported—what is now the Co-operative Housing Federation (CHF), which facilitated the development of extensive educational and training programs for people involved in housing co-operatives—indeed, one of the best such programs ever developed within the English-Canadian movement.[6]

All of these initiatives, both rural and urban, tended to emerge out of the social and economic needs of communities, whether conceived of as a geographic area (for example, the Kensington Market district of Toronto) or a community of interest (for example, the dairy farmers of Vancouver Island or eastern Nova Scotia). The people most involved tend to be understandably very proud of what their co-ops have accomplished, and they generally understand them in local terms. The result is that many co-ops, while generally interested in the development of central organizations that serve immediate, practical needs (for example, lobbying governments, purchasing supplies at reduced levels, helping with the marketing of goods), are not easily involved in organizations or initiatives of less immediate benefit. Thus, general-purpose co-operative organizations—the provincial or national apex institutions—in most instances have had to struggle for support. In the co-operative world, the local and the immediate tend to overwhelm the broad and the distant. There is always a need for perspectives that engage the larger issues that co-operatives address locally, but also need for ones that consider what Moses Coady, the most famous of the leaders from the Antigonish Movement (see Box 2.1), used to call "the Big Picture."[7] (See Lionais and Johnstone in this volume for a development of the importance of place.)

Coady was suggesting that the co-operative movement was about much more than simply trying to secure a loaf of bread or a better price for a can of milk at the farm gate. He was raising the possibility of developing co-operative enterprises through a community-based activism concerned with how the major changes of the day were shaping the way in which people were living—or were forced to live. His was one of the most ardent and articulate voices in a long line of Canadian co-operative thinkers. He also possessed one of the movement's most intense and committed social visions.

The English-Canadian perspectives on the role and place of the Canadian co-operative movement have drawn on many sources, but three stand out. One of them was the series of agrarian movements that began in the latter part of the 19th century with the appearance of the Patrons of Husbandry in the 1870s, continued through the multifaceted progressive move-

BOX 2.1 The Antigonish Movement

The Antigonish Movement was a co-operative social movement located in maritime Canada—Cape Breton Island and Nova Scotia—that was active roughly from the start of the 20th century until the mid to late 1950s. The movement is strongly associated with two Catholic priests, Jimmy (J.J.) Tompkins and Moses Coady, whose tireless efforts to explain and develop co-operatives as an ethical economic alternative left a lasting legacy in the area and, indeed, in Canada as a whole. The movement was famous for its use of adult education (see Sousa in this volume) in "kitchen meetings" to inform various populations about the possibilities that the co-operative form offered for economic and social self-help. Central to the movement was the idea of community or micro credit and linkage between co-operatives in a particular area. A core belief in self-help drove the Antigonish Movement. Specifically, adherents believed that out of a community's own resources of land, labour, and capital could come a sustainable and humane economic system in the control of those communities. The strength of these ideas has left a legacy in the Maritimes, including a tradition of co-operative educa-tion—for example, in the Moses Coady Institute at St. Frances Xavier Univer-sity—and a vibrant culture of economic innovation in community economic development—for example, New Dawn Enterprises (see Lionais and John-stone in this volume).

ments of the early 20th century, the pooling movements of the 1920s, the back-to-the-land movements of the 1930s and 1960s, and the current movements of rural revival.[8] This perspective has been responsible for rais-ing issues about the sustainability of rural economies and communities, the plight of rural women, youth, and seniors, and the need for improved access to educational facilities in rural areas. More recently, it has been associated with various efforts to encourage the local production of food and to mini-mize impact on the environment. There is, therefore, a continuity of con-cerns over the responsible stewardship of resources—a recognition of environmental limits of the land and a concern over the consequences of bad agricultural practices. (See Mook and Sumner in this volume for fur-ther development of the idea of sustainability.)

This is not to suggest that the co-operative movement has functioned perfectly in all respects in its stewardship of rural production, but it does mean that it possesses an ingrained capacity and need to perform responsi-bly, even when the costs may be high. Thus, agricultural co-operatives have traditionally encouraged better practice among their members—as "better practice" has been understood at a given time. People wishing to encourage new forms of husbandry—new ways to raise crops or animals—have often turned to co-operative institutions and arrangements because they are based—or should and can be based—on values that are synergistic. As such, people wishing to create economic entities that are less hierarchical, for example in the distribution of food, can find within the co-operative tradition ways to do so. In an overpoweringly urban society, it is easy to forget or underestimate the strength of rural visions, past and present, and this is nowhere more true than in the English-Canadian co-operative movement. These are also visions that have strong social dimensions derived from the challenges confronting rural communities and rural culture.

A second important perspective for the English-Canadian movement shares roots with the adult education (AE) and community economic development (CED) movements (see Faris 1975), a pattern one can find in countries such as the United Kingdom and the United States as well. In its sharing of such roots, the Canadian movement has historically advocated for the centrality of education and knowledge and links these with individual and community action. The best-known example of this kind of synergy was to be found at St. Francis Xavier University within the university's Extension Department where its Antigonish Movement was located,[9] but, in various ways, the same kind of approach can be found within other educational institutions at various times as well. It can also be found within the history of the co-operative movement in the use of "fieldmen" training programs for elected leaders and support for research/teaching at some universities (see MacPherson 1986). Its spirit can even be seen as continuing in the service learning practices that have been underdevelopment in faculties of education in Canada (see Sousa in this volume).

In essence, this approach often features co-operatives as a particularly useful way in which people in communities can shape their own destiny. It is an open-ended approach that can usefully pursue a wide range of community-based objectives. In the modern period, it has become particularly concerned with issues associated with problems in rural and remote communities, in single-resource towns that are losing their economic base, in pockets of urban decay where such problems as homelessness and under-employment are evident, and in the general issues associated with environmental and energy changes.

The third common perspective emanates from the diverse and complex heritage of the international co-operative movement.[10] This viewpoint reflects the many and varied ways in which people around the world have used co-operatives to respond to social and economic needs. It is a rich tradition that includes several hundred kinds of co-operatives. It is a tradition that

BOX 2.2   Mondragón

The Mondragón Cooperative Corporation is the world's largest worker co-operative, with total assets in excess of 32 billion euros ($52 billion Cdn). Mondragón developed under harsh conditions in General Franco's (1939–1975) Fascist Spain. Its formation was inspired by the teachings of a Catholic priest, José María Arizmendiarrieta. Father José arrived in the Basque area (a unique cultural group in Europe whose traditional territory includes parts of northeastern Spain and southwestern France) in 1941, and two years later set up a professional school to facilitate the spread of technical and social knowledge. In 1956, five of his students formed Mondragón's first worker co-operative, manufacturing paraffin (gas) stoves and heaters. In 1959, again under the guidance of Father José María, the Caja Laboral (the Credit Union of Mondragón) was founded, giving Mondragón a stable source of credit. The Caja precipitated the rapid growth of the co-operative by ensuring that the wealth created by Mondragón stayed in the Basque region and under co-operative control. In the same year, Mondragón founded Lagun-Aro, a social security co-operative built to provide benefits to co-operative members. (The Fascist government of General Franco had passed a law denying co-operative members state welfare benefits.) As a result of these innovations, by the end of the 1960s the number of co-operatives associated with Mondragón had grown to 41, and by 1990 exceeded 100. The success of Mondragón continued beyond the collapse of Fascism in 1975, through the changes brought about by the European Union (including the adoption of the euro currency) and globalization. Mondragón has shown that a social economy organization can operate on a global scale without sacrificing the needs of its members or its social purpose. Mondragón's success as a worker co-operative is evident in its levels of employment; in 2007 Mondragón had a workforce of over 100,000 for the first time in its history.

Further information about Mondragón can be found on its website at http://www.mcc.es/ing/index.asp (where much of the information above was sourced) or in the chapter by Lionias and Johnstone in this volume.

has developed differently in different countries, one that is often associated with other kinds of movements, that has been supported variously by different kinds of governments, and that is constantly being adapted. Historically, the English-Canadian movement has drawn particularly on the experiences of northern Europe (the United Kingdom, Scandinavia, and Germany). In the last few decades, however, it has demonstrated considerable interest in the movements in Spain and northern Italy. Regardless of where they have emerged, however, the perspectives of the international movement have been grounded in social as well as economic change: the class struggles of industrialism, the extensive migration of peoples, and the dislocations caused by disasters, both human-made and natural.

The Co-operative Movement and the Social Economy

It can be argued, therefore, that the English-Canadian co-operative movement is a significant force in the national life; that it has strong and integrated social dimensions as well as economic purposes; and that it has a multifaceted intellectual heritage derived from social and economic circumstances and associations with many groups in Canadian life and with international associations. One way of comprehending what this means is to consider the relationships, real and potential, with the social economy.

BOX 2.3   Intentional Communities

Intentional communities are communities that are consciously constructed to meet a particular need, reach a particular goal, or to serve an identified group. Unlike communities that develop as a result of general socio-economic forces (such as migration for employment purposes), intentional communities are first formed conceptually—they are the result of an idea. Examples of these communities are as various as the ideas of how people should live, but can range from eco-villages to land trusts or communes to housing co-operatives. Famous historical intentional communities would include the kibbutz, the communes of the medieval period as well as the 1960s, and the housing co-operative movement. Especially important for intentional communities, and indeed the social economy, is the fact that these communities rely on a significant level of co-operation and shared vision. As living arrangements, intentional communities combine to a significant degree economic and social concerns.

The idea of the social economy as a concept has historically emerged as a way to understand how people at times reacted to the advent of industrialism, rapid urbanization, and extensive rural change in the 19th century— the process that Karl Polanyi called "the great transformation" (see Polanyi 1944). Typically, advocates of the social economy began with concerns over social issues and the negative consequences of the economic changes wrought by the development of the market economy.[11] They emphasized the ways in which people could organize to overcome such adversities by resisting changes or, just as often, by harnessing those changes for mutual and reciprocal benefit. They championed the development of such structures as worker co-operatives, profit-sharing businesses, trade unions, consumer co-operatives, intentional communities, and stronger municipal governments. The social economy is an approach that, although it also attracted the interest of some advocates of the unregulated market and of moderate socialism, was distinct in its emphasis on dispersed, local control over economic activities and the value of social mobilization. It reacted against using purely economic criteria to measure the success and effectiveness of economic change. It believed in the capacity of what might be called group economic activism derived from such social values as solidarity, reciprocity, and mutuality (see McMurtry in this volume for further development of these ideas.)

As it developed in the 19th and early 20th centuries, the best-known advocates of the social economy were to be found in France, though there were also important leaders in Belgium, Italy, Spain, Portugal, and Greece.[12] The fact that support for the social economy developed in several countries led to somewhat different ideas about what it meant and hindered the development of an international consensus—the same kind of tendency one finds readily enough in the European co-operative movements.[13] The divisions were further intensified by the emergence of the Union of Soviet Socialist Republics (USSR), the First and Second World Wars, the Great Depression, and competition among intellectuals wanting to define the essence of what we now call the social economy approach. Like the co-operative movement itself, the idea of the social economy was buffeted badly by the course of history in the 20th century.

The creation of the European Union (EU) in 1993, along with a general, worldwide reconsideration of the roles of the state, also encouraged a reconsideration of the nature of the international co-operative movement and a growing interest in the possibilities of the social economy. Canadian co-operators were particularly involved in the former process, which culminated in the adoption of a "Statement on the Co-operative Identity" in 1995 (International Co-operative Alliance 2009b). It articulated historic co-operative commitments to the organizational values of self-help, self-responsibility, democracy, equality, equity, and solidarity and the ethical values of honesty, openness, social responsibility, and caring for others. Most important, the "Statement" also gave voice to a deep-seated commitment by co-operators to "the sustainable development of their communities through policies approved by their members" (International Co-operative Alliance 2009b, principle seven).

In the same time frame, some Canadians, especially in Quebec, were following closely the development of the social economy in Europe. The

BOX 2.4 Seven Co-operative Principles

The seven principles of co-operation are the result of over a century of nego-tiations within the International Co-operative Alliance (ICA), which was founded in 1895. The idea of principles comes from the Rochdale Co-operative, founded in 1844, which is often cited as the first modern co-operative. In fact, when the principles were first formalized by the ICA in 1937, they were called "The Rochdale Principles of Co-operation." In their original articulation, there were seven formal and three less formal principles. The principles were revised in 1966 and reduced to six basic principles under the title "Principles of Co-operation." Further revision in 1995 raised the number of principles back to seven. They are:

- Voluntary and open membership
- Democratic member control
- Member economic participation
- Autonomy and independence
- Education, training, and information
- Co-operation among co-operatives
- Concern for community

Full details of these principles and more information about the Inter-national Co-operative Alliance can be found on the ICA website at http://www.ica.coop/al-ica/.

creation of the EU stimulated, much more than did the North American Free Trade Agreement (NAFTA) of the same year, an intense debate over the impact of free trade on social and cultural policies. Many Europeans were concerned that the union would emphasize economic development without concern for social consequences. They wanted to ensure that local communities had the capacity to respond to change and mobilize resources—group as well as individual—in order to meet economic and social needs—in other words, to develop social economy organizations. They lobbied the European Parliament for support of the social economy, leading to the creation of the Social Economy Intergroup, a watchdog and promotional network within the bureaucracy of the European Union. It pays particular attention to the roles that social economy organizations are playing and could play in confronting such issues as those associated with social cohesion, social protection, health, insurances, social services of general interest (SSGI), competition, corporate social responsibility (CSR), and employment practices.[14] In particular, the Social Economy Intergroup emphasizes that the social economy is a key participant, an active agent, in the European economy, not just a caretaker for whatever is left over when the main course of market activities has been run. One of its most important projects has been to understand the nature and extent of the social economy in Europe. The Intergroup commissioned a study in 2006 by the International Centre of Research and Information on the Public, Social and Cooperative Economy (CIRIEC), located in Liège, Belgium; CIRIEC is the main international organization for research into the social economy (Centre International de Recherches et d'Information sur l'Economie Publique, Sociale et Coopérative 2007).[15] The Social Economy Intergroup provides a valuable survey upon which people within the social economy and those responsible for creating policies for its development can visualize opportunities while planning for future growth.

The observers from Quebec, many associated with *Le chantier de l'économie sociale* under the leadership of Nancy Neamtan, plus a cluster of academics, notably Benoît Lévesque, Yves Vaillancourt, Marie Bouchard, Jean-Marc Fontan, and Marjorie Mandell, built on the lessons learned and undertook a systematic analysis of the European, particularly the French, social economy experience. Collaborating with a number of community *acteurs* drawn from a wide variety of organizations and the older established co-operative movement, such as the *Mouvement Desjardins*, they helped develop an increasingly integrated approach to the growth of the social economy in Quebec. It is an approach that has gained the support of the provincial and federal governments and one that has become increasingly integrated within the programs of municipal and local governments. It is a model that English Canadians could profitably examine and perhaps in some ways adapt. The co-operative experience is, in both the Quebecois and European experiences, an important touchstone on which the social economy has been built.

Finding Intersecting Circles of Influence

One can argue, therefore, that the times are propitious for considering creatively how the co-operative movement in English Canada could engage with the social economy approach. The movement possesses a background of social engagement that permeates its history. It has intellectual roots that suggest the possibilities of synergy. The social economy is as valid a range of associations and point of comparison for the movement as are the private companies in the same lines of business—the yardstick with which co-operatives are most often measured and understood. It is one way in which the co-operative movement's social side can be fully engaged, opportunities perceived, and important connections made. It can be a way to reach out to segments of the population, for example, young people, that are important for the movement's future. It can lead to associations in communities that will stand co-operatives in good stead: a way to demonstrate "they walk the walk as well as talk the talk." It can provide opportunities for learning about diverse ways in which institutions with strong social purposes can be managed and for relating to their communities; there are striking examples of effective management techniques among non-profit and mutual organizations. It can contribute a strong economic edge, possibilities for escaping structural, multigenerational dependency on the welfare system that otherwise might expand if the current economic crisis deepens and continues. It can more clearly demonstrate to the public and to governments how effective the co-operative approach can be in addressing an even wider range of issues than it currently does, thereby significantly affecting public policy.

Developing such relationships, however, is not as simple as one might assume. It is only in recent years that the social economy approach, so well established on the European continent and particularly in countries bordering the Mediterranean, has been considered seriously in the northern countries from which so many of the English-Canadian co-operative traditions emanate. The association has not been developed without complexities, past and present (see, for example, Wuelker 1995), so one should not expect it to take place without controversy in English Canada. It has, however, already stimulated some remarkable successes in the United Kingdom and Sweden. On a very fundamental level, this move toward a more *social* economy will mean that many Canadians will have to rethink how the economy can best function. For the last 30 years, most English Canadians have been attracted to the idea that an unregulated market based on individual self-interest will create wealth at such levels that social and economic problems will be dealt with either directly or indirectly. Many very powerful voices articulate those views and, indeed, there is some reason for believing that socially motivated adjustments within the private sector can indeed be helpful in meeting social and economic problems (see, for example, Yunus 2007).

The recent economic problems, however, suggest that there is also a need to give greater appreciation to the possibilities that community-based approaches can bring—in fact, have brought—to English Canadians for generations. They also have demonstrated that community-based enterprises, such as co-operatives, while less likely to engage in rapid expansion, are more likely to avoid the problems that overstimulation can bring. Organizations operating in the economy on the values underlying the co-operative movement or the social economy in general offer ways to mobilize community resources to meet social and economic needs and to undertake economic activities that individuals alone cannot—and that the mainstream economy might not—visualize as sustainable. Many co-operative organizations have been developed amid such doubt. Indeed, one might say that almost all of the successful co-operatives today began that way—they were not taken seriously at first except by their proponents.

Associations between co-operatives and the social economy have also to be pursued in a spirit of openness and mutual respect. If one approaches the possibilities of greater cohesion among the three most readily understood institutional forms (the non-profit sector, co-operatives, and mutuals), it is important to understand that they have developed in their own ways in English Canada; that they do have differences in structures and interests that deserve respect; that any notion that the three would suddenly coalesce into some kind of completely integrated "force" is naive; or that the rapid emergence of some supra social economy organization is hardly realistic—or perhaps not even desirable. There is value in difference, both for what might be accomplished and, more important, for what communities might choose to do.

The goal should not be an alternative hierarchical system, but rather a series of circles of influence and experience that intersect when useful and that remain in regular and frequent communication with one another. In fact, one reason for pursuing the social economy approach should be to understand more thoroughly the differences among community-based alternatives to economic and social development, and to explore more systematically how they can most effectively operate, what kinds of benefits they can create, and how they can be most effectively supported through government, foundation, and academic involvement. There is a need to work together systematically to develop ongoing, tended research bases so that advocates of the social economy can respond effectively to the intellectual challenges associated with other forms of economic development; so that they can build effective educational programs; and so that they can engage meaningfully in public policy discussions.

Conclusion

The social economy approach elsewhere cannot be studied and then applied like a blanket over or even as a model for English Canada, as inspiring as it might be to read about such endeavours or, better still, to visit them. There are, of course, great benefits to be had in examining social economy experiences in other countries, as Quebec has demonstrated in its study of its European predecessors. But, in the final analysis, each society must develop its own ways of understanding which institutions and practices of the social economy can be most effectively undertaken in its own context. There is a need, then, for the collection of information, but also for careful reflection and prudent application. There is a need for appreciating, even encouraging, differences. There is value in not ascribing to any one form of the social economy organization a primacy of place or influence, as hard as that is in the North Atlantic world among proponents of each form or among academics generally. There is no need to have someone in first place.

The gathering social and economic clouds of our times, as with other periods of human history, warrant more consideration than has been recently evident in general in English Canada about how community-based, socially concerned initiatives can be harnessed for the common good. It is an old story for which new chapters have to be prepared and written. Reflecting on the insights and possibilities of the social economy framework and stimulating collaboration among its enthusiasts and organizations would be a helpful way to begin to do so.

Glossary

Agricultural co-operative   A co-operative that defines its membership as agricultural producers (and therefore is often called simply a producer co-operative). Some of the economic needs met by this type of co-operative are access to markets, better prices for goods, and economies of scale for smaller producers. Some of the social needs met by this type of co-operative are sustainable rural communities, food security, and member empowerment.

Consumer co-operative   A co-operative that defines its membership as its consumers. These co-operatives have their roots in the Rochdale Co-operative, founded in 1844. Some of the economic needs met by this type of co-operative are quality or hard-to-source goods at affordable prices. Some of the social needs met by this type of co-operative are community decision making, quality control, and member empowerment.

Co-operative   A democratic, member-owned and -operated organization whose primary goal is to the membership's economic and social needs. "Member-owned" means that the members (not outside investors) control the organization economically, and "member-operated" means that members also manage the affairs of the organization, either directly or through oversight. Membership may be defined in various ways that modify the concept of co-operative, but membership control is a co-operative's defining feature.

Worker co-operative   A co-operative that defines its membership as its workers. Some of the economic needs met by this type of co-operative are wages and sustainable and meaningful work. Some of the social needs met by this type of co-operative are employment and member empowerment.

Notes

1. As early as the 1780s Loyalist farmers in Lower Canada (Quebec) were collaborating to export grains. In the 1820s and 1830s, discussions about organizing a co-operative store as well as the co-operative marketing of farm produce took place in Upper Canada (Ontario). The most commonly used starting points for the co-operative movement, however, were the formation of the first consumer co-op in Stellarton, Nova Scotia in 1864 and the development of cheese factories at about the same time.

2. Information on the great variety of new co-operatives can be found on the websites of the Centre for the Study of Co-operatives, University of Saskatchewan (see Centre for the Study of Co-operatives 2009) and the British Columbia Institute for Co-operative Studies (see British Columbia Institute for Co-operative Studies 2009).

3. For information on co-operatives in indigenous communities, see Hammond-Ketilson and MacPherson (2001).

4. For a series of articles that refer to the social dimensions of co-operatives, see MacPherson and McLaughlin-Jenkins (2008), especially the chapters by Roger Spear, Leslie Brown and Viola Winstanley, Panu Kalmi, Stephen Yeo, and Ian MacPherson.

5. There is no history of the national credit union movement, though one is in process of being written by the present author. Two provincial histories in which the theme of credit union contributions to the suburbanization of Canada is dealt with in passing can be found in Purden (1980) and MacPherson (1995).

6. See Cole (2008, 82–83) for a very brief survey of the program.

7. See Welton (2001) and Laidlaw (1971).

8. See MacPherson (1979) (in which the rural dimensions of co-operative development are pervasive themes), Fulton and Sanderson (2005), and Tunnicliffe (2008).

9. See Welton's book *Little Mosie from the Margaree* (2001) for the most recent examination of the Antigonish movement, albeit through the eyes of Moses Coady. Further references to the rich historiography of the movement can be found in this book's references and bibliography.

10. See the chapters in MacPherson and McLaughlin-Jenkins (2008), especially those by Stephen Yeo, Rita Rhodes, Jean-François Draperi, and Ian MacPherson. See also MacPherson (2008).
11. There have been numerous efforts to analyze the development of the social economy. See, for example, Bidet (1997), Defourny and Develetere (1997), Defourny and Campos (1992), and Laville (2003). For a global perspective, see Defourny and Develtere (1999). See also Smith and McKitrick (forthcoming).
12. For example, see Desroche (1991) and Moulaert and Ailenei (2005).
13. These tensions can be readily observed in Watkins (1970), Birchall (1995), and Rhodes (1995).
14. See Social Economy Europe (2009).
15. For a summary of the report, see European Economic and Social Committee (2009).

Discussion Questions

1. How do co-operatives change in form and focus to reflect the changing nature of Canadian society economically and demographically?
2. What features of co-operatives make them form an "intersecting circle of influence" with the social economy? How are they distinct?
3. To what extent is it possible to call the co-operative movement "Canadian," as opposed to "western," "Ontarian," "francophone," or "maritime"? What issues does this raise?

Suggested Further Readings and Resources

Birchall, J. 1995. *The international co-operative movement*. Manchester: University of Manchester Press.

Cole, L. 2008. *Under construction: A history of co-operative housing*. Ottawa: Borealis.

Fairbairn, B. 1989. *Building a dream: The co-operative retailing system in western Canada, 1928–1988*. Saskatoon: Western Producer Prairie Books.

Laidlaw, A. 1971. *The man from Margaree: Writings and speeches of M.M. Coady*. Toronto: McClelland and Stewart.

MacPherson, I. 1979. *Each for all: A history of the co-operative movement in English-Canada, 1900–1945*. Toronto: Macmillan.

References

Bidet, E. 1997. *L'économie sociale*. Paris: Le Monde-Éditions.

Birchall, J. 1995. *The international co-operative movement*. Manchester: University of Manchester Press.

British Columbia Institute for Co-operative Studies (BCICS). 2009. Homepage. http://www.bcics.org.

Centre for the Study of Co-operatives, University of Saskatchewan. 2009. Homepage. http://www.usaskstudies.coop.

Centre International de Recherches et d'Information sur l'Economie Publique, Sociale et Coopérative (CIRIEC). 2007. The social economy in the European Union. Liège: Université de Liege. http://www.ciriec.ulg.ac.be.

Cole, L. 2008. *Under construction: A history of co-operative housing*. Ottawa: Borealis.

Co-operatives Secretariat. 2007. *Co-operatives in Canada*. Ottawa: Co-operatives Secretariat.

Co-operatives Secretariat. 2008. *Co-operatives in Canada*. Ottawa: Co-operatives Secretariat.

Credit Union Central of Canada. 2009. The credit union difference. http://www.cucentral.ca/FirstsQuickFacts.

Defourny, J., and M. Campos. 1992. *Économie sociale: Third sector*. Brussels: De Boeck Université.

Defourny, J., and P. Develetere 1997. Jalons pour un clarification des débats sur l'économie sociale. http://www.globenet.org/horizon-local/ada/9721.html.

Defourny, J., and P. Develtere. 1999. The social economy: The worldwide making of a third sector. In *Social economy: North and south*, ed. J. Defourny, P. Develtere, and B. Fonteneau, 25–56. Brussels: De Boeck Université.

Desroche, H. 1991. *Histoire d'économie sociale*. Paris: Syros.

Emmanuel, J., ed. 2007. *A passion for possibilities: Co-operatives and communities in British Columbia*. Victoria: British Columbia Institute for Co-operative Studies.

European Economic and Social Committee (EESC). 2009. *Social economy*. Brussels: EESC. http://www.eesc.europa.eu/groups/3/index_en.asp?id=1405GR03EN.

Fairbairn, B. 1989. *Building a dream: The co-operative retailing system in western Canada, 1928–1988*. Saskatoon: Western Producer Prairie Books.

Faris, R. 1975. *The passionate educators: Voluntary associations and the struggle for control of educational broadcasting in Canada, 1919–1952*. Toronto: Peter Martin.

Fulton, M., and K. Sanderson. 2005. *Co-operatives and farmers in the new agriculture*. Occasional paper series. Saskatoon: Centre for the Study of Co-operatives, University of Saskatchewan.

Hammond-Ketilson, L., and I. MacPherson, eds. 2001. *A report on aboriginal co-operatives in Canada: Current situation and potential for growth.* Saskatoon: Centre for the Study of Co-operatives. http://www.usaskstudies.coop.

International Co-operative Alliance (ICA). 2009a. Homepage. http://www.ica.coop/al-ica.

International Co-operative Alliance (ICA). 2009b. Statement on the co-operative identity. http://www.ica.coop/coop/principles.html.

Laidlaw, A. 1971. *The man from Margaree: Writings and speeches of M.M. Coady.* Toronto: McClelland and Stewart.

Laville, J.-L. 2003. A new European socioeconomic perspective. *Review of Social Economy* 61 (3): 289–405.

MacPherson, I. 1972. The origins of the Canadian co-operative movement. *Historical Papers.* Canadian Historical Association.

MacPherson, I. 1979. *Each for all: A history of the co-operative movement in English-Canada, 1900–1945.* Toronto: Macmillan.

MacPherson, I. 1986. Missionaries for rural development: The fieldmen of the Saskatchewan Wheat Pool, 1925–1945. *Agricultural History* 60 (2): 73–96.

MacPherson, I. 1995. *Co-operation, conflict and co-ordination: B.C. Central and the credit union movement in British Columbia to 1995.* Vancouver: BC Central Credit Union.

MacPherson, I. 2007. *One path to co-operative studies: A selection of papers and presentations.* Victoria: British Columbia Institute for Co-operative Studies.

MacPherson, I. 2008. The co-operative movement and the social economy traditions: Reflections on the mingling of broad visions. *Annals of Public and Co-operative Economy* 79 (3–4): 625–642.

MacPherson, I., and E. McLaughlin-Jenkins. 2008. *Integrating diversities within a complex heritage: Essays in the field of co-operative studies.* Victoria: New Rochdale.

Moulaert, F., and O. Ailenei. 2005. Social economy, third sector and solidarity relations: A conceptual synthesis from history to the present. *Urban Studies* 42 (11): 2037–2053.

Polanyi, K. 1944. *The great transformation: The political and economic origins of our time.* Boston: Beacon.

Purden, C. 1980. *Agents for change: Credit unions in Saskatchewan.* Regina: Saskatchewan Co-operative Credit Society.

Rhodes, R. 1995. *The International Co-operative Alliance during war and peace.* Geneva: International Co-operative Alliance.

Smith, J., and A. McKitrick. Forthcoming. Current conceptualisations of the social economy in the Canadian context. Victoria: Social Economy Hub, Canadian Social Economy Research Partnerships.

Smith, J., R. Puga, and I. MacPherson. 2006. *Youth reinventing co-operatives.* Victoria: British Columbia Institute for Co-operative Studies.

Social Economy Europe (2009). Social Economy Intergroup. http://www.socialeconomy.eu.org/spip.php?rubrique60.

Tunnicliffe, R. 2008. *Saanich Organics: A model for sustainable agriculture through co-operation.* Occasional paper series. Victoria: British Columbia Institute for Co-operative Studies.

Watkins, W.P. 1970. *The International Co-operative Alliance, 1895–1970.* London: International Co-operative Alliance.

Welton, M.R. 2001. *Little Mosie from the Margaree: A biography of Moses Coady.* Toronto: Thompson Educational.

Wilson, K. 2005. *Practical dreamers: Communitarianism and co-operatives on Malcom Island.* Victoria: British Columbia Institute for Co-operative Studies.

Wuelker, H.D. 1995. The social economy and co-ops: A German perspective. Geneva: International Co-operative Alliance. http://www.uwcc.wisc.edu/icic/orgs/ica/pubs/review/vol-88-2/21.html.

Yunus, M. 2007. *Creating a world without poverty: Social business and the future of capitalism.* New York: Public Affairs.

CHAPTER THREE

The Social Economy in Quebec and Canada: Configurations Past and Present

YVES VAILLANCOURT

Introduction

I well remember in the late 1990s the assertions in public talks of Nancy Neamtan (a leader in community economic development in southwestern Montreal), in a manner rather like Molière's character who unknowingly spoke in prose, that she had long been doing social economy without realizing it. In speaking that way, this well-known social economy leader was expressing a common feeling. Indeed, while the social economy has existed de facto in Quebec for more than a century and a half, it has been referred to explicitly in public discourse for less than 20 years. As we documented in a literature review (Jetté et al. 2000), it was from 1995 onward that the concept of social economy began to be used by a significant number of practitioners, decision-makers, and researchers.[1] Prior to that, the expression was rarely used. Quebecers were doing social economy without realizing it.[2]

In the past, I have often written papers on the social economy, but this is the first opportunity I have had to write a chapter on the social economy in Quebec that will appear in English in a book on the social economy in Canada and intended for a primarily English-speaking readership. This context encouraged me to find a way of covering the social economy in Quebec while seeking to establish a dialogue with English-Canadian readers. Thus, this chapter has a preoccupation with comparisons between the Quebec and Canadian contexts.

In this paper, I shall use the concept of social economy in its broad, inclusive sense, as I have done elsewhere, and very much along the lines of the definition proposed by the Groupe de travail sur l'économie sociale (GTES, Working Group on the Social Economy) at the Quebec Summit on the Economy and Employment in the fall of 1996 (GTES 1996). At that time, this inclusive definition had not only been proposed by the GTES at the summit, it had also been accepted by the socio-economic partners and the Quebec government. As a result, it subsequently became an official definition that was often repeated by the Chantier de l'économie sociale (CÉS, Task Force on the Social Economy), sometimes with minor variations (CÉS 2001, CÉS et al. 2005).

It is worthwhile to examine this type of broad, inclusive definition used, among others, by the CÉS since 1996. Here is an example from a paper drafted in 2005 by the CÉS in co-operation with the Canadian Community Economic Development Network (CCEDNet) and the Alliance de Recherche Universités-Communautés en économie sociale (ARUC-ÉS, Community-University Research Alliance in the Social Economy) (CÉS et al. 2005, 17):

> As a whole, the social economy refers to the set of activities and organizations stemming from collective entrepreneurship, organized around the following principles and operating rules: 1) the purpose of a social economy enterprise is to serve its members or the community rather than to simply make profits; 2) it operates at arm's length from the state; 3) it promotes a democratic management process involving all users and/or workers through its statutes and the way it does business; 4) it defends the primacy of individuals and work over capital in the distribution of its surpluses and revenues; 5) it bases its activities on the principles of participation and individual and collective empowerment. The social economy therefore encompasses all co-operative and mutual movements and associations. The social economy can be developed in all sectors that meet the needs of the people and the community.

Like others in the same vein produced over the years by the CÉS, this definition emphasizes values—democracy, autonomy, empowerment—and draws on theoretical contributions from Belgium. It represents an *ideal type*—that is, an ideal to be constantly pursued, even if it is never fully achieved. It builds on the conjunction of deeply entwined economic and social goals. We describe it as broad and inclusive, insofar as it includes not only enterprises, but also organizations and activities. In other words, this definition makes room not only for market components—enterprises selling goods and services on the market—but also for non-market components funded from public subsidies and private philanthropic giving that provide their goods and services without charge (Vaillancourt et al. 2004; Vaillancourt 2006). As we shall see below (in the "1990–2008" section), this broad, inclusive definition allows us to put forward the idea that the social economy in Quebec currently includes 14,775 organizations and enterprises—including 8,000 community organizations or non-market associations—representing some 167,541 jobs.[3]

Since 1996, this type of definition has often been repeated by the CÉS and a number of its partners in the field and in research. But this does not mean it is always used consistently,[4] nor that it is the subject of consensus among stakeholders, decision-makers, and researchers. Nevertheless, it represents a good reference for the debate (see issue number 1 in the summary section below), and we shall use it as the underlying thread in this chapter.

This chapter has three main sections. In the first, I take as my own the timeline recently produced by Benoît Lévesque (2007, 2008a) concerning five successive "dominant configurations of the social economy" over the century and a half of history of social economy in Quebec. In the second, referring to the last three stages in Lévesque's timeline, I compare Quebec's historical legacy in the social economy field with the English-Canadian legacy, and this prompts me to express some thoughts on what I shall call Quebec's missed date with social democracy. In the third, I examine six specific issues with respect to the social economy in Quebec.

Five Dominant Configurations in the History of the Social Economy in Quebec

To summarize the history of the social economy in Quebec, I begin with the contribution of a researcher who has long been interested in the history of the social economy in Quebec, North America, and Europe. I refer in particular to two recent papers in which Benoît Lévesque (2007, 2008a) proposes an original interpretation of 150 years of the development of the social economy in Quebec. In his analysis, Lévesque distinguishes five "dominant configurations of the social economy." I very much like this concept of dominant configurations. On the one hand, it allows us to review the history of the social economy, less with a view to producing a *quantitative mapping* of the social economy than with the intention of *identifying the dynamic relations of the social economy with other elements in its sociohistorical environment*—social movements, the state, the market, churches, international networks, and so on. On the other hand, by looking at the dominant configurations of the social economy over a given historical period, one recognizes that there are also, at the same time, "dominated configurations."

In recalling the five dominant configurations identified by Lévesque, I have two pedagogical aims. On the one hand, I echo a rereading of the history of the social economy in Quebec that I find well documented and well packaged and likely to be helpfully enlightening to readers in English who might not otherwise have access to his work. On the other hand, I provide a historical point of reference that I can use for discussion in the rest of the chapter.

1. 1840–1900: Mutual Aid Societies—Social Economy Independent of Traditional Elites

In the 1840–1900 period, the dominant configuration in the social economy field was marked by the emergence of mutual aid societies in working-class urban areas. During the 19th century, no fewer than 253 mutual aid societies appeared in Quebec. In the early 20th century, Lévesque (2008a), on the basis of research by historian Martin Petitclerc (2007), stated that mutual societies had 150,000 members, or approximately 35 percent of adult urban males. These mutual societies promoted values of autonomy, solidarity, and self-management within working-class social strata in urban settings. They enabled the workers and their families who belonged to these societies, in exchange for a social rather than a commercial contribution,[5] to acquire protection covering them against the risks of unemployment, illness, accident, disability, age, fire, and so on. These societies developed in the manner of an autonomous social movement as against the influence of the traditional French-Canadian Catholic elites. The societies' autonomy was also manifested in relation to the state, which did not intervene in social policy. The societies predated the labour unions, but when the Knights of Labour were at their height during the 1880s, they would promote these societies just as much as they promoted production and distribution co-operatives (Lévesque 2007, 5–6).

At the same time, in rural environments, there was another configuration, but a *dominated* one, that promoted the formula of farming co-operatives. Unlike the dominant configuration, this one involved a more conservative social economy subject to the influence of the clerical elites. In terms of its international contacts, this configuration was tied in with networks fostering the conservative vision of the social economy specific to the French, Catholic school of Frédéric Le Play, which stood out from other more secular and socialist schools.

2. 1900–1930: Patron-Led Social Economy

In the 1900–1930 period, the configuration of the social economy became dominated by the traditional elites associated with the Catholic Church, not only in rural but also in urban areas. There was a rise in the number of mutual societies, but the mutualist movement lost the autonomy it enjoyed in the preceding period with respect to traditional elites. The influence of the French social economy school of Le Play and the social doctrine of the Catholic Church increased. It was implemented in the province by the Société canadienne de l'économie sociale de Montréal (SCÉSM), founded in 1888, and the Jesuits' École sociale populaire (ÉSP), set up in 1911. Farm co-operatives remained important in rural settings. The first Caisse populaire d'épargne et de crédit (savings and credit union) was founded in Lévis in 1900 by Alphonse Desjardins, himself a member of the SCÉSM. But the Mouvement des caisses populaires would begin to spread from the second decade of the 20th century on, "with the explicit support of the Catholic Church. In 1920, out of the 160 credit unions, 140 had a priest as leader and 116 as chairman" (Lévesque 2008a, 5). Thus, the emergent social economy within this dominant configuration at this time was "built on the patronage of social authorities" (Lévesque 2008a, 3).

3. 1930–1960: Social Economy Embedded in the Corporatist Doctrine

The dominant configuration of the 1930–1960 period follows the vein of the previous period. To respond to the problems of the economic crisis of the Great Depression and stem the contagion of anti-capitalist ideas and movements coming from the rest of Canada, in particular the western provinces, the traditional elites first grouped together in March 1933 around the Jesuits of the ÉSP, and launched a "social restoration" program (ÉSP 1934).

In fact, the social restoration program was drawn up in two stages. The first went back to a study day held on March 9, 1933 and led to the ÉSP's first program. On that day, emphasis was placed on doctrinal and moral dimensions, and the resource persons involved were 13 priests and prelates.[6] The second stage occurred in September 1933, and took the form of a second study day in which the resource people were a dozen secular individuals, including Esdras Minville from the École des Hautes études commerciales (HÉC). Emphasis was placed on socio-economic dimensions, and the presentations were subsequently to constitute ÉSP's second program. In the following months, the first and second programs brought together a large number of organizations from civil society at large.[7] This even led to the birth of a new political party, Action libérale nationale (ALN), headed by Paul Gouin.[8]

The ideas from the two ÉSP programs are central to the corporatist configuration that dominated the period. This configuration:

- was explicitly based on the Catholic Church's social doctrine (including Pope Pius XI's encyclical Quadragesimo Anno, issued in 1931);

BOX 3.1   Desjardins

The Desjardins Group (Mouvement des caisses Desjardins in French) is Canada's largest financial co-operative (credit union). With over 5 million members and $152 billion in assets in 2008, it is the largest credit union association in North America, the sixth largest financial institution in Canada, and the largest financial organization in Quebec. Because of its size and co-operative nature, Desjardins is intricately intertwined with the history of Quebec in the 20th century, and is specifically important to the history and development of the social economy in that province. Inspired by the credit union movement in Europe, Alphonse Desjardins founded the first "caisse populaire" in Lévis, Quebec on December 6, 1900 (it became operational the next year). Originally, Desjardins focused on developing a national credit union movement, and he lobbied the Canadian government for legislation to govern financial co-operatives. Ultimately, however, Desjardins was unsuccessful in his efforts. Not one to be easily discouraged, Desjardins turned his attention toward his home province of Quebec, where recognition for credit unions was given in 1906 through the *Loi concernant les syndicats coopératifs* (the Act respecting cooperative organizations), placing the caisse under provincial jurisdiction. With this recognition, Desjardins founded 146 individual caisses populaire from 1907 to 1914. After his death on October 31, 1920 these individual co-operatives, under Desjardins' inspiration, formed themselves into a federation in 1921, and the modern basis for the organization was laid. Desjardins has been central in the development of the social economy in Quebec because of its role in providing financing, logistical, and political support throughout the 20th century, as is outlined in the rest of this chapter. It is interesting to note that English Canada has had no single parallel institution to encourage and support the growth of the social economy.

FIGURE 3.1
Mouvement Desjardins Statistics

Assets: $144 billion

Employees: 40,000, including 3,000 outside Quebec

Quebecers doing business with Desjardins: 5.8 million

Transactions performed by close to 2 million users: 672 million

- advocated a socio-political blueprint for social corporatism, building on intermediary institutions so as to curb more effectively the need to resort to state intervention in economic and social development, and culminating in virulent anti-statism;
- denounced the abuses of capitalism, including foreign (that is, English-Canadian and American) monopolies that ignored the common good;
- defended the principle of private property, notably of the means of production;
- was against communism and socialism, in both the Marxist form and the social democratic or labour form;[9]
- built on a preservationist nationalism based on protecting the specific French-Canadian, Catholic nature of Quebec society, clearly differentiated from the specific Anglo-Saxon, Protestant nature of English-Canadian society (Angers 1955, 176–179, 370–373); and
- set store by the social economy, in the form of mutual societies, producer and consumer co-operatives, and charitable organizations, provided, though, that these social economy initiatives followed the benchmarks of the corporatist, nationalist, Catholic project.

This period was marked by "exceptional" growth in the co-operative movement, not only in agriculture, savings, and credit, but also in such new areas as consumer protection, fisheries, housing, electricity, telephones, and the student world. The advances in the social economy of the time did not enjoy smooth sailing, though, but took place alongside tensions and conflicts.

It was during this period, in 1939, that Father Georges-Henri Lévesque (on whom, see note 6) founded the Conseil supérieur de la coopération (CSC, Superior Council of Co-operation) (Lévesque 2008a, 6), the forerunner of today's Conseil québécois de la coopération et de la mutualité (CQCM). The CSC of the time represented a more secular trend within the social economy, in contradiction to the Catholic religious character with which the dominant configuration was heavily imbued. This was expressed in the CSC manifesto, which advocated non-denominational co-operatives (Lévesque 2007, 18–21; 2008a, 6–7). This choice led to divisions within the co-operative family, as Benoît Lévesque (2008a, 7) points out:

> In 1942, the Fédération des caisses populaires withdrew from the CSC, owing to opposition from the Union régionale de Montréal, which feared outside interference and was against the principle of non-denominationality. This dispute, which intensified in 1945, revealed two different conceptions of co-operation, nationalism, and the place of religion in the economy. For the

Quebec City School of Social Science, co-operation represented an end in itself owing to its rules, whereas, for the supporters of corporatism [more rooted at that time in the Montreal area], it was a means toward collective emancipation. (translation)

These divisions among trends within the large social economy family manifested themselves not only with respect to issues internal to Quebec society. They were also manifested in debates concerning the links to be fostered with social economy stakeholders in the rest of Canada and in other countries. For instance, with the rise of co-operatives that were close to a social democratic party, such as the Co-operative Commonwealth Federation (CCF) in Saskatchewan, the question was whether co-operative groups in Quebec could meet with leaders of co-operatives visiting Quebec (Lévesque 2008a, 7). The perception of different interests both within and outside Quebec led to a fractured social economy "movement" in the Canadian context (see MacPherson and McMurtry in this volume). This fracturing has continued to some degree up until today (for examples, see Guy and Heneberry in this volume).

In short, during these years, social economy circles were one of many settings for the expression of significant ideological struggles in Quebec society. The viewpoint espoused by G.-H. Lévesque and the School of Social Science at Laval University, one more favourable to the separation of church and state and more open to state intervention in social development, was a minority view during the period 1938 to 1945. But following the Second World War, the hegemony of the corporatist configuration began to decline, as can be seen in organizations that previously stood in line with this configuration, such as the Confédération des syndicats catholiques du Canada (CTCC), the Fédération des unions industrielles du Québec (FUIQ), the newspaper Le Devoir, and various Catholic social movements (Clavette 2005, chap. 15; Vaillancourt 1988, chap. 3). A rise in pluralistic ideas and projects took place. In short, the social economy was no longer reduced to operating largely along conservative lines, as had been the case during the golden age of the corporatist configuration.

4. 1960–1990: Social Economy Embedded in Economic Nationalism

During the 1960s and 1970s, the traditional corporatist and nationalist current ceased to dominate, but it did not disappear.[10] A new dominant configuration emerged, marking the evolution of the social economy toward an environment characterized by greater pluralism with respect to ideas and values.

The new configuration that emerged and dominated during the period bore, according to Lévesque (2007, 2008a), the following characteristics:

- the rise of a new, modern nationalism manifested not only on the cultural and social fronts, but also on the economic and political fronts, in both urban and rural areas;
- value was given to state intervention in social and economic development, leading to cases of nationalization (Hydro-Québec) and the establishment of several Crown corporations, including the Société générale de financement (SGF) in 1963 and the Société de développement coopératif (SDC) in 1967; these corporations would act along the lines of joint ventures involving linkages between state, private, and co-operative capital, with participation from Mouvement Desjardins (Lévesque 2007, 25–28);
- ambivalence on the part of the co-operative and community movement toward the state and the new economic nationalism; two socio-economic currents were present during the 1980s: "first, the dominant current of co-operation embedded in economic nationalism, then the current of emerging co-operatives contesting economic nationalism in favour of democratizing the economy" (Lévesque 2008a, 8);
- increased involvement of the public sector in several areas of collective life, in particular social policy and education;
- assertion of the autonomy of the state and civil society in relation to the church (secularization, de-denominalization); and
- desire for joint action with the state on the part of a section of co-operatives and associations; growing segments of the co-operative and non-profit sectors demanded Quebec government support for local development, employment, and services (Favreau and Lévesque 1996).

The evolution of the social economy in this configuration in Quebec at this time can be summarized as follows:

- remarkable growth in Mouvement Desjardins, through the support of the Quebec government, which amended the legislation concerning co-operatives and authorized the creation of new tools to facilitate Desjardins' participation in economic development, including Société d'investissement Desjardins (SID) (Lévesque 2007, 26–28);
- the emergence from 1965 onward of the Associations coopératives d'économie familiale (ACEF) movement, and from the 1970s of the non-profit child-care-centre movement;

- the development, from the 1970s, of associations and co-operatives in the culture and communications field (for example, community radio stations);
- an increase in the number of housing co-operatives and Quebec government policy to support them;
- a loosening of the policies around saving banks, which were adapted to the needs of labour unions and which represent an alternative model to the credit unions (caisses populaires) tied to the parish (Lévesque 2007, 20–21);
- recognition on the part of the Quebec government through financial support, from the late 1970s onward, of community and volunteer organizations that look after the elderly, women, young people, and so on (Jetté 2008);
- difficulties imposed on many co-operatives by the 1980s financial crisis, including the bankruptcies of Pêcheurs-Unis and Magasins Co-op (Lévesque 2007, 31–32); other co-operatives came out intact by opting to restructure with state assistance; and
- the appearance of a new economic militancy on the part of unions and community organizations; this militancy was expressed in local and regional development and the struggle to create and maintain jobs, and was also seen in the creation in 1983 of the Fonds de solidarité FTQ (Solidarity Fund QFL [Quebec Federation of Labour]) and in the rise of community economic development corporations (CEDCs) and community development corporations (CDCs).

Inasmuch as it stretched over a 30-year period (1960s–1980s) marked by rapid social change, this period was not homogeneous in certain respects. As a result, subperiodization is required in order to clarify what occurred at the beginning or end of the period. For instance, the welfare state was developing rapidly across Canada in the 1960s and 1970s, but was in crisis and undergoing transformation from the 1980s onward. Furthermore, in terms of the development of ideology, social democratic ideas emerged clearly in public discourse during the second half of the 1960s, especially in social movements.

Crucially, the rift between social democracy and Marxist socialism widened during the 1970s, and recognition of this is central to an understanding of the evolution of debates within social movements. To begin with, Marxism, understood as an analytical tool, made significant inroads in social movements, and certain progressive circles dedicated themselves to researching, spreading information about, and training social actors in this theoretical approach. From about 1973 or 1974, Marxism was influential as a tool for guiding action to transform society. There was an emergence and rise of Marxist and Leninist political groups of various stripes (Stalinist, Maoist, Trotskyist, etc.), along with divisive debates on the famous "correct line" for creating revolution. Far-left groups would have an influence in union, community, co-operative, feminist, and student movements, as well as in CEGEPs (colleges of general and vocational education in Quebec—community colleges—but attendance at which was required as a step to enter university), universities, and progressive Christian organizations. Beginning in the 1980s, this far left reached its nadir and began petering out in a context marked by the clear victory of the "No" side in the 1980 Quebec sovereignty referendum and especially by the crisis in

---

BOX 3.2   Sovereignty Movement in Quebec

One might locate the origin of the sovereignty movement in Quebec in France's surrender of its territory in North America to Britain at the end of the Seven Years' War (1756–1763). From this point onward, French-speaking communities have felt, to varying degrees, under threat of cultural annihilation in the face of a large and growing English (and later non-French) population. This fear has been periodically expressed in different ways—perhaps most famously in the Lower Canada Rebellion of 1837.

The contemporary sovereignty movement in Quebec has its roots in the 1960s and the Quiet Revolution (see Box 3.4). Out of this period of turmoil emerged two important social and political forces. The first was the Front de libération du Québec (FLQ), a revolutionary organization combining the appeals of socialism and independence. Broad sympathy for the political convictions of this organization within Quebec served as a significant barometer of the desire for sovereignty. Although the FLQ collapsed rapidly after they kidnapped and killed Pierre Laporte (a provincial Cabinet minister) in 1970, the idea of Quebec as an occupied society remained in the popular consciousness. The second significant, and longer-lasting, social force to emerge from this period was the Parti Québécois (PQ). This social-democratic political party was founded in 1968 in a merger of two other parties, and was famously led by René Lévesque until 1985. The Parti Québécois has embodied the ideas of Quebec sovereignty, leading the province's two attempts to achieve independence through referendum and, importantly for the social economy, numerous projects in support of the unique social and cultural aspirations of the population of Quebec. Support for the party, and sovereignty itself, continues to be high in Quebec, ranging from around 30 to 45 percent.

the welfare state and public finances more generally, which intensified from the 1981–82 fiscal year onward.

These new ideological and political rifts during the 1970s and part of the 1980s led to a host of sterile conflicts not only in social movements but also in the co-operative and community components of the social economy. The Conseil de la coopération du Québec (CCQ) was not free of such debates (Lévesque 2008a, 8). In this context, a segment of the progressive forces tended to distrust the social economy.[11] Some even ended up criticizing the co-operatives, reproaching them for being an obstacle to socialism.

5. 1990–2008: Recognition of the Social and Solidarity Economy

The dominant configuration in this period featured a more formal recognition of the social and solidarity economy. This recognition stemmed from both civil and political society. It was shared by the different components (co-operative, mutual society, and community) and by the different generations (old and new). But this did not mean that all the players who belong *objectively* to the social economy recognized themselves *subjectively* in the concept of social economy. With increasing recognition, the social economy during the period became more diversified, dynamic, and pluralistic. It posted significant progress, leading in turn to further upheaval, tension, and conflict. These tensions arose among various components, or families, of the social and solidarity economy (the latter being a component of the social economy more focused on social justice and a critique of capitalism) that competed among one another for a better place in the sun. Tensions also arose between the large family of the social and solidarity economy on the one hand and stakeholders in the public and the private economy on the other. In fact, recognition of the social and solidarity economy was disruptive insofar as it led to the breakdown of the dominant frameworks for binary analysis that tended to see only the state and the market—frameworks that for decades had dominated public discourse in Quebec as well as the rest of Canada.

In his analysis of the dominant configuration of the fifth period, Lévesque identified 1996 as a pivotal year for recognition of the social and solidarity economy in Quebec in reference to the decisions made at the two socio-economic summits organized by the new Parti Québécois (PQ) government under Lucien Bouchard that had been elected in January 1996. Lévesque pointed out that the long-term preparation of the two 1996 summits, quite as much as their staging, were not the outcome of some modern corporatist approach in which the government was held hostage to interest groups (Esping-Andersen 1990, 1999), but rather were the product of *democratic co-construction* (Lévesque and Mendel 1999, 2005; Lévesque 2007, 57; Vaillancourt 2008b).[12] This co-construction was made possible by two factors: on the one hand, through the participation of elected officials and a variety of players from the labour world (unions and employers' organizations) and civil society (community organizations, universities, churches, etc.); on the other hand, because the deliberations that took place between these various socio-economic and socio-political players led to public policy decisions that took the shape of *institutionalized compromises* in line with the general interest.[13]

Lévesque emphasized as a crucial factor the *preparation for the summits* during the 1990s by social economy organizations. This led him to identify a series of initiatives from civil society that challenged various public authorities, notably the Quebec government. Among the initiatives mentioned were:

- the Employment Forum in the early 1990s;
- the symposium on community action organized by the Victoriaville Community Development Corporation in 1986;
- the 1989 symposium on community economic development organized by the Programme économique de Pointe-St-Charles, which would later become Regroupement économique et social du Sud-Ouest (RÉSO) (Group for the Economic and Social Recovery of Southwestern Montreal);
- the États généraux des communautés rurales (Assembly of Rural Communities) in 1991, which would give birth to Solidarité rurale (Rural Solidarity);
- the États généraux de la coopération (Assembly of Co-operation) launched by the Conseil de la coopération du Québec (CCQ), whose province-wide convention was held in 1992;
- the creation of trade union investment funds (fonds syndicaux de travailleurs) by the QFL in 1983 and the Confédération des syndicates nationaux (CSN) in 1996; and
- the Bread and Roses March in May and June 1995.[14] This women's march led to debate and awareness of the social economy and to the establishment of regional social economy committees (Lévesque 2008a, 11).

THE TWO 1996 SUMMITS

The idea of convening two socio-economic summits was broached by the Parti Québécois government. The first Conférence sur le devenir social et économique du Québec (Summit on the Social and Economic Future of Quebec) was held in March 1996 and had two goals: to establish a plan to achieve a balanced budget (or zero deficit) and trigger a recovery in employ-ment. The first goal was attained with an agreement between summit attendees to achieve a zero deficit within four years. But the treatment of the second goal that concerned employment was postponed to the second summit that had been scheduled for the fall.

In the context of the first summit, a number of working groups were set up to prepare the debates and decisions on employment planned for the second summit. These groups included the Groupe de travail sur l'économie sociale (GTES, Working Group on the Social Economy), chaired by Nancy Neamtan (see Neatman 2003). The GTES was notable for the originality of its composition and the expectations it elicited in connection with the preparation of the economic and employment summit that was scheduled for late October 1996. This working group comprised representatives of the social economy (including the co-operative world), the community sector, and the public and private sectors. After six months' work, it produced the paper "Osons la solidarité!" (GTES 1996), a report that became an important document for referral and debate at the fall summit. It proposed both an inclusive definition of the social economy and a social economy development plan in 20 or so sectors, in particular in local services, local development, and social housing, and for labour market entry (Lévesque 2008a, 11).

The second economic and employment summit was indeed held in the fall of 1996. It was at this summit that what Lévesque calls a "founding compromise" was reached concerning an inclusive definition of the social economy mentioned above (2008a, 11). The terms proposed by the GTES (1996) were well received by the participants and had a significant impact on the decisions reached by the summit. This does not mean that the open-ness toward the social economy shown by some participants was not accompanied by the expression of certain fears and reservations. For instance, the union representatives attending the summit insisted that the new jobs in home-care services created by the social economy should be sustainable, quality jobs that would not replace public sector jobs.

AFTER THE SUMMITS[15]

In the wake of the 1996 summits, the support provided for the social economy by the Quebec government has been expressed in two ways: first, through the adoption of sectoral public policy that gives preference and even exclu-sive access sometimes for the social economy in the implementation of certain areas of public policy. This is happening, for instance, in the areas of:

- *family social policy*, with the decision to use primarily non-profit child-care centres to create 150,000 new places in ten years for children aged six and under (Lévesque 2007, 53–54; Vaillancourt and Tremblay 2002; Vaillancourt 2003).
- *social housing*, with the AccèsLogis policy, which gave preference to housing co-operatives and non-profit organizations (NPOs) for the creation of 20,000 new housing units between 1997 and 2007 (Lévesque 2007, 53–54; Bouchard and Hudon 2005; Vaillancourt and Ducharme 2001; Vaillancourt 2008a, 2008b).
- *home-care services*, where 101 new entreprises d'économie sociale en aide domestiques (EESADs, home-care social economy enterprises) emerged between 1997 and 2000 (Vaillancourt, Aubry, and Jetté 2003; Jetté, Aubry, and Vaillancourt 2005).

The second mode of government support has been through the adoption of geographical area-specific public policy that indirectly leads to recognition and development of social economy initiatives by supporting the development of local and regional organizations:

- strengthening the Quebec government's policies (in place since the 1980s and 1990s) of support for the Coopératives de développement régional (CDRs, regional development co-operatives), which help the development of co-operatives in Quebec's administrative regions, with priority to job creation (Lévesque 2007, 33, 51; Favreau 2008, 46);
- building on the rise over the past 30 years of Groupes de ressources techniques (GRTs, technical resource groups), which help social economy and public economy players in the development of new housing projects, taking advantage of provincial and federal programs (Bouchard and Hudon 2005; Vaillancourt 2008b); and
- the devolopment since 1997 of 112 Centres locaux de développement (CLDs, local development centres), which support economic and social development in cities and regional county municipalities across Quebec (Comeau et al. 2001; Favreau 2008, 53–58). The CLDs are enabled through a Fonds de développement des entreprises de l'économie sociale (FDEÉS, social economy enterprise development fund).[16]

Other instruments for enabling the social economy include Carrefours jeunesse emploi (CJEs, the youth employment forums), Services spécialisés de main-d'œuvre (SEMOs, specialized labour services), and several innovative financial tools. In addition to the collective tools created by the Quebec government, there is also an important tool under federal government responsibility: the 67 community futures development corporations (CFDCs), which participate in the field of local development in rural Quebec (out of a total of 268 CFDCs across Canada). The CFDCs have provided support to 473 Quebec social economy organizations over the past few years (Favreau 2008, 51–54).

Lévesque (2007, 43–48) identified four main components of the social economy in terms of its status at the end of Period 5:

- *Mutual societies.* There are 39 mutual societies, with the two largest being SSQ Groupe financier and La Capitale.

TABLE 3.1   Social Economy in Quebec in 2005

Components	Number of organizations	Number of employees
Mutual societies	39	4,875
Co-operatives	2,795	82,586
Market associations	3,941	45,080
Non-market associations	8,000	35,000
Total	14,775	167,541

Sources: Quebec Ministry of Economic Development, Innovation and Export Trade (MDÉIE) (2007, 9 and 16); Vaillancourt et al. (2004); Lévesque (2007, 47–48); Jetté (2008, 2; 2009); Chantier de l'économie sociale (2003, 6); D'Amours (2006, 20). See also Favreau (2008, 85).

TABLE 3.2   Chantier de l'économie sociale Trust

Startup capital: $52.8 million
- Federal government: $22.8 million
- Quebec government: $10 million
- QFL Solidarity Fund: $12 million
- Fondaction (CSN): $8 million

Governance: board of directors with nine (9) members
- 4 members named by the Chantier de l'économie sociale
- 1 member named by the Conseil québécois de la coopération et de la mutualité
- 1 member named by the federal government
- 1 member named by the Quebec government
- 1 member named by the Fonds de solidarité du Québec
- 1 member named by Fondaction (CSN)

Sources: CÉS (2006b); K. Lévesque (2006); and Chantier de l'économie sociale Trust (2007).

- *Co-operatives.* There are 2,834 co-operatives in some 40 sectors but concentrated in a few, including agri-food and financial services. Co-operatives come in various forms, including solidarity co-operatives, labour co-operatives, producer co-operatives, and shareholding worker co-operatives. Obviously, as discussed above, Mouvement Desjardins represents a very significant segment within this component of the Quebec social economy (see Box 3.1).

- *Associations with economic activities* (in the sense of production of goods and services). After pointing to the complexity and stumbling blocks that make it difficult to count the number of associations—for example, the difficulty of establishing a clear boundary between associations that have commercial activities and those that do not—Lévesque provides an estimate of 10,000 associations, an estimate that does not include those that lack salaried staff. In so doing, he keeps his distance from two types of estimates. On the one hand, he stands back from the generous estimate of Imagine Canada's national poll, which counted 46,000 non-profit and voluntary organizations in Quebec out of a total of 161,000 in Canada (Hall et al. 2004). On the other hand, he distances himself from the CÉS's conservative estimate of a mere 2,461 NPOs in 2001 (CÉS 2001, 5) and only 3,941 in 2003 (CÉS 2003, 6). In arriving at the figure of 10,000 for associations, Lévesque did not count those that sell or charge for goods and services—such as child-care centres charging Cdn$7.00 a day per child. In line with the inclusive definition of the social economy that he has often put forward (see, for example, Lévesque and Mendell 2005), Lévesque counts associations that provide their services without charge, including many that balance their budgets through donations from foundations and grants from United Way/Centraide organizations and public authorities, in particular the Quebec government (Lévesque 2007, 47–48). While adjusting the figure upward, we have taken account of Lévesque's estimate of 10,000 associations in preparing Table 3.1 on the magnitude of the social economy in Quebec in 2005.[17]

- *Workers' funds and other financial tools.* First, there is the Quebec Federation of Labour's Solidarity Fund (Fonds de solidarité FTQ), set up in 1983 and specializing in job maintenance and creation through investment in small and medium-sized enterprises (SMEs). There is also the CSN's Fondation (Fonds de développement de la CSN pour la coopération et l'emploi, CSN Development Fund for Co-operation and Employment), set up in 1996 and specializing in investment that fosters workers' participation and sustainable development. Lévesque identifies these two union venture capital funds as "social economy enterprises" and as successful social innovations (2007, 45). In 2006, the Solidarity Fund "had 573,086 shareholders and assets of $6.6 billion, including $3 billion invested in 1,681 Quebec companies" (2007, 45) while, also in 2006, Fondaction had 64,000 shareholders and $442 million in assets (2007, 46). Furthermore, the two union funds, along with the governments of Canada and Quebec, are participants in the total capitalization of the new Chantier de l'économie sociale trust (Social Economy Trust) (see Table 3.2).[18] To complete the list of financial tools, the Réseau d'investissement social du Québec (RISQ, Social Investment Network of Quebec) must be added.[19]

In closing, it is important to note that at the end of the fifth period—from 2003 to 2008—a number of changes occurred concerning the government's recognition of and support for the social economy. These changes took place with a new government in Quebec City—that of Jean Charest in 2003—and then in Ottawa with the government of Paul Martin in December 2003, and finally, with Stephen Harper's government in January 2006 (see item number 4 in the summary section below).

Links Between Social Economy and Social Democracy: Contrast Between the Quebec Legacy and the Canadian Legacy

As this chapter is the only one covering Quebec in a work devoted to the social economy in Canada, I feel it is worthwhile to compare Benoît Lévesque's five dominant configurations of the social economy to the English-Canadian tradition. I shall do so by focusing on the three most recent configurations, which together cover more than 75 years of history (1930–2008).

The first astonishing fact that results from this comparison is that *the encounter between the social economy and social democracy*[20] *was historically more recent in Quebec than in the rest of Canada.* Over the period covered by the last three of Lévesque's five dominant configurations, social democracy had difficulty taking root in Quebec because it was dominated by its right "wing" during the third period (1930–1960) and by its left "wing" during the fourth period (1960–1990). In fact, it is during the current, fifth period that social democracy in Quebec has found more fertile ground for its realization in the social economy, reflective of the fact that Quebecers and English Canadians hold social democratic values even if they do not realize it. This unrecognized social democratic value basis among Canadians is worthy of reflection. In fact, my hypothesis is that of all of the dominant configurations historically experienced by and currently available to the social economy, one that could develop within a renewed social democracy would be the most appropriate and promising for realizing the full potential of the social economy.

During Period 3, Social Democracy Was Critiqued from the Right

Using this focus on social democracy and given the "astonishing fact" above, I want to review the period when the dominant configuration in Quebec was corporatist and traditional nationalist—that is, from 1930 to 1960—in comparison with trends in the rest of Canada at that time. I want to investigate why Quebec has emerged as a leader in social democracy and economy given its corporatist roots, while the rest of Canada has become more conservative based on its strong social democratic and economic roots (see MacPherson in this volume for details on English Canada). While the corporatist configuration reigned in Quebec, in some other regions of Canada, the western provinces in particular, *the dominant configuration concerning the social economy was social democratic, or socialist in the labour mode.* Not only was 1933 the year when the ÉSP's first and second programs of social restoration in a context of economic crisis were launched, it was also the year in which, in that same context of economic crisis, the Regina Manifesto was issued in western Canada and became the platform of a new Canadian social democratic party, the Co-operative Commonwealth Federation (CCF).[21] Unlike the Communist Party of Canada (CPC)—which was founded in 1921 but never made any headway in the Canadian Parliament, but had in the 1930s and 1940s managed to increase its influence substantially in several ways, including in the union movement, unemployed workers' committees, and collectives for peace—the CCF was not a Marxist-type socialist party advocating the abolition of all private ownership of the means of production.[22] It was a socialist party within the labour family or, more accurately, a social democratic party that accepted the market economy while advocating strong government regulation in economic and social development. The CCF focused on democratic change without resort to violence.[23] It advocated state control or nationalization of some, but not all, means of production.

Unlike the socialist parties in the social democratic tradition from other European countries, in particular France and Belgium, the CCF, influenced by the labour tradition of the United Kingdom, had no conflictual relationship with Christianity.[24] Many of the CCF's top leaders (Woodsworth,

Coldwell, Douglas, Knowles, and so on) and its seminal texts identified with progressive Protestantism—that is, a social gospel-type radical social Christianity.[25] Using Christian principles as a basis, CCF members who shared these beliefs could support social democratic and anti-capitalist-type social

BOX 3.3   Co-operative Commonwealth Federation

The Co-operative Commonwealth Federation (CCF) was founded in 1932 in Calgary by a number of political forces—farmers' organizations, progressive academics, "ginger" (socialist) parliamentarians, and the emerging labour movement. In 1933 in Regina, at its first national convention, the CCF elected its first leader, J.S. Woodsworth, and adopted a policy document called the Regina Manifesto. J.S. Woodsworth was a Christian minister and a strong believer in the "social gospel" (a belief that Christianity had much to offer in the way of solutions to the various problems of an increasingly industrial society) and had been a member of Parliament since 1921. He was influential in ensuring that the CCF held to principled positions throughout his term as party leader—most famously, a pacifist position during the Second World War and a belief in the possibility, and moral validity, of social democracy.

The Regina Manifesto, the backbone of the CCF's policy, called for the replacement of the capitalist system with a more equitable economic order, and it pledged that the basis of this new order would be democratically controlled co-operatives. The manifesto stated: "We aim to replace the present capitalist system, with its inherent injustice and inhumanity, by a social order from which the domination and exploitation of one class by another will be eliminated, in which economic planning will supersede unregulated private enterprise and competition, and in which genuine democratic self-government, based upon economic equality will be possible. ... [These goals are to be achieved, in part, through] the encouragement by the public authority of both producers' and consumers' cooperative institutions" (http://economics.uwaterloo.ca/needhdata/Regina_Manifesto.html).

Membership in the CCF grew from about 20,000 in 1938 to about 30,000 in 1942, peaked at more than 90,000 in 1944, the year that the CCF under Premier Tommy Douglas was elected to power in Saskatchewan, and declined in the years following the war. In 1956 the Regina Manifesto was replaced by the Winnipeg Declaration, and in 1961 the CCF was disbanded and replaced by the New Democratic Party.

As Canada's first political party to support sustained development of the social economy as a principle of social democracy, the CCF left a strong legacy. Among the programs advocated by the CCF were universal health care, unemployment insurance, and workers' compensation—programs now enshrined in federal and provincial legislation.

and political commitments (Pelletier and Vaillancourt 1975, 69–76; Vaillancourt 1988, 75–76). So, unlike Quebec social Catholicism, social Christianity (primarily Protestant, but also Catholic), as conceptualized and practised in English Canada during this corporatist period, was open to social democracy.[26] In other words, during the 1930s in particular, there was no doctrinal problem for a Christian holding membership in the CCF in English Canada, but there certainly was such a problem in Quebec. This factor alone does not explain the historical difficulties long encountered in Quebec by the CCF-New Democratic Pary (NDP) tradition,[27] but it is a factor that slowed the rise of social democracy during the corporatist period.

The concept of social economy as such was not used in the CCF's program. But the reality of the social economy was implicitly recognized and supported. As indicated by the party's name, the CCF was very interested in co-operation and co-operatives. In the Regina Manifesto, adopted at the 1933 congress, and which remained the CCF's platform until 1956, the co-operative formula was promoted in several places. In section 4 of the manifesto (CCF 1933), the section devoted to agriculture, "encouragement of producers' and consumers' co-operatives" was central (CCF 1933, 5); in section 6, the co-operative formula was encouraged in broader terms:

> co-operative organization can be extended into wholesale distribution and into manufacturing. Co-operative enterprises should be assisted by the state through appropriate legislation and through the provision of adequate credit facilities.

It is not my intention here to analyze in greater depth the place of the social economy in the history of the federal or provincial parties and governments in the CCF-NDP tradition in Canada from the 1930s onward. My point here is to underscore the existence of a social democratic configuration of the social economy in English Canada at the same time as the social economy stood in a corporatist configuration in Quebec. Indeed, one can talk of a *social democratic configuration* that was the dominant configuration for the social economy in English Canada, since the social democratic project was highly influential both in the federal Parliament, some provincial legislatures in the prairie and western provinces,[28] urban and rural social movements, and many institutions and organizations of civil society in Canada. The social democratic influence on the Canadian scene was maintained when the CCF party was superseded by the NDP in 1961.

Let us return now to the differences and links between the corporatist configuration of social economy that dominated in Quebec and the social democratic configuration of social economy that dominated in the rest of

Canada. For the corporatist period, Lévesque emphasizes that this configuration aimed to counter the penetration of communist (or Marxist-type
socialist) ideas and projects in Quebec society, a society characterized at the
time as French-Canadian and Catholic. Further, the elite in Quebec were
also strongly anti-social democrat; witness the Catholic position adopted
at the time against the CCF doctrine. Further, the corporatist current pre-
vailing in Quebec was even opposed to liberal democracy and Keynesianism,
the latter two being seen as Anglo-Protestant and not adapted to the French-
Canadian Catholic culture that was dominant in the province at that time.
This explains the criticism directed at the Beveridge and Marsh reports on
social policy by Quebec corporatist intellectuals during the Second World
War.[29] This opposition was reaffirmed in the 1950s by such corporatists as
François-Albert Angers of the HÉC, who helped bring the ideas of the Beveridge and Marsh reports into the Liberal Party of Canada and who openly
worried that the presence of the CCF was helping "socialist intellectuals" to
infiltrate "the universities and the bureaucracy" (Angers 1955, 178–179).[30]

It is interesting to observe that the vision of the social economy and
social Christianity that emerges in the corporatist configuration dominant
during the third period in Quebec was more conservative than that which,
during the same period, cohabited with the social democratic configuration
in English Canada. The advent of the Quiet Revolution marked the end of

BOX 3.4   The Quiet Revolution

The Quiet Revolution was a period in Quebec that lasted from 1960 (with
the election of the Liberal premier Jean Lesage) to 1970 (with the October
Crisis of the FLQ—see Box 3.2 on the sovereignty movement). During this
period there was a transformation of social control of key public institutions
from the Catholic Church to the provincial government. Previously, services
such as health care and education had been under the purview of the Roman
Catholic Church—marking the "corporatist" period mentioned in this chapter.
Just as important as this transference of social control, however, was the new
"nationalistic" or sovereignty spirit that dominated Quebec during this
decade. To help foster the Quebec nation, significant investment was made
in the provincial economy, from infrastructure and education to the nationalization of the energy sector. Provincial unions were also given a greater role
in society, notably through the unionization of public servants. The Quiet
Revolution therefore significantly altered Quebecois conceptions of the role
of the state in the economy, and specifically the role of the social economy
in creating and maintaining a viable society.

the domination of the corporatist configuration, but did not mean the abrupt disappearance of corporatist ideas. On the contrary, from 1960 to 2008, certain areas of collective life would continue to be imbued with such ideas.[31]

During Period 4, Social Democracy Was Critiqued from the Left

While social democracy was criticized from the right during the third period, it was not long before it was criticized by the left during the fourth period. Paradoxically, in Quebec, unlike in the rest of Canada and other countries, social democracy was not chosen, experienced, and reflected on in a lasting manner by a large number of individuals, organizations, and political parties. Prior to the Quiet Revolution, the social democratic perspective was present in Quebec society, but its advances had been hampered by the domination of the corporatist and traditional nationalist configuration.[32] In short, the influence of the CCF-NDP tradition remained marginal in Quebec compared with that in the rest of Canada.

With the Quiet Revolution began the period of economic nationalism we summarized earlier. During the 1960s, social democratic perspectives made substantial headway in Quebec, particularly in the second half of the decade. This headway was manifested in new political formations, such as the Rassemblement pour l'indépendance nationale (RIN) and the PQ. But, unlike the NDP, the PQ would not be clearly a social democratic party. Rather, it would be a party where a social democratic tendency lived alongside other more centrist, conservative tendencies. But the penetration of social democracy would be felt more clearly in social movements and civil society—for example in the citizens' committees of 1963–1970 and the trade union movement, which became more radical from 1966 onward. Thus, the second half of the 1960s represented an intense period of consolidation by the social democratic movement in Quebec society.

But during the 1970s and part of the 1980s, as mentioned above (see section 4), the radicalization of ideologies and socio-economic and socio-political projects continued, with a large proportion of progressives becoming infatuated with Marxism understood as an instrument for analysis and action. This adoption of Marxism took place at high speed in a great variety of settings, particularly in the social movements. From 1973, several new Marxist political groups arose, each competing to see which would be the most revolutionary, or indeed the most Marxist-Leninist (or Maoist). This dissemination of the Marxist and Leninist ways of seeing and doing was quickly accompanied by a strong inclination to sectarianism and dogma-tism. This led in particular—and this is important for the social economy—to suspicions and denunciations of everything that could be identified with social democracy by a significant portion of the new supporters of socialism with Marxist leanings. These struggles between supporters of Marxism and supporters of social democracy raged for a good part of the period 1975–1985, leaving scars among the protagonists in the years that followed. The struggles weakened the alliances that should have developed further between the left of the PQ and the left of the social movements as the first PQ gov-ernment (1976–1981) was putting forward several social democratic-style reforms. This difficulty in cementing alliances was especially tangible at the time of the 1980 referendum on sovereignty.

For the social economy, the implications of the above were considerable. In fact, the infatuation with Marxism, indeed Marxism-Leninism and Stalinism, also affected several social economy organizations—the ACEF, child-care centres, food counters, and so on. In short, the cohabitation between the Marxism of the time and the social economy was not as smooth as the cohabitation that can occur between social democracy and the social economy. As easily as the social economy can tie in with a social democratic vision, it has had (and has) difficulty doing so with a Marxist socialist or anti-capitalist vision cut through by the dogmatism that flourished in the late 1970s not only in Quebec, but also in several regions of Canada and in other northern and southern countries. Why was this? Because with the structuralist Marxism of the time, it was impossible to talk of capitalism in the plural, and even more so of socialist alternatives in the plural (Favreau 2008, 132–134). Capitalism and the alternatives always had to be talked of in the singular. As a result, the social economy was often criticized as being the "Trojan horse of capitalism" (Favreau 2008, 21–22) because it mirrored reforms without leading to the abolition of the capitalist control of the means of production, or the elimination of the principles of the market economy.[33]

During Period 5, Social Democracy Is Back on the Agenda

During the period 1990–2008, the pendulum had begun to swing back from rejection to respect for social democracy, at least within Quebec. The fall of the Berlin Wall in 1989 symbolized the difficulties in the construction of "real socialism" inspired by the Marxist and Leninist traditions. In both northern and southern countries, in Quebec and the rest of Canada, in intellectual milieux, social movements, and left-wing political parties (except among a few hard-core members), there was a greater hesitation to declare one's support for communism, Marxism, Marxist-type socialism, and even anti-capitalism, since these labels had become the orphans of the historical models that inspired them. In short, the social democrats, who had been placed on the defensive owing to Marxist radicalization during the 1970s and 1980s, were now in a situation more conducive to articulating the value of their position. Furthermore, many who identified with Marxist socialism during previous decades distanced themselves, formally or informally, from these positions, falling back de facto on social democracy. Finally, for the young generations whose awareness was built on new struggles in the fields of alter-globalization, sustainable development, solidarity-based funding, fair trade, and so on, social democracy became a more attractive current than it had been in the 1970s and 1980s. But many progressives continue to be reluctant to identify with social democracy.[34]

Lévesque's fifth period (and configuration) therefore opens the intellectual space for understanding the social economy within a blueprint for a social democratic society, something not possible in the previous two periods and configurations. But a problem remains for a close association between social democracy and social economy. While not as discredited as the Marxist-type socialist model, social democracy, to prove attractive in the new millennium, has to free itself from a number of limitations that appeared when it was in power, both in the North and in the South, in the past 25 years.[35] In other words, it needs to renew itself. Hence the importance of taking into account the debate on the *refounding* of social democracy that has arisen in France since the presidential elections of spring 2007.[36]

Closer to home, in Canada and Quebec, the refounding of social democracy is also necessary. It implies among other things a critical look at the historical failings of the CCF-NDP tradition as it was expressed in political parties and social movements in Canada and Quebec. These failings primarily include *centralization* (anything good for the general interest in economic and social terms must originate in Ottawa and the federal state) and *government control* (good public policy is constructed by the state and its experts alone). In other words, if the weight of the corporatist project was a factor that historically stemmed the spread of the CCF's ideas during the third period, that does not mean that the faults of the CCF of that time—notably, its propensity for centralization and government control—did not also contribute to its lack of success in Quebec. This critical reflection on the limitations of centralization and statism is necessary, not only in reference to the CCF-NDP tradition in Canada and Quebec, but also to the social democratic visions conveyed, since the Quiet Revolution, in certain parts of Quebec social movements and, at times, in certain public policy put forward by the Quebec government headed by the Quebec Liberal Party or the PQ.[37]

In Quebec, in the current climate and also over the next few years, opportunities appear to be emerging for a more harmonious, explicit conjunction between the social economy and a renewed social democracy. This new model—or configuration—has been germinating in the evolution of Quebec society since the 1990s (see the fifth period above). But certain conditions are needed for it to grow and take stronger root in the face of the corporatist and neo-liberal models with which it often cohabits in the development and implementation of public policy. I conceptualize these not as simple conditions, but as complex issues that need to be thought through if the social economy is to develop and flourish in this new period.

Summary: Six Key Issues for the Future of the Social Economy in Quebec

1. Defining and Mapping the Social Economy

Some people, often on the pretext of being attached to tangible things, prefer not to spend time on questions of definition, yet attempt to map the social economy anyway. To approach things in this way is to set oneself up for failure. To map the social economy, one first has to know what one is talking about, and so must start by defining it. It is for this reason that I took a position in favour of a particular broad and inclusive definition of the social economy, because this definition includes both market and non-market components (see Table 3.1). However, over the past ten years decision-makers, stakeholders, and researchers have not unanimously adopted this definition. Many in government and social research and many conducting research prefer to hold to a more restrictive definition of the social economy. This is the case with researchers such as Favreau (2008), who, for example, excludes non-market components from his definition. In short, in Quebec as in other parts of the world, there is no consensus on the definition of the social economy. Such disagreement is good, however, for it generates discussions that are healthy, provided that all parties take the trouble to clarify their positions. If the social economy is to emerge stronger from the current period, open and vigorous debate on the definition and resulting "maps" must be undertaken.

2. Tension Between the State and Social Movements

Particularly since 1996, one of the specific features of the social economy in Quebec concerns the fact that, particularly since 1996, it has received special recognition from the Quebec government. How can this recognition be explained? Was it a gift from the public authorities? Or was it rather a victory achieved by civil society and social movements? Our answer is that political recognition of the social economy is like an *institutionalized compromise*. It represented at least a partial government response to demands from civil society and labour market stakeholders, in particular those directly or indirectly involved in development of the social economy as examined above (Vaillancourt and Favreau 2001). For example, the women's movement, with the Bread and Roses March, has been identified as having made an outstanding contribution to forcing the Quebec government to recognize the social economy (Corbeil, Descarries, and Galerand 2002). Recognition of the social economy then appears as the fragile product, not "permanently locked in," of the *co-construction* of public policy with which the social economy itself is associated (Vaillancourt 2008a and 2008b). If the social economy is going to continue to survive in the new configuration in Quebec, it must continue to demonstrate its importance and connection to social movements.

3. Transforming and Reforming Capitalism

In this subsection, the important contribution of the social economy to the transformation of society is examined. It is important to acknowledge that, like the definition of the social economy, the positions taken by stakeholders and researchers about its transformative role are diversified. Researchers from Quebec (Fontan and Shragge 2000) and Canada (Loxley and Simpson 2007; Loxley 2007), however, have stressed that there are two general currents of thought concerning the transformative potential of the social economy and one of its components, community economic development. Fundamentally, the first current of thought is content with *reforming* capitalism, whereas the second aims to *transform* it—that is, to *replace* it. This issue implicitly resumes the old debate between reformism (or social democracy) and revolution (or socialism in the Marxist tradition); many of us in Quebec stand outside these two positions because we forward the idea that the dominant position within Quebec's social economy movement, influenced by the theoretical contributions of Créer et diffuser l'innovation sociale (CRISES) and the International Centre of Research and Information on the Public, Social and Cooperative Economy-Canada (CIRIEC-Canada), signifies its preference for a social economy capable of fitting in with a perspective of profound social change. The impetus of this position is that change targets not the end of capitalism, but a different capitalism. This transformation of capitalism, however, in the vein of a renewed social democracy, promotes a *plural economy* in which there is room for a new balance between recognition of the principles of the solidarity economy (giving and reciprocity), the public economy (redistribution), and the market economy (CIRIEC-Canada 1998; Lévesque, Bourque, and Forgues 2001). A view of the social economy as a partner in the development of social democracy, not as a force of anti-capitalist revolution, is important to develop in this period of history in Quebec.

4. Relations with Government

While acknowledging the importance of relations between local government and the social economy, this subsection restricts itself to discussing the relations involving the Quebec government and the federal government. Simply put, the social economy was more strongly recognized and supported by PQ than by Quebec Liberal governments (the evidence for this claim are to be published in a forthcoming paper). While there were many setbacks during the period of the various PQ governments, nevertheless there was continuity concerning the recognition by the state of the social economy during their time in office. This continuity continued under the recent Liberal minority government owing to the provincial Liberals' desire to differentiate themselves from the more right-leaning Action démocratique du Québec (ADQ).

Concerning the various federal governments from 1993 to 2008, it is important to highlight three important moments for the social economy. The first is the fact that the Chrétien government in 1999, toward the end of its rule, was interested in the non-market component of the social economy with the Voluntary Sector Initiative (VSI). The two Martin governments (in the space of 26 months, from December 2003 to January 2006) built on this initiative and put forward a formal policy of recognition of the social economy for the first time in Canadian federal government history. Finally, after this brief moment of recognition, this policy was quickly disowned and largely sabotaged by the minority Harper governments of 2006–2009, reminding one of the hostility of the corporatist regimes in Quebec many years ago (Vaillancourt and Thériault 2008). The social economy needs to think through its relationships with provincial and national governments carefully if it is going to continue to develop. This is an especially difficult area for the social economy as changes in government can rapidly and severely alter the possibilities for development (see Guy and Heneberry in this volume). However, social economy actors and the movement as a whole must stay true to its principles despite this difficult reality and work towards a consistent relationship with government as happened with the PQ in Quebec.

5. Links with Research and Universities

The links between social economy stakeholders and researchers have been ongoing and significant in Quebec over the past 40 years, but have intensified over the past 15. Already in the 1970s and 1980s, there were university research agencies interested in co-operatives. Among them were CIRIEC-Canada (founded in 1966), the University of Sherbrooke's IRECUS (founded in 1967), HÉC Montreal's Desjardins Centre for Studies in Management of Financial Services Co-operatives (founded in 1975), and CRISES (founded in 1986). The 1990s and the following decade saw the addition of several new research bodies, including LAREPPS (founded in 1992), the University of Quebec in Outaouais (UQO) Canada Research Chair in Community Development (established in 1995), ARUC-ÉS (founded in 2000), and so on. Over the years, Quebec's research apparatus has become impressive. It is characterized by three characteristics: those research bodies interested in the social economy are interdisciplinary; they value research in partnership (Vaillancourt 2007; ARUC-ÉS and RQRPÉS 2007; Favreau 2008, 238–240); and they had an influence on the policy decisions made by the Martin government in 2004 concerning the social economy (Lévesque and Mendell 2005; CÉS et al. 2005). This relationship between social economy actors and organizations and the academy is one of the key strengths of the movement and needs to be continued and expanded if the social economy is going to continue to emerge as a serious social player in Quebec and across the country.

6. Networking of Social Economy Stakeholders

Another characteristic specific to the Quebec social economy movement concerns its dynamic tradition of networking. This networking is engaged in within Quebec through the contribution of two provincial groups, the Conseil québécois de la coopération et de la mutualité (CQCM), created in 1939, and the Chantier de l'économie sociale (CÉS), created in 1996. Certainly, until 2004, one might have had the impression that the CÉS was the only provincial group or "network of social economy networks" insofar as the CQCM and several older co-operatives hesitated to identify themselves as social

TABLE 3.3   Quebec Tools for Promoting the Social Economy Internationally

- DID: Desjardins International Development (created in 1970)
- SOCODEVI: Société de coopération pour le développement international (created in 1985 and associated with the CQCM)
- UPA-DI: Union des producteurs agricoles-Développement international (created in 1993)
- GESQ: Groupe d'économie solidaire du Québec (created in 2001)
- Solidarity Fund QFL (Quebec Federation of Labour) (created in 1983)
- CIRIEC-Canada (created in 1966)
- Caisse d'économie solidaire Desjardins (created in 1971)
- International co-operation agencies that give priority to promoting the social economy in southern countries (Development and Peace, CECI [Centre d'éducation et de coopération internationale], CUSO, OXFAM, Alternatives, etc.)
- Fonds Solidarité Sud (created by Development and Peace in 2007)

Sources: Lévesque (2008b) and Favreau (2008, 115–117, 206–218).

economy organizations. But in the wake of work by Favreau (2005 and 2006), which shook up perceptions, the labelling changed and co-operatives clearly now identify themselves as part of the social economy (CQCM 2007).

Networking is also engaged in with and within English Canada. Certainly, the various components of the Quebec and Canadian social economy (co-operatives, associations, and mutual aid societies) have long been in touch with each other. But it is the community economic development stakeholders who, with encouragement from the CÉS, from 2003 in particular, have developed a strategic Quebec/Canada networking plan that led to the emergence of the Martin government's policies in favour of the social economy (Neamtan 2004, 26). Finally, there is the international networking in which Quebec's social economy stakeholders have long been participating, using a variety of tools with which they have equipped themselves (see Table 3.3). Here again, CIRIEC-Canada, through its links with CIRIEC International, played a key role, particularly in the past 20 years (Lévesque 2008b). Also worth mentioning is the role of the Groupe d'économie solidaire du Québec (GESQ), which since 2001 has mobilized and brought about the participation of Quebec social economy stakeholders in international and intercontinental activities, fostering the connection with the the Réseau Intercontinental de Promotion de l'Economie Sociale et Solidaire (RIPESS, the Intercontinental Network for the Promotion of the Social Solidarity Economy), at gatherings in Quebec City in 2001, Dakar in 2005 (Favreau,

Lachapelle, and Larose 2003; Salam Fall, Favreau, and Larose 2004; Favreau and Salam Fall 2007), and in Luxembourg in 2009. Networking on the provincial, national, and international levels is an important activity for the social economy to be engaged in, both to encourage wider and more sophisticated practice, but also to embed social economy activity in the consciousness of citizens around the world.

Conclusion

The originality of the preceding sections on the social economy in Quebec, in my view, lies in the fact that they were written primarily with an English-Canadian readership in mind. This has encouraged me to highlight the differences and similarities between the social economy in Quebec and in the rest of Canada. As I did so, the specific nature of recent history and the current reality of the social economy in Quebec became clearer. In expressing myself in these terms, I am taking for granted that the main point of *similarity* emerging from a comparison between the social economy in Quebec and in the rest of Canada is the fact that, *objectively*, it has long existed in both societies. While Lévesque (2007) spoke of at least "a century and a half of social economy in Quebec," specialists in the history of the social economy in Canada could make quite similar statements in reference to what occurred in Canada outside Quebec (see MacPherson in this volume).

The *differences* between the social economy in Quebec and in the rest of Canada begin to emerge when one takes into account the subjective perceptions and the time when the concept of social economy began to appear in public discourse in Quebec and the rest of Canada. Even though, in Quebec as in the rest of Canada, we have been doing social economy without realizing it for several decades, the moment when we realized *subjectively* that we were doing so came earlier in Quebec than in the rest of Canada. In fact, the turning point concerning the use of the concept of social economy in public discourse occurred in about 1995 in Quebec. In the rest of Canada, it occurred in December 2003, when Paul Martin took over from Jean Chrétien as head of the federal Liberal government.

But the differences between the social economy in Quebec and Canada emerge even more clearly when one looks at the *configurations*—or sociohistorical contexts—in which it operated at various moments in the history of the two societies. It is important to look at the "dominant configurations" because the issue to be focused on has less to do with the quantity of social economy activity than the type of relations established between the social economy, the state, the market, social movements, civil society, ideologies, churches, international networks, and so on. This explains the choice I made in devoting the first section of my chapter to the five dominant configurations in which the social economy stood historically over the past 160 years, while paying greater attention to the last three successive configurations over the past 75 years. I did so by taking Benoît Lévesque's recent work into account, while adding my thoughts based on my own work.

In sum, here are several of these dominant configurations:

- The third dominant configuration in which the social economy operated (from 1930 to 1960) was characterized by the encouragement of a social corporatism based on the social doctrine of the Catholic Church and a traditional Quebecois nationalism, alongside a virulent anti-statism; it distrusted not only the federal state (owing corporatism's position against centralization), but also the Quebec provincial state (owing to its anti-statist position). Certainly, visceral anti-statism was the major weakness of the corporatist and traditional nationalist project. Paradoxically, this weakness had a silver lining by way of leaving room for participation in development by players from civil society and the market. Along the way, the national question constituted, over the decades, a central dimension that lives on in various configurations of the social economy in Quebec. The social economy was a lever for fostering the socio-economic and socio-cultural growth of the Quebec nation.
- The fourth dominant configuration emerged from 1960 to 1990. It was characterized by the affirmation of a modern economic nationalism that remained critical of initiatives from the federal state, but was differentiated from traditional nationalism in valuing intervention by the Quebec state in economic and social development and promoting a strong public sector. During this period, the social economy was sometimes split between asserting its autonomy vis-à-vis the state and seeking an alliance with the state and the state public machinery such that the latter two would contribute to economic, social, and sustainable development. Those 30 years witnessed ascendant ideological and political currents that were rapidly evolving in Quebec society, particularly in the social movements. In those movements and also in milieux interested in the social economy, an increase in social democratic perspectives took place during the 1960s, in turn superseded by an increase in Marxist socialist perspectives during the 1970s. The 1980s were marked by the crisis of the welfare state and public finances, and by the exhaustion of the Marxist *projets de société* (blueprints for society), whereas the social economy

appeared to cohabit more easily with social democracy than with the Marxist socialist approaches during the period.

- The fifth dominant configuration appeared in the 1990s and 2000s and was characterized by the pursuit and acquisition of a degree of recognition of the social and solidarity economy on the part of public authorities, the Quebec state in particular. This is the configuration that prevails at present. It coincides with the return of the social economy to a social democratic project that is trying, with difficulty, to renew itself. This social democratic renewal is made harder by the fact that it is taking place in an environment where other socio-political and socio-economic stakeholders are also interested in the social economy. Such renewal may in fact not be social democratic but rather involve a neo-liberal configuration (with a social economy subservient to the market) or a social-statist configuration (with a social economy instrumentalized by the state and the public sector), or a modern corporatist configuration in which state participation is sought, but in complicity with the participation of only certain socio-economic stakeholders, such as labour unions and management organizations. The dominant current of the social economy movement in Quebec, however, favours a democratic, solidarity-based configuration in line with a blueprint for renewed social democracy.

The second section of this chapter introduced a critical discussion by comparing the configurations that were dominant in Quebec and in the rest of Canada from the 1930s onward. This analysis underscored the fact that the Quebec social economy has long had more difficulty than the social economy in English Canada in coming into line with a social democratic configuration. In short, the opportunity for Quebec's social economy to enter into an open, productive dialogue with social democracy has reappeared since the mid-1980s. From the 1930s to 1980, the conjunction between the social economy and social democracy in Quebec only encountered more favourable conditions during the 1960s. But both before and after the latter decade, it came up against less conducive conditions. This was the case from 1930 to 1960, when traditional nationalist and corporatist ideas hampered the possibility of interest in social democracy. This was the case again between 1970 and 1985, when the rise of Marxist and Leninist ideas in social movements and left-wing milieux curbed the possibility of interest in social democracy and the social economy at the same time. In English Canada, the opportunity for a meeting between social democracy and the social economy arose more quickly and with greater force than in Quebec owing to the weight of the CCF-NDP tradition from the 1930s

onward. *Objectively*, the social economy was operating in a social democratic configuration in English Canada insofar as, de facto, social and political
organizations in the CCF-NDP tradition have always been sympathetic
toward co-operatives. But, *subjectively*, this conjunction between social
democracy and the social economy was never taken on board by organizations and parties of the CCF-NDP persuasion. Today, in English Canada as
in Quebec, the conditions for a creative meeting between the social economy and social democracy could be more strongly present. But, to be productive, both in Canada and in Quebec, this meeting requires reflection and
a refounding effort moving toward renewed social democracy. That means
a social democracy concerned with reconciling state intervention with participation by stakeholders from civil society and the market, one that in our
terminology entails opportunities for participation by the social economy
in the co-construction of public policy.

With the Quebec national question, there is a difference that is likely to
remain for a long time between a social economy in Quebec (supported by
the state) and the social economy that exists in the rest of Canada. The point
is that in Quebec, the state—indeed the nation-state—is first of all the
Quebec state; only secondarily is it the federal state. In the rest of Canada,
so far at least, the opposite holds; the state is first of all the federal state, and
then the provincial and territorial states. The point, then, is that in Canada,
there is more than one nation. The social economy, however, while emerging from different histories in these two nations, crosses boarders in practice and values and might in time bring them closer together.

Glossary

Corporatist The control of a state, province, or institution by large, defined
interest groups. In the case of Quebec, the interest group would be the
Catholic Church.

Keynesianism A theory of economics based on the work of John Maynard
Keynes (1883–1946) that emphasizes the importance of economic policy
responses of the public sector to stabilize the inefficiencies and boom–bust
cycles of the private sector. Often this term is used as a byword for the
welfare state.

Parti Québécois A social democratic political party in Quebec focused on
Quebec independence. The party was formed in 1968 as a result of a merger
between the Mouvement Souveraineté-Association (led by René Lévesque,
who later became the first leader of the Parti Québécois) and the Ralliement
national (led by Gilles Grégoire).

Social democracy   A political belief that argues for a peaceful and democratic transition to a more socially focused society. This would mean more state involvement and funding of key social sectors such as health care, education, and public welfare.

Solidarity economy   A concept (often employed in Quebec) that, while contested, indicates an economy focused on community well-being and co-operation in opposition to the individualistic focus of capitalism. While there are a number of potential overlaps between this concept and the social economy, solidarity economy is usually thought to indicate a more political focus.

Notes

1. Prior to 1995, a number of Quebec researchers occasionally used the concept of social economy. For instance, Benoît Lévesque and Marie-Claire Malo had produced in the early 1990s a fine chapter on the social economy in Quebec that was published in a collective work by CIRIEC International on the social economy and the third sector (Lévesque and Malo 1992).
2. Indeed, could it not be said that English Canada, until even more recently, was doing social economy without realizing it?
3. This social economy count does not include organizations and enterprises without a paid workforce.
4. The fact that the Chantier de l'économie sociale (CÉS) and other government and social stakeholders have often used this definition does not, however, imply that subsequently they have always acted consistently with respect to this definition. For example, in mapping the social economy in the past few years, the CÉS has often forgotten to count non-market components. See, for example, CÉS (2001, 5).
5. Social contributions are differentiated from commercial insurance firm premiums as follows: the commercial premium is established on the basis of the risk incurred. In the commercial mindset the higher the risk—of unemployment, for example—the higher the insured's premium. In contrast, in a mutual society, the contribution is established on the basis of the collective ability to pay off all the individuals insured, with members providing solidarity by making the risk mutual. Historically, the formula of social contributions in mutual societies paved the way for the mandatory, public social insurance programs that developed with the advent of the social policy of the welfare state. So the mutualist movement historically pointed the way to the social state (Favreau 2008, 24–25).
6. I would add a clarification concerning ÉSP program number 1 and the organization of the study day which led to its drafting on March 9, 1933. The program for this study day was based on two main talks. One was given by

Father Georges-Henri Lévesque, a Dominican. He had just returned to Canada from studying sociology at the Catholic University in Lille and was teaching philosophy and social theology at the Dominican College in Ottawa. Father Lévesque's lecture concerned the program of the new socialist political party that had been recently created in western Canada, the Co-operative Commonwealth Federation (CCF). The purpose of this lecture was to determine whether a Catholic could espouse the doctrine of the CCF. The second talk was given by Father Louis Chagnon, a Jesuit, and presupposed for all practical purposes that the answer to the question covered in the morning by Father Lévesque would be that a Catholic could not support the CCF. In fact, the goal of Father Chagnon's lecture was to present a sort of counterprogram of reforms that a Catholic could support. It was this second lecture that was to give birth to the social restoration program based on a corporatist doctrine. But there is an interesting point to be emphasized concerning this March 1933 study day in that the first speaker, Father Lévesque, expressed a hesitant, qualified view of the CCF. Certainly he ended up concluding that a Catholic could not support the CCF. Nonetheless, as he relates in his memoirs (Lévesque 1983, 222–238), he did so rather backwards, as if he did not wish to displease the ÉSP Jesuits who had organized the day and had as it were given him an "order" (ÉSP 1934, 1–3; Pelletier and Vaillancourt 1975, 129–136). In the years that followed, especially from 1938 onward, and when he was for 25 years a professor of social science and then dean of the Faculty of Social Science at Laval University, G.-H. Lévesque modified his positions concerning the CCF, as he clearly explained in his memoirs (Lévesque 1983, 222–238). He gradually distanced himself from the traditional corporatist and nationalistic positions of the ÉSP Jesuits—hence, the controversial position he was to take and defend in the 1940s and 1950s on the non-denominational nature of the co-operatives. In other words, the vision of co-operatives and the social economy conveyed by Father G.-H. Lévesque from 1936 onward was different from the one he had defended at the ÉSP study day in March 1933. Therefore, G.-H. Lévesque was part of the corporatist dominant configuration in 1933, but from the mid-1930s he was no longer part of it, insofar as the vision of co-operatives he had been advocating since 1936 belonged to an emerging, more progressive configuration. This accounts for the distinction made by Lévesque in his memoirs between his "opinions on the CCF in 1933–1936" (1983, 227 and 229) and his opinions thereafter.

7. These included the HÉC, the Faculty of Social Science at the University of Montreal, the periodicals *Action nationale* and *Relations*, the Association catholique de la jeunesse canadienne-française (ACJC), the Société Saint-

Jean-Baptiste, the Union catholique des cultivateurs (UCC), the Confédération des travailleurs catholiques du Canada (CTCC) from before 1946, and so on (see Pelletier and Vaillancourt 1975, 103–111).

8. The ALN's leaders were courted and its ideas taken up by Maurice Duplessis during the 1936 provincial election campaign. Once elected premier, though, Duplessis left the ALN's members on the sidelines, along with those of their demands that most symbolized change (Pelletier and Vaillancourt 1975, 143–167).

9. This point is not made formally and explicitly by Benoît Lévesque in his papers (2007, 2008a), but it is important to do so here in order to prepare the ground for some reflections on social democracy and social economy that we shall be putting forward in sections 2 and 3.

10. This current continued to imbue a number of institutions, organizations, and periodicals, including *Relations* (until 1968) and *L'Action nationale*.

11. This fearful, negative representation of the social economy survived to this day within part of the traditional left, as some of the literature demonstrates (Piotte 1998; Boivin and Fortier 1998). Over time, a number ended up modifying their positions. For example, in his latest book, Jean-Marc Piotte (2008) has made a significant shift in writing more constructively of the social economy and its potential for transformation of society.

12. On the meaning of the concept of co-construction of public policy, see Vaillancourt (2008b).

13. In presenting a painstaking analysis of the long-term preparations for the 1996 summits, Benoît Lévesque answered the analysts who criticized the summits, either for approximating modern corporatism (see Lise Bissonnette's critique in *Le Devoir* in fall 1996), or for having been made possible by the betrayal of union leaders who renounced the practice of "combative unionism" (see Jean-Marc Piotte's critique, 1998, 257–269).

14. On the spring 1995 Bread and Roses March, see Lorraine Guay (1997) and Martine D'Amours (2006). This march was instrumental in bringing the concept of social economy into the public debate and in linking it with "social infrastructure" to create jobs for women. It was a major event, one that heavily influenced Jacques Parizeau's PQ government in June 1995. The premier reacted by setting up a task force consisting of civil servants and activists from the women's movement. In May 1996, the task force submitted its report, "Entre l'espoir et le doute" (Between Hope and Doubt) (Comité d'orientation et de concertation sur l'économie sociale [COCES] 1996). Between the Women's March of spring 1995 and the socio-economic summit in fall 1996, the question of the social economy was debated within the social movements, leading to the drafting of several working papers (Aubry and Charest 1995; CSF 1996).

15. In this part of the chapter concerning the evolution of the social economy following the fall 1996 Summit, we are adding to Benoît Lévesque's contribution that of other researchers, without excluding our own work. This at times allows us to update the evolution of the social economy movement in Quebec over the past few years.

16. Mendell and Rouzier (2006, 2) commented on this fund as follows: "Through this fund, the CLDs give grants that rarely exceed or reach $50,000 to social economy organizations. The grants are used to cover the start-up costs, but can also serve for the consolidation of social economy organizations. In 2001, the average amount available for the FDEÉS in 55 CLDs out of 111 was $105,065."

17. In Table 3.1, we have taken into account Benoît Lévesque's figure of 10,000 associations, which comes from adding 4,000 market associations and 6,000 non-market associations (excluding those which use no salaried staff). For our part, while taking Lévesque's general approach as our own, we feel his estimate of 6,000 non-market associations is too conservative. We prefer to work with the hypothesis of a minimum of 8,000 non-market associations, giving us a total of 12,000 associations, when we add together market and non-market associations and exclude, as Lévesque does, those not using salaried staff. The figure of 8,000 non-market associations is higher than the 4,000 we had previously put forward (Vaillancourt et al. 2004, 317), which was taken up by Martine D'Amours (2006, 20). It is also higher than the 6,000 suggested by Lévesque. In putting forward the approximate figure of 8,000 non-market associations and 35,000 jobs, we are taking into account the figures suggested by Christian Jetté (2008, 2; 2009) who, limiting himself to non-market associations funded by the Quebec government, identified 5,000 associations representing 22,000 full-time equivalent (FTE) jobs. To these 5,000 associations and 22,000 jobs, we estimate an additional minimum of 3,000 non-market associations (representing 13,000 jobs) that are not recognized and supported financially by the Quebec government.

18. Also worth mentioning is the participation since 1993 of the QLF Solidarity Fund in the capitalization of the 86 Sociétés locales d'investissement et de développement de l'emploi (SOLIDES, local investment and job development corporations), the latter being regional development funds to which various levels of government contribute, the Quebec government among them. On the various venture capital funds and the role of the SOLIDES in particular, see Favreau (2008, 48–50), Mendell and Rouzier (2006), and Bourque et al. (2007).

19. "At the beginning of 2003, RISQ represented a $10.3-million venture capital fund devoted strictly to social economy organizations, of which 60% comes from the Quebec government. ... RISQ had invested more than $8.3 million

at the end of June 2005: $7.4 million in capitalization and $930,486 in technical assistance" (Mendell and Rouzier 2006, 3).

20. It is important to draw attention to some characteristics of social democracy as embodied for instance in the British Labour tradition or the Scandinavian social democratic tradition in the 20th century. For the individuals, social organizations, political parties, and governments describing themselves as social democratic, the name social democracy implies: (1) special—often organic—relations with social movements; (2) government intervention in the form of regulations to achieve full employment, progressive taxation, and income redistribution; (3) pursuit of the general interest; (4) access to decent living conditions for a majority of citizens; and (5) participation by the majority of citizens in the democratization of society (Esping-Andersen 1990, 1999). Unlike the socialist project of the Marxist variety, the social democratic project does not advocate the abolition of the market economy (or the capitalist system). Rather, it seeks its profound transformation via, among other things, the socialization (or state ownership) of certain strategic means of production in the general interest of the population.

21. During the 1930s, 1940s, and 1950s, the CCF was a political party active at the federal and provincial levels dedicated to the democratic transformation of Canadian society from capitalism to a "co-operative commonwealth." In 1961, the party disbanded and was replaced by the New Democratic Party (NDP).

22. It has to be acknowledged, however, that the CCF's first program, the Regina Manifesto, had strong Marxist leanings. In the second paragraph of the manifesto, the following goal was expressed: "We aim to replace the present capitalist system, with its inherent injustice and inhumanity, by a social order from which the domination and exploitation of one class by another will be eliminated, in which economic planning will supersede unregulated private enterprise and competition" (CCF 1933, 1). Moreover, the last paragraph of the manifesto began as follows: "No CCF Government will rest content until it has eradicated capitalism" (1933, 8). But the program remained social democratic, rather than fully socialistic, inasmuch as it advocated socialization of the "principal means of production and distribution" and not of all means of production (1933, 2).

23. The Regina Manifesto made the following commitment: "We do not believe in change by violence" (CCF 1933, 2).

24. In his memoirs, G.-H. Lévesque (who had lived in France and Belgium in the early 1930s) acknowledged that in 1933, when he stated that a Catholic could not support the CCF doctrine, he was unaware of the differences between the French and Belgian socialist tradition, on the one hand, and the British labour tradition and the Scandinavian social democratic tradition,

on the other. This prompted Lévesque to write: "During my time studying in Europe, my practical knowledge of socialism mainly, if not solely, concerned the Belgium and French versions of socialism, both fiercely anticlerical and antireligious. ... So it is not surprising that I should entertain serious misgivings and even aggressiveness toward our homegrown socialist party [that is, the CCF]. It is true that the British Labour Party, which officially flew the socialist flag, proved to be, in line with the Anglo-Saxon mentality, much less doctrinaire or radical than its Continental colleagues and that, in concrete terms, there was nothing antireligious about it" (Lévesque 1983, 231).

25. On the ideas front, the history of the CCF during the 1930s was inseparable from that of a collective of progressive intellectuals, the League for Social Reconstruction (LSR), whose main leaders were from the University of Toronto and McGill University. The Montreal group included King Gordon, a professor of Christian Ethics at United Theological College in Montreal (Horn 1986, xvi–xix, in Pelletier and Vaillancourt 1975, 70).

26. In his work on Catholics and Canadian socialism, which dealt with the relationship between Catholics and social democracy, Gregory Baum thoroughly documented the fact that, during the 1930s and 1940s, there were also Catholics who had social democratic-type commitments. But they were an exception (Baum 1980).

27. The CCF program was highly centralizing and statist, and showed a lack of sensitivity to the Quebec "national question." The Regina Manifesto advocated constitutional changes to the *British North America Act* to reinforce the federal government's powers to run the economy (CCF 1933, section 9). In addition, the manifesto placed great emphasis on a "National Planning Commission consisting of a small body of economists, engineers and statisticians assisted by an appropriate technical staff" (CCF 1933, section 1).

28. For example, the CCF was in power in Saskatchewan from 1944 to 1961.

29. See on this topic the three articles published against the Marsh report by Father Émile Bouvier, a Jesuit economist highly representative of the corporatist perspective, in the April, June, and September 1943 issues of *Relations*. See also our comments in Vaillancourt (1988, 126–128).

30. But Angers was an ardent promoter of co-operation and corporatism. With other Catholic intellectuals belonging to the same current—Émile Bouvier, Richard Arès, and Esdras Minville among them—he liked the social economy, provided it remained rooted in a conservative, anti-statist configuration.

31. For example, this corporatist current remained strong in *Relations* until 1968. Over the ensuing years, this Jesuit periodical became more pluralistic,

opening up to contributions of a social democratic and even Marxist bent, and adhering to liberation theology.

32. Suzanne Clavette (2005, 505) mentions the support given in 1957 by certain progressive union figures such as Gérard Picard, Pierre Vadeboncoeur, and Michel Chartrand to the Parti socialiste démocratique (PSD), the Quebec wing of the CCF.

33. My criticism of Marxism's difficulty in showing openness toward the social economy is aimed at the intransigent structuralist Marxism we experienced in Quebec (and the rest of Canada) from 1970 to 1985. It does not refer to all forms of Marxism. So there is room for imagining a perspective to be developed concerning a more harmonious articulation between Marxism and the social economy. But I cannot develop this point here.

34. The left's current reticence to identify with social democracy struck me when I read "Douze contributions pour un renouvellement de la gauche au Québec" (Twelve Contributions for Renewal of the Left in Quebec), recently published in *L'avenir est à gauche* (*The Future Is on the Left*) and edited by Pierre Mouterde (2008). In fact, the political position of most of the authors contributing to that book falls *objectively* under social democracy. But *subjectively*, these authors do not dare label themselves social democrats. The great majority of them stand apart from neo-liberalism or "neo-liberal capitalism." Some—Jacques B. Gélinas, for example—reproach the PQ for never having been social democratic and for moving even farther away from social democracy during the time of Bouchard and Landry. Jacques Gélinas and Françoise David are critical of Pauline Marois for having launched the idea of modernizing social democracy. These descriptions and others like them imply that these left-wing personalities are implicitly defined as being social democratic. But one observes a malaise that prevents a significant part of today's left wing in Quebec from acknowledging that they belong to the world of social democracy.

35. Consider, for example, the difficulties of the social democratic governments in France from 1981 to 1995 under President Mitterrand, in Chile from 2000 to 2008 under socialist presidents Lagos and Bachelet, and in Brazil since the election of Lula's Workers' Party (PT) government in 2003. Or the difficulties in Canada of the episodes of provincial NDP governments of Bob Rae in Ontario in the early 1990s and Gary Doer in Manitoba since the late 1990s.

36. These debates on the refounding of France's socialist party may be followed in various French progressive publications, in particular *Le nouvel observateur*. In that weekly, Jean Daniel and Jacques Julliard on several occasions in the past two years have returned to the idea that the socialist party in France should remove the ambiguity involved in calling officially for a break with capitalism whereas, in reality—and very clearly since 1983—

that political formation has drawn its inspiration from social democracy inasmuch as it does not claim to break with the market economy, unlike, for example, the goal of a Marxist-type socialist project (see Daniel 2008, 20–21; Julliard 2007).

37. I refer here to a way of seeing socio-economic reforms that build on government intervention without making room for participation by civil society stakeholders and the labour market (Vaillancourt 2008b).

Discussion Questions

1. What are the five periods of Quebec social economy history?
2. What role has sovereignty played in the development of a distinct vision of the social economy in Quebec?
3. What similarities and differences are there between the development of the social economy in Quebec and in English Canada?

Suggested Further Readings and Resources

D'Amours, M. 2006. *L'économie sociale au Québec: Cadre théorique, histoire, réalités et defies.* Montreal: Éditions Saint-Martin.

Favreau, L. 2006. Social economy and public policy: The Quebec experience. *Horizons* 8 (2): 7–15.

Favreau, L. 2008. *Entreprises collectives: Les enjeux sociopolitiques et territoriaux de la coopération et de l'économie sociale.* Quebec City: Presses de l'Université du Québec.

Jetté, C. 2008. *Les organismes communautaires et la transformation de l'État-providence: Trois décennies de coconstruction des politiques publiques dans le domaine de la santé et des services sociaux.* Quebec City: Presses de l'Université du Québec.

Lévesque, B., and M.-C. Malo. 1992. L'économie sociale au Québec: Une notion méconnue, une réalité économique importante. In *Économie sociale: Entre économie capitaliste et économie publique/ The third sector: Cooperative, mutual and non-profit organizations,* ed. J. Defourney and J.L. Monzan Campos, 385–446. Brussels: De Boeck Université.

Lévesque, B., and M. Mendell. 2005. The Social economy: Diverse approaches and practices. *Journal of Rural Cooperation* 33 (1): 22–45.

Lévesque, B. 2007. *Un siècle et demi d'économie sociale au Québec: Plusieurs configurations en présence (1850–2007).* Montreal: CRISES, ÉNAP, and ARUC-ÉS. http://www.crises.uqam.ca.

Neamtan, N. 2004. The political imperative: Civil society and the politics of empowerment. *Making Waves* 15 (1): 26–30.

Shragge, E., and J.M. Fontan, eds. 2000. *Social economy: International debates and perspectives.* Montreal: Black Rose.

Simard, H. 2004. The co-operative movement of Quebec: A dynamic and diversified movement. Powerpoint. Quebec City: Conseil de la cooperation du Québec.

Vaillancourt, Y. 2008. Social economy in the co-construction of public policy. Fall. Occasional papers series. Victoria: Canadian Social Economy Hub, University of Victoria.

Vaillancourt, Y., and L. Tremblay, eds. 2002. *Social economy: Health and welfare in four Canadian provinces.* Halifax: Fernwood.

References

Alliance de recherche universités-communautés en économie sociale (ARUC-ÉS) and Réseau québécois de recherche partenariale en économie sociale (RQRP-ÉS). 2007. *La recherche partenariale: Le modèle de l'ARUC-ÉS et du RQRP-ÉS.* Montreal: ARUC-ÉS and RQRP-ÉS, UQAM.

Angers, F.-A. 1955. Appendix 3: La sécurité sociale et les problèmes constitutionnels. *Report of the Royal Commission of Inquiry on Constitutional Problems,* vols. I and II. Quebec City: Royal Commission of Inquiry on Constitutional Problems.

Aubry, F., and J. Charest. 1995. Développer l'économie solidaire: Éléments d'orientation, document déposé au Conseil confédéral de la CSN les 13, 14 et 15 septembre 1995. Montreal: Confédération des syndicates nationaux (CSN).

Baum, G. 1980. *Catholics and Canadian socialism: Political thought in the thirties and forties.* Toronto: James Lorimer.

Boivin, L., and M. Fortier (eds). 1998. *L'économie social: L'avenir d'une illusion.* Montreal: Fides.

Bouchard, M.J., and M. Hudon. 2005. Le logement coopératif et associatif comme innovation sociale émanant de la société civile. C-2005-01. April. Montreal: Chaire de recherche en économie sociale, UQAM.

Bourque, G.L., B. Lévesque, M. Mendell, A. De Serres, F. Hanin, R. Rouzier, A. Lauriault, T. Zerdani, and R. Milot. 2007. *Portrait de la finance socialement responsable au Québec.* Montreal: Fonds de développement de la CSN pour la coopération et l'emploi (Fondaction).

Chantier de l'économie sociale (CÉS). 2001. *De nouveau, nous osons ... Document de positionnement stratégique.* Montreal: Chantier de l'économie sociale.

Chantier de l'économie sociale (CÉS). 2003. *L'économie sociale en mouvement.* November. Montreal: Chantier de l'économie sociale.

Chantier de l'économie sociale (CÉS), in collaboration with the Canadian Community Economic Development Network (CCEDNet) and Alliance de recherche universités-communautés en économie sociale (ARUC-ÉS). 2005. *Social economy and community economic development in Canada: Next steps for public policy*. September 21. Montreal: Chantier de l'économie sociale.

Chantier de l'économie sociale (CÉS). 2006a. $52.8 million to develop the social economy: Launch of the Chantier de l'économie sociale Trust. Press release. January 11. Quebec City: CÉS.

Chantier de l'économie sociale (CÉS). 2006b. 10 M$ pour le soutien de l'économie sociale. March 13. Press release. Quebec City: CÉS.

Chantier de l'économie sociale Trust. 2007. *2007 annual report*. Montreal: Chantier de l'économie sociale Trust.

CIRIEC-Canada. 1998. *Appel pour une économie sociale et solidaire*. May. Montreal: CIRIEC-Canada.

Clavette, S. 2005. *Les dessous d'Asbestos*. Quebec City: Presses de l'Université Laval.

Comeau, Y., L. Favreau, B. Lévesque, and M. Marguerite. 2001. *Emploi, économie sociale, développement local*. Quebec City: Presses de l'Université du Québec.

Comité d'orientation et de concertation sur l'économie sociale (COCES). 1996. *Entre l'espoir et le doute*. Quebec: COCES.

Conseil québécois de la coopération et de la mutualité (CQCM). 2007. *Rapport d'activités 2006*. La coopération: des valeurs à transmettre. Quebec City: CQCM.

Co-operative Commonwealth Federation (CCF). 1933. *The Regina manifesto*. First CCF National Convention. July 19–21. Regina, Saskatchewan. http://www.sasknpd.com/assets/file/history/manifest.pdf.

Corbeil, C., F. Descarries, and E. Galerand, eds. 2002. *Actes du colloque L'économie sociale du point de vue des femmes*. Cahiers du LAREPPS, 02-02. Montreal: CRISES and ARUC-ISDC.

D'Amours, M. 2006. *L'économie sociale au Québec: Cadre théorique, histoire, réalités et defies*. Montreal: Éditions Saint-Martin.

Daniel, J. 2008. Libéral, disent-ils. *Le nouvel observateur* 2273 (May 29–June 4): 20–21.

Defourny, J., and L. Monzon Campos, eds. 1992. *Économie sociale: Entre économie capitaliste et économie publique / The third sector: Cooperative, mutual and nonprofit organizations*. Brussels: CIRIEC and De Boeck Université.

Defourny, J., P. Develtere, and F. Bénédicte, eds. 1999. *L'économie sociale au Nord et au Sud*. Paris: De Boeck Université.

École sociale populaire (ÉSP), ed. 1934. *Le programme de Restauration sociale expliqué et commenté*. Montreal: ÉSP.

Enjolras, B., ed. 2008. *Gouvernance et intérêt général dans les services sociaux et de santé*. Brussels: P.I.E.-Peter Lang.

Esping-Andersen, G. 1990. *The three worlds of welfare capitalism.* Cambridge: Polity.

Esping-Andersen, G. 1999. *Les trois mondes de l'État-providence: Essai sur le capitalisme moderne.* Paris: Presses Universitaires de France.

Favreau, L. 2005. *Les regroupements nationaux d'économie sociale au Québec: Essai d'analyse politique.* Canada Research Chair in Community Development, research report 36, May. Gatineau: University of Quebec in Outaouais. http://www.uqo.ca/crdc-geris.

Favreau, L. 2006. Social economy and public policy: The Quebec experience. *Horizons* 8 (2): 7–15.

Favreau, L. 2008. *Entreprises collectives: Les enjeux sociopolitiques et territoriaux de la coopération et de l'économie sociale.* Quebec City: Presses de l'Université du Québec.

Favreau, L., and B. Lévesque. 1996. *Développement économique communautaire: Économie sociale et intervention.* Quebec City: Presses de l'Université du Québec.

Favreau, L., and A. Salam Fall, eds. 2007. *L'Afrique qui se refait: Initiatives socioéconomiques des communautés et développement en Afrique noire.* Quebec City: Presses de l'Université du Québec.

Favreau, L., R. Lachapelle, and G. Larose. 2003. Social movements, social and solidarity economy, democracy and development: The key aspects of an equitable globalization. *Économie et solidarités:* 4-15.

Fontan, J.-M., and E. Shragge. 2000. Tendencies, tensions and visions in the social economy. In *Social economy: International debates and perspectives,* ed. E. Shragge and J.-M. Fontan, 1–15. Montreal: Black Rose.

Groupe de travail sur l'économie sociale (GTES). 1996. *Osons la solidarité!* October. GTES report submitted to the Summit on the Economy and Employment. October. Montreal.

Guay, L. (ed.). 1997. *Du néolibéralisme à l'économie solidaire: Le combat des femmes.* Proceedings of the second international seminar on the solidarity economy. June 10, 11, and 12, 1996, June 1997. Montreal.

Hall, M.H., et al. 2004. *Cornerstones of community: Highlights of the national survey of nonprofit and voluntary organizations.* Catalogue no. 61-533-XPE. Ottawa: Statistics Canada, Canadian Centre for Philanthropy, and seven partners.

Horn, M. 1986. Introduction. In F.R. Scott, *A new endeavour: Selected political essays, letters, and addresses,* ed. M. Horn. Toronto: University of Toronto Press.

Jetté, C. 2008. *Les organismes communautaires et la transformation de l'État-providence: Trois décennies de coconstruction des politiques publiques dans le domaine de la santé et des services sociaux.* Quebec City: Presses de l'Université du Québec.

Jetté, C. 2009. Quand l'État fait appel au "tiers secteur": le cas de la santé et des services sociaux. *L'état du Québec 2009*, 391–394. Montreal: Fides.

Jetté, C., F. Aubry, and Y Vaillancourt. 2005. L'économie sociale dans les services à domicile: Une innovation davantage institutionnelle qu'organisationnelle. *Économie et solidarités* 36 (2): 129–151.

Jetté, C., B. Lévesque, L. Mager, and Y. Vaillancourt. 2000. *Économie sociale et transformation de l'État-providence dans le domaine de la santé et du bien-être: Une recension des écrits (1990–2000)*. Sainte-Foy: Presses de l'Université du Québec.

Julliard, J. 2007. Réinventer la gauche. *Le nouvel observateur* 2219 (May 17): 20–21.

Klein, J.-L., and D. Harrisson, eds. 2007. *L'innovation sociale: Émergence et effets sur la transformation des sociétés*. Quebec City: Presses de l'Université du Québec.

Lévesque, B. 2004. *Le modèle québécois et le développement régional et local: Vers le néolibéralisme et la fin du modèle québécois?* May. ET0405. Montreal: CRISES.

Lévesque, B. 2007. *Un siècle et demi d'économie sociale au Québec: plusieurs configurations en présence (1850–2007)*. Montreal: CRISES, ÉNAP, and ARUC-ÉS. http://www.crises.uqam.ca.

Lévesque, B. 2008a. Aperçu des relations internationales de l'économie sociale au Québec sur plus d'un siècle et demi (1840–2008). Paper submitted in spring 2008 to *Globe: Revue internationale d'études québécoises*.

Lévesque, B. 2008b. Le CIRIEC-Canada (1966–2006): Quarante ans de partenariat en recherche sur les entreprises publiques et d'économie sociale. August. Draft. Montreal: UQAM and CRISES.

Lévesque, B., and M.-C. Malo. 1992. L'économie sociale au Québec: Une notion méconnue, une réalité économique importante. In *Économie sociale: Entre économie capitaliste et économie publique / The third sector: Cooperative, mutual and non-profit organizations*, ed. J. Defourney and J.L. Monzan Campos, 385–446. Brussels: De Boeck Université.

Lévesque, B., and M. Mendell. 1999. Éléments théoriques et empiriques pour le débat et la recherché. *Lien social et politiques* 41: 105–118.

Lévesque, B., and M. Mendell. 2005. The social economy: Diverse approaches and practices. *Journal of Rural Cooperation* 33 (1): 22–45.

Lévesque, B., and W.A. Ninacs. 2000. The social economy in Canada: The Quebec experience. In *Social economy: International debates and perspectives*, ed. E. Shragge and J.-M. Fontan, 130–158. Montreal: Black Rose.

Lévesque, B., G.L. Bourque, and É. Forgues. 2001. *La nouvelle sociologie économique: Originalité et tendances nouvelles*. Paris: Desclée de Brouwer.

Lévesque, G.-H. 1983. *Souvenances 1: Entretiens avec Simon Jutras*. Montreal: La Presse.

Lévesque, K. 2006. Près de 53 millions pour développer l'économie sociale. November 23. *Le Devoir*.

Loxley, J. 2007. *Transforming or reforming capitalism: Towards a theory of community economic development.* Halifax: Fernwood.

Loxley, J., and D. Simpson. 2007. Government policies toward community economic development (CED) and the social economy in Quebec and Manitoba. April, amended October. Report prepared for the Canadian CED Network.

Mendell, M., and R. Rouzier. 2006. Some initiatives that enabled the institutionalization of Quebec's social economy: Civil society's crucial role and the state's essential role. Paper produced for the CURA on Social Economy, December 6. Montreal: Concordia University.

Mouterde, P. (ed.). 2008. *L'avenir est à gauche: Douze contributions pour un renouvellement de la gauche au Québec.* Montreal: Écosociété.

Nadeau, M. 2008. La nouvelle présidence veut redonner le pouvoir aux caisses. *Forces* 154: 30–34.

Neamtan, N. 2003. Social and solidarity economy in North America: The Quebec experience. Special edition. *Économie et solidarités:* 184-189.

Neamtan, N. 2004. The political imperative: Civil society and the politics of empowerment. *Making Waves* 15 (1): 26–30.

Pelletier, M., and Y. Vaillancourt. 1975. Les années 30. Vol. 2 of *Les politiques sociales et les travailleurs.* Montreal.

Petitclerc, M. 2007. *Nous protégeons l'infortune: Les origines populaires de l'économie sociale au Québec.* Montreal: VLB Éditeur.

Piotte, J.-M. 1998. *Du combat au partenariat: Interventions critiques sur le syndicalisme québécois.* Montreal: Nota Bene.

Piotte, J.-M. 2008. *Un certain espoir.* Montreal: Éditions Logiques.

Quebec Council for the Status of Women (CSF). 1996. *L'économie sociale et les femmes: Garder l'œil ouvert.* Quebec City: CSF.

Quebec Ministry of Economic Development, Innovation and Export Trade (MDÉIE). 2007. *Coopératives du Québec: Données statistiques (édition 2007).* Quebec City: MDÉIE.

Salam Fall, A., L. Favreau, and G. Larose, eds. 2004. *Le Sud ... et le Nord dans la mondialisation: Quelles alternatives? Le renouvellement des modèles de développement.* Quebec City: Presses de l'Université du Québec and Karthala.

Shragge, E., and J.M. Fontan, eds. 2000. *Social economy: International debates and perspectives.* Montreal: Black Rose.

Vaillancourt, Y. 1988. *L'évolution des politiques sociales au Québec, 1940–1960.* Montreal: Presses de l'Université de Montréal.

Vaillancourt, Y. 2003. The Quebec model in social policy and its interface with Canada's social union. In *Forging the Canadian social union: SUFA and beyond,* ed. S. Fortin, A. Noël, and H. St-France, 157–195. Montreal: Institute for Research on Public Policy.

Vaillancourt, Y. 2006. Le tiers secteur au Canada, un lieu de rencontre entre la tradition américaine et la tradition européenne. *Canadian Review of Social Policyy/Revue canadienne de politique sociale* 56: 23–39.

Vaillancourt, Y. 2007. Democratizing knowledge: The experience of university–community research partnerships. In *Building local and global democracy*, 63–79. Toronto: Carold Institute. http://www.carold.ca.

Vaillancourt, Y., with P. Leclerc. 2008a. *Note de recherche sur l'apport de l'économie sociale dans la coproduction et la coconstruction des politiques publiques.* January. Cahiers du LAREPPS 08-01. Montreal: CRISES and ARUC-ISDC. http://www.larepps.uqam.ca.

Vaillancourt, Y. 2008b. *Social economy in the co-construction of public policy.* July. Occasional papers series, 3. Victoria: Canadian Social Economy Hub, University of Victoria.

Vaillancourt, Y. 2008c. *L'économie sociale au Québec et au Canada: Configurations historiques et enjeux actuels.* October. Cahiers du LAREPPS 08-07. Montreal: CRISES and ARUC-ÉS.

Vaillancourt, Y., and L. Favreau. 2001. Le modèle québécois d'économie sociale et solidaire. *RECMA: Revue internationale de l'économie sociale* 281: 69–83.

Vaillancourt, Y., and L. Tremblay, eds. 2002. *Social economy: Health and welfare in four Canadian provinces.* Halifax: Fernwood.

Vaillancourt, Y., and M.-N. Ducharme, with R. Cohen, C. Roy, and C. Jetté. 2001. *Social housing—A key component of social policies in transformation: The Quebec experience.* September. Ottawa: Caledon Institute of Social Policy. http://www.caledoninst.org.

Vaillancourt, Y., F. Aubry, and C. Jetté (eds). 2003. *L'économie sociale dans les services à domicile.* Quebec City: Presses de l'Université du Québec.

Vaillancourt, Y., F. Aubry, M. Kearney, L. Thériault, and L. Tremblay. 2004. The contribution of the social economy towards healthy social policy reforms in Canada: A Quebec viewpoint. In *Social determinants of health: Canadian perspectives*, ed. D. Raphael, 311–329. Toronto: Canadian Scholars' Press.

Vaillancourt, Y., and L. Thériault. 2008. *Social economy, social policy and federalism in Canada.* Fall. Occasional paper, 4. Victoria: Canadian Social Economy Hub, University of Victoria.

CHAPTER FOUR

Building the Social Economy Using the Innovative Potential of Place

DOUG LIONAIS AND HARVEY JOHNSTONE

Introduction

The social economy is an emerging phenomenon that is composed of numerous responses to the negative socio-economic impacts of neo-liberal capitalism. It is broadly understood to include any number of economic and quasi-economic activities that are pursued with the intent to create social benefits rather than to maximize profits. With increased interest in the social economy within academic, practitioner, and particularly policy circles, there has also been increased scrutiny and critical assessment of the sector. Two broad perspectives regarding the social economy, with their respective criticisms, have emerged from the diverse number of approaches that operate under the guise of this term.

Fontan and Shragge (2000) characterize these two perspectives as *pragmatic* and *utopian*. In the pragmatic reform approach, the social economy fills in for the welfare state by servicing unmet and undermet needs. This is the third-sector approach wherein services are provided neither by government nor by conventional private business. In the radical utopian approach, the social economy is seen as a separate (often non-market) circuit of capital. This form of "alternative" economy specifically establishes itself outside the mainstream market.

While there are specific criticisms of both perspectives, there are also problems associated with the social economy account as a whole. For example, the relationship between the social economy and wealth creation is problematic. While at times the literature promoting the social economy mentions wealth creation, there is little evidence to suggest that a priority is placed on creating wealth and economic value. When it is present as a stated goal, wealth creation tends to be subordinated to other (often conflicting) priorities. Furthermore, accounts of the social economy tend to overemphasize the local—often depicting communities as bounded territories within which both the causes of and solutions to depletion are to be found. This exposes a limited understanding of the role that geography plays in the genesis of depletion and social exclusion. Similarly, the potential role that geography might play in any solution frequently goes unrecognized. Consequently, accounts of the social economy often underestimate the complexity of depletion and exclusion by presenting simple, unidimensional solutions to systematic, institutional, complex problems. In our view, the expectations placed on the social economy are too onerous for the tools currently being used to fix problems, and this suggests that there is need for further innovation—innovations that are rooted in a deeper understanding of the role that geography plays.

In this chapter, we examine the role of place-based business as a viable tool for creating wealth within a geographical perspective on depletion and exclusion. We suggest that place-based businesses represent an innovative approach to development in economically distressed regions. To demonstrate these ideas, we examine two cases: the Mondragón Corporación Cooperativa (MCC, Mondragón Cooperative Corporation) and New Dawn Enterprises Limited (NDE).

The Social Economy Debate

Interest in the social economy rises with crises in society (Moulaert and Ailenei 2005; Ninacs 2002; Fontan and Shragge 2000). The collapse of Fordism, subsequent market turmoil, and the re-emergence of regional and class-based economic divergence have contributed to the current interest in alternative social economies (Moulaert and Ailenei 2005). In the past few decades a multitude of economic experiments have been undertaken in an attempt to service unmet and undermet needs of those excluded by mainstream capitalism. These socio-economic innovations are often developed by local people living in places we have characterized as depleted communities (Johnstone and Lionais 2004); they are driven to experiment with alternative development practices as the mainstream economy and mainstream development techniques lose grounding within peripheral areas.

These "socially guided" responses to the deficiencies of neo-liberal capitalism are loosely bound together in the term social economy, a term that is gaining currency in policy and academic circles. However, debate on what exactly we are talking about when we discuss the social economy continues. Gide (1912) identified the social economy as an activity that improves the condition of people. This focus on social rather than private benefit of economic activity has continued into contemporary uses of the term. Neamtam (2005), for example, characterizes the social economy as the set of economic organizations that are neither private for profit nor public, while Amin, Cameron, and Hudson (2002, 1) simply identify the social economy as "not-for-profit activity geared towards meeting social needs."

Moulaert and Nussbaumer (2005) distinguish between essentialist and holistic methods of defining social economy. For them, an essentialist definition includes:

1. the satisfaction of basic and sustainable needs;
2. the democratic institutionalization and organization (governance) of production systems; and
3. reciprocity and redistribution in production and exchange relationships.

Holistic definitions, they argue, are more contextualized (in terms of the social, cultural, and economic context within a given time and space) and may include essentialist definitions as a guide for analysis; but analysis may also reshape the essentialist definition.

Alternative approaches have identified shifts in the way that change agents have thought about and contributed to the social economy. For example, Ninacs (2002, 4) divides thought on the social economy between "old" and "new." The old social economy, he argues, "focused on the development of the cooperative as an alternative model of business enterprise," while the new social economy is "seen as a fundamental part of a new socioeconomic regulatory mechanism." Along the same lines, Moulaert and Ailenei (2005) further break down that which Ninacs labels the old social economy into three generations, each related to the socio-economic context of the time:

1. unions and mutual associations emerged in the 1840s and '50s, as the economy shifted from craft guilds to wage labour, in order to protect massed workers from dangerous working conditions, retaliations against labour action, and extreme exploitation;
2. agricultural and savings co-operatives (credit unions) emerged near the end of the 19th century in response to the industrialization of agriculture and the need to protect small producers; and

3. consumption and housing co-operatives emerged as a result of the Great Depression—that is, as a response to the material needs of blue-collar workers and the unemployed.

The new social economy, by contrast, is seen as a response to the collapse of Fordism beginning in the 1970s, a collapse that Moulaert and Ailenei (2005) characterize as a simultaneous crisis of the mass-production system and the welfare state. It is characterized by a small (local) business focus and the emergence of worker co-operatives and non-profit organizations. As such, the social economy, both old and new, can be seen as a response to the changing context of capitalist growth and the associated social conflicts brought on by changes in the capitalist economy. The social economy is a response to the needs arising in the wake of capital expansion and growth.

In contrast to this historical approach, others have made distinctions based on the different ways of addressing needs within the social economy. A number of authors have distinguished between more radical approaches to the social economy and more pragmatic reform approaches (Zografos 2007; Amin et al. 2002; Fontan and Shragge 2000). Fontan and Shragge argue that much of the "new" social economy is a part of the pragmatic reform vision because it fills in the gaps left by permanent structural unemployment in the market and the withdrawal of the state from social service provision. Thus, the pragmatic reform approach is associated with the rise of the "third sector" as an arena of activity that is neither market nor state. This form of the social economy is composed of new associational governance structures that operate beyond the state (Swyngedouw 2005) and in this way are purported to represent a new regulatory mechanism (Ninacs 2002). However, Amin et al. (2002, 123), among others, warn that this approach can be read as a "subtle abandonment of the universal welfare state under the guise of partnership, efficiency of service delivery, and local targeting" in which the social economy becomes a "poor form of welfare for the poor." Fontan and Shragge (2000, 8) argue that the potential for social transformation through such an approach is "an illusion." This approach to the social economy can be conceptually linked to the neo-liberal economy as a support structure rather than an alternative to it.

A prominent arm of the pragmatic reform approach emphasizes enterprise as a key element of the social economy. Social enterprises are promoted as mechanisms for achieving social goals and serving the excluded as well as being financially sustainable. Defourny (2001) describes social enterprises as the outcome of a new form of social entrepreneurship that innovates new means of providing for social need. Defourny identifies the socialization of production surpluses as the defining characteristic of a social enterprise. For Amin et al. (2002), however, the enterprise approach to the social economy is suspect. The enterprise ethos, they argue, is a means to legitimate the social economy to sponsors (primarily public sector ones) by adopting market-driven forms. For them, this approach is problematic; they argue that the commitment made by social enterprises to social empowerment of and service to the excluded actually hobbles their ability to be efficient producers of profit. Social goals and profitability (and, therefore, sustainability) are in conflict, often resulting in a trade-off of one for the other. Thus, social enterprises suffer from isomorphic tendencies, moving either to the commercial or to the non-profit end of the spectrum at the cost of the other (Laville and Nyssens 2001).

On the other side of the debate are conceptualizations of the social economy as a radical alternative to mainstream capitalism. Radical forms of social economy thus seek to replace capitalism with new forms of socioeconomic organization. A review of such alternative economic practices is contained in the volume *Alternative Economic Spaces* edited by Leyshon, Lee, and Williams (2003). Radical approaches to social economy in this volume include local credit unions, worker-ownership enterprise models, local exchange trading systems (LETS), back-to-the-land self-provisioning, and black market and mutual aid systems. Such radical attempts at local economic development are often (desperate) attempts at regeneration made only after conventional approaches have failed. Furthermore, because of the depleted nature of the locality, these regeneration strategies often fail. Such alternative circuits of capital often rely on primary capitalist circuits for the production of wealth, which is then recirculated in the alternative economy. Thus, although such alternative circuits may redistribute capital with fewer leakages, they are still dependent on the wealth-creating capacity of the primary circuits. Lee and Leyshon (2003) conclude that these alternative economic practices are perhaps more effective in terms of their political capital than in terms of their material reproducibility. That is, while they may not all be effective as material economies, they do demonstrate different ways of thinking and acting and, therefore, hold the potential for an alternate economy or for a diversity of coexisting economies.

Criticisms of the Debate

Beyond the specific advantages and disadvantages of each approach to the social economy mentioned above, there are a number of general issues that the social economy needs to address if it is to become a significant form of socio-economic organization. We will now turn to issues that are pertinent to our study.

The first issue is a concern with the wealth-creating ability of the social economy. At the root of criticisms regarding the pragmatic reform approach to the social economy is the lack of wealth production. In the absence of a strong welfare system, the pragmatic "third sector" approach is organized as a mechanism for redistributing wealth, rather than a mechanism for creating it. Radical alternatives often remain dependent upon the mainstream economy for primary wealth creation (as in LETS, back-to-the-land movements, recycled retailing, etc.). However, where profitability *is* a main concern of the social economy, as in the enterprise approach, internal conflicts between the competing demands of social goals on the one hand and economic viability and competitiveness on the other often result in failures either as a business entity or in maintaining social goals. In practice, Hayton (2000) reports that many organizations adopt the rhetoric of enterprise in order to legitimize their activities and access targeted funding programs, but in reality never approach (nor intend to approach) the self-sufficiency ideal of social enterprise.

Lack of wealth creation is problematic because without a mechanism for producing wealth, the social economy is doomed to remain a marginal economy on the periphery of capitalism; as such, it would not represent an alternative to the mainstream, but rather would remain dependent on it. As Leyshon and Lee (2003, 8) note, all economies and their geographies "must (always) be constrained by the requirements of materially effective circuits of consumption, exchange and production." Materially effective circuits require creation of a surplus. A social economy that fails to create a surplus is incapable of reproducing itself and must remain reliant on the (dominant) mainstream system. Such a social economy would remain a poor, second-rate system trapping the poor and the excluded and offering few means for individuals to escape from one system to the other.

Too often a focus on social needs narrows the debate to the *symptoms* of unconstrained capitalism (that is, exclusion and poverty) while ignoring the *causes* of these social problems. Thus, the social economy is predominantly concerned with addressing the unmet and undermet needs of those who are currently excluded from mainstream circuits of the economy but has had little to say about the *production* of those inequalities. The focus has been on redistribution of wealth rather than on the ways in which the production of wealth and value creates inequalities in the first place. In contrast to this approach, we feel that the social economy would be better served by examining the possibilities of production with a social goal of arresting the depletion of localities. This is not necessarily the same thing as undertaking to serve the social needs of the excluded. There are important distinctions between causes and symptoms of depletion and exclusion. Much of the social economy focuses on symptoms rather than on causes. While assisting those groups and individuals who are experiencing impoverishment and exclusion is an important social task, there also needs to be attention paid to the causes of depletion. Thus, there is a need for explorations of how wealth can be produced in more socially equitable ways.

This ties in to the second issue of concern with respect to current social economic debates. While debates about the social economy are often grounded in localities, they lack an understanding of the role of geography in creating social exclusion and uneven development. The causes of deprivation, poverty, and exclusion to which the social economy dedicates itself are themselves often the products of spatial forces within the economy (Hudson 2001; Harvey 1996; Massey 1995). This suggests that any redress of these problems will include a spatial component and will indeed require a concern for "the local," particularly those places that have been abandoned by mainstream circuits of capital. The locales in which the social economy is most active—that is, in depleted communities—are the products of uneven development.

Geographers are also concerned with how the term "local" is understood in conceptualizations of the social economy. Amin, Cameron, and Hudson (2003, 32), for example, argue that "the local" is used uncritically in social economy debates; it is usually meant to refer to "a small, definable territory and a homogenous resident population." In this context, the social economy is a means for local (depleted) communities to use their own resources to address their own distinct territorial problems. The assumption here is that local problems and their solutions are rooted in the locality. As Amin (2005) comments, there is a perverse logic in this approach. Communities that are suffering from the socio-economic impacts of depletion are being told, on the one hand, that they are in decline because they lack the right "social" mix, while on the other hand, that the only way for them to develop is through the use of their "social" resources. Amin et al. (2003) argue that such a localized social economy, wherein the "social" is associated with localized areas of poverty and exclusion, is less likely to result in a "socialized economy" and is more likely to lead to the establishment of a "second-class economy" on the periphery of capitalism.

Alternatively, geographers would argue that the causes of local depletion are rooted in the shifting dynamics of the global economy and the uneven development of capitalist accumulation (Massey 1995; Hudson 2001).

Similarly, localities are not bounded territories but relational entities that are defined not by their socially constructed boundaries but by the numerous internal and external relationships that coalesce around particular places. Nor are such places homogenous. Rather, places consist of multiple identity groups with contrasting visions for their location. Thus, while location certainly plays a role in combatting uneven development and the socio-economic problems it causes, social economic practices need not—and more prescriptively, *should* not—be constrained by territory. Rather, the key process of economic development is the (re)building of relationships that lead to greater connectivity not only within the local, but also between the local and the external. Furthermore, such relationship building will happen on the part of a variety of actors in a multitude of ways and will be contested as different visions and politics come into play.

The final issue we wish to deal with relates to the complexity of social exclusion. In our view, debates within the social economy tend to oversimplify the problems of poverty, chronic unemployment, and exclusion. The enterprise approach to the social economy, for example, suggests that one can create profitable enterprises that simultaneously include and address local issues of poverty and exclusion. This is to be accomplished by creating businesses that both service those unmet needs and include the excluded in the management and provision of those services. Within this context, there is a whole host of expectations placed upon social enterprises operating in these depleted communities. According to Amin et al. (2002), the expectations of the social economy include:

1. meeting the needs of the excluded in areas where the state and/or the market have pulled out;
2. increasing civic engagement by building social capital;
3. empowering the "grassroots" to pursue social justice; and
4. supporting a counterculture of needs-based economics opposed to individualism and the pursuit of profit.

In addition to these expectations, social enterprises are expected to be self-supporting, efficient, and businesslike. This sets a mighty high bar. Given these criteria for success, it should not be surprising that many social enterprises fail to meet the expectations placed upon them (Amin et al. 2002). At issue here is whether business organizations are the proper social mechanism for dealing with established groups of impoverished and excluded individuals. As Blackburn and Ram argue (2006, 85), social exclusion has "overwhelming geographic, family, education and labour market aspects which entrepreneurship can do little to address." While Blackburn and Ram are discussing more traditional forms of business and entrepreneurship, it is difficult to understand how social enterprises, given the constraints of their localities (that is, as depleted communities) and the expectations placed upon them, will fare any better in addressing all aspects of social exclusion.

On the one hand, issues of exclusion are complex and need to be properly addressed by institutional arrangements beyond the firm. On the other hand, efforts looking to remedy specific manifestations of social exclusion (such as poverty, unemployment, deprivation, and crime, etc.) are approaches that often ignore the *root causes* of socio-economic depletion. Those root causes are often based outside the region. Not only are social enterprises poorly equipped to remedy specific manifestations of social exclusion, they may also be operating with a misdirected purpose from the outset. To confront the causes of uneven development and local depletion, there should be greater interest in the ways in which social enterprise can operate "outside of the local" and can ground circuits of capital to the locality. Efficient social enterprise, we argue, should address the underlying forces that create exclusion rather than exclusion itself.

Each of these critiques is related in that each questions the possible effectiveness of current modes of thought in the social economy. They question the ways in which the social economy produces value and the ways in which it is social. In the next section, we examine an innovative place-based model of social enterprise that responds to some of these criticisms.

Place as the Basis of Innovation in Social Enterprise

Given the discussion above, we are interested in innovations within the social economy that explore the relationship between social enterprise and critical understandings of geography and place. While we emphasize enterprise, our approach is different from the traditional "social enterprise approach" as critiqued by Amin et al. (2002). Amin et al. are critical of an "enterprise approach" that is "forced" on the third sector, which traditionally has operated in a wealth redistribution role. Demanding self-sustainability and wealth creation of such entities is in direct contradiction to their purpose, which is to assist those excluded from participation in mechanisms of wealth creation by redirecting wealth from other sectors. The redistributive role of such organizations (whether public or third sector) is important; but forcing inconsistent goals on such organizations would seem to constrain rather than improve their ability to fulfill that role.

At the enterprise level, we are concerned with the ways in which a firm can create wealth while simultaneously addressing the causes of depletion and exclusion through place-rootedness. This, however, raises the question whether an enterprise can be focused on wealth creation and be "social." Social enterprises are commonly understood to be social in that they address unmet or undermet needs of particular groups. By definition, this indicates a substitution of a redistributionist mechanism for the market mechanism. It is one thing to ask such organizations to be businesslike in terms of professional management practices, which certainly may help operational effectiveness. It is quite another to ask such organizations to be self-sufficient wealth creators, which suggests the use of market mechanisms, when the very need for their existence is due to market failure. Thus, to be a "social" enterprise in this sense seems to be a contradiction in terms.

However, there are other ways to be "social." In contrast to the approach to social enterprise just outlined, our interest is in firms that have wealth creation as their central organizing factor. Our argument is that there *are* spatial approaches to the social. As indicated above, although the causes of depletion and exclusion are multifaceted, one important factor is the spatial patterns of economic forces. Poverty and exclusion tend to be concentrated within local areas. Thus, it is suggested here that one avenue for innovation within the social economy is to explore ways to purposefully ground circuits of capital in local (depleted) areas. Entities using the business form to ground wealth creation in local areas we call "community-based" or "place-based" business. In this sense, "place" rather than "meeting social needs" becomes the social component of enterprise. By locally rooting wealth creation, place-based businesses become "social" in that their purpose is to create an economy where one was lacking and in so doing address the *causes* of depletion and exclusion. Place-based business, thus conceived, provides an avenue for (at least part of) the community to materially reproduce itself by becoming involved in meaningful relationships of exchange. Place, institutionalized within the business structure, becomes an innovative way to create a social component of the business form. In the next section we explore ways in which firms can be grounded in place or become locally rooted.

In What Ways Can a Wealth-Creating Business Be Locally Rooted?

Businesses are inherently geographic; their activities have spatial impacts. Even "global" businesses are grounded; production and consumption must take place somewhere. The various activities that a business undertakes occur in specific geographies.

TABLE 4.1 Mechanisms That Ground Business in Place

Grounding mechanism	Description
Labour	Location of labour; spatial division of labour
Management	Location of management functions (headquarters, etc.)
Markets	Location of markets served
Capital assets	Location of built infrastructure
Supply	Supply chain groundings
Knowledge	Geographies of knowledge development
Investment and financing sources	Location of financial partners
Ownership	Location of the owners of the business
Governance structures	Location of control
Profit distribution	Location of profit distribution and accumulation

In Table 4.1 we outline the numerous ways in which a business is grounded. Businesses are grounded through their labour and management functions; the spatial division of labour within a firm has different geographic implications (Massey 1995). Each business has a geographic impact through the markets it serves and through the supply chains it uses. Geographies of knowledge and learning also mark the spatial impact of firms (Amin and Cohendet 2005). Businesses are also grounded concretely by means of their built capital (buildings, equipment, etc.). Businesses are grounded through their mechanisms of investment and ownership (where the investment comes from and where the owners are located). Governance structures ground businesses to certain locations. Finally, and related to the last three, businesses are grounded through the distribution of their profits. By following capital flows of all of these functions, we can map out the spatial impacts of a firm.

While Table 4.1 demonstrates the myriad ways in which any business is geographically grounded, we are interested in particular forms of "place-based" business. Place-based businesses differ from mainstream businesses in that the former are deliberately "rooted" to a particular place. Mainstream businesses, within the context of the profit maximization imperative of capitalism, evaluate location in terms of profitability and competitive advantage. In addition to the necessity of profitability, place-based businesses also value local places for social purposes connected to sense of place and community.

The difference is both in intent and in practice. Place-based firms are purposefully locally rooted; they are rooted to place for social reasons (community development, for example) rather than for reasons of "pure" economic rationality. They are intentionally located in a particular place. Place-based firms differ in practice in that they formally anchor one or more grounding mechanisms to the locality. A place-based firm may confine itself to the local labour pool or serve only local markets. For example, a place-based firm could formally state, through its articles of incorporation or bylaws, that it would only employ local residents. Given these characteristics, we define a place-based business as one that is deliberately rooted to place through one or more grounding mechanisms. It is "rooted" in that it elects to limit at least one of its grounding mechanisms to the local area. In contrast to traditional businesses, which may have numerous groundings in various localities, a place-based business is purposefully rooted to a local area.

To emphasize the differences further, we can compare the location decisions of a place-based firm with those of a traditional firm. Traditional businesses, particularly in a classical economic analysis, tend to locate their activities (finance, production, markets, etc.) in locations that have economic advantages. Thus, the motivating intention of traditional business concerning its choice of location is to maximize profitability. The intent of a place-based business is different in that its decisions as to where to locate are not exclusively or even primarily based on profitability but on other social motivations. Place-based businesses locate one or more of their functions in a *particular* place for specific *social* reasons.

The location of business activities for mainstream firms, however, does not always follow rational economic motivations of profit maximization. Entrepreneurial firms, for example, often choose locations based on social factors (such as proximity to family, environment, etc.) rather than rational economic factors (Lionais 2008). Such firms, therefore, would trade economic rationalities of profitability for social factors. Entrepreneurs may tie their firms to particular places for social reasons, but they do not necessarily formalize the ties; they are intentionally place-specific, but only through the decision making of the entrepreneur. Place-based businesses, in contrast, create formal structural ties to the locality in which they root themselves.

Place-based businesses are place-specific because of social motivations and exhibit their spatial choice by formally "rooting" themselves to particular locations through formal mechanisms. In the following section, we use Mondragón Cooperative Corporation and New Dawn Enterprises as two examples of place-based businesses and their rooting mechanisms.

Mondragón Cooperative Corporation

The Mondragón Cooperative Corporation (MCC) is a system of integrated worker co-operatives in the Basque region of Spain. Of its 103,700 employees, 63 percent are located outside the Basque region and 16 percent are located outside Spain (MCC 2008). In terms of markets, a significant portion of MCC's revenues come from international markets. MCC's operations are also global. When possible, the MCC locates its production facilities (and, therefore, its labour) within the Basque region. If competitiveness requires it, however, the MCC does not hesitate to move outside the region. Therefore, at a glance, the MCC appears to be a geographically dispersed global company.

TABLE 4.2 MCC Grounding Mechanisms

Grounding mechanism	MCC
Labour	Forty-four percent of MCC's workforce is in the Basque region. The policy is to return work to the Basque region whenever feasible, especially through technological innovation.
Management	MCC management functions are located primarily in the Basque region. Six international corporate offices are maintained.
Markets	MCC markets extend throughout Europe and the world.
Capital assets	The majority of MCC's assets are in the Basque region, though they have 65 production facilities located throughout the world.
Supply	MCC's supply chains are not localized.
Knowledge	MCC maintains its own university (Mondragón University), polytechnic (Txorierrii), management training centre (Otalora), and research and development centres (such as Ikerlan).
Investment and financing sources	MCC's investments primarily come from worker–owner contributions and retained earnings. Finance is managed through the MCC bank, the Caja Laboural. MCC has started to finance some activities using other external financing tools.
Ownership	Ownership in MCC is attributed to the worker-owners who are primarily located in the Basque region.
Governance structures	The MCC body is based in the Basque region.
Profit distribution	Profit distribution is the rooting mechanism for the MCC. All profits are cycled back to the Basque region for reinvestment in the mandated social purposes of the corporation.

On closer examination, the MCC has many aspects that ground it in the locality. Table 4.2 outlines MCC groundings in the Basque region. While the table outlines the numerous groundings of the MCC in the Basque region, MCC's geographic reach is actually global. In fact, MCC routinely goes outside the Basque community in order to satisfy many of these functions. The MCC, however, is rooted in the local community through its surplus distribution system, which is formalized through its contract of association in which member co-operatives agree to the regulations of the MCC parent body. The "Congress Regulations" stipulate how member firms must distribute their surplus.

TABLE 4.3   MCC Profit Distribution

Fund	Percentage
Education and Co-operative Promotion Fund	10% (minimum)
Reserve Fund	20% (minimum)
Co-operative Returns (dividends)	70% (maximum)

Table 4.3 outlines the profit distribution requirements of MCC. The reserve fund and the education and promotion fund are both requirements of Basque co-operative legislation. At least 20 percent of the surplus is retained by the co-operative for reserves. At least 10 percent is put into the Education and Co-operative Promotion Fund. The remainder is distributed through a dividend payment to the owner-workers' individual accounts. In 2007, 50 percent of surplus went into reserves. The Reserve Fund ends up on the equity side of the balance sheet. As of 2007, the reserves accounted for over half (52.9 percent) of the equity in MCC (MCC 2008). The Reserve Fund serves to anchor the co-operative in the Basque community. The fund is used to pursue the objectives of the organization. The co-operative reserve in MCC is associated with the purpose of the organization. The MCC mission statement identifies the organization as being deeply rooted in the Basque region and tasked with generating wealth through business and job creation:

> Mondragón Corporación Cooperativa (MCC) is a socioeconomic reality of a business nature *with deep cultural roots in the Basque Country*. It was created by people and for people, inspired by the Basic Principles of our Co-operative Experience. It is committed to the environment, competitive improvement and customer satisfaction in order to generate wealth in society by means of business development and job creation. (MCC 2001, emphasis added.)

The MCC's regulations thus tie a portion of its surplus to its community purpose: local wealth creation. Thus, although the MCC does not geographically limit its labour, operations, management, markets, investment, ownership, and other functions, it is rooted in the community through its profit structure.

The scale of MCC enables further forms of local embeddedness. Because it is now a complex with significant capacity, MCC can develop new forms of rootedness such as the Ikerlan research centre. The benefits of centres like Ikerlan are directed to the "place" through new enterprise development and continual change and innovation in existing businesses. This is not likely to be true of individual place-based businesses, which are less able to invest in research and development (R&D).

The MCC, through its structure, has developed a mechanism that roots it within the Basque community. This enables the MCC to focus foremost on successful business operations and subsequently on its role in the community. The structure of the MCC, however, ensures that by focusing on business operations, the complex brings benefits to the community.

New Dawn Enterprises

On an entirely different scale from the Mondragón complex are long-standing place-based institutions such as New Dawn Enterprises (NDE). While much smaller than the MCC, New Dawn demonstrates the same approach.

New Dawn Enterprises is a Canadian place-based business located in Cape Breton, Nova Scotia. New Dawn was founded in 1976 and was developed as a response to the limitations experienced by the Cape Breton Association for Cooperative Development, a registered charity that was developing housing and commercial real estate. New Dawn's founder, Greg MacLeod, found that organizing as a society rather than as a business constrained the growth and threatened the sustainability of the organization. As a remedy, MacLeod sought ways in which an organization could create wealth but have that wealth rooted in the community and also work for social purposes.

New Dawn, an umbrella organization, operates a number of companies including divisions in commercial and residential real estate, health care services, and vocational training. It currently has assets of over Cdn$12 million and over 150 full-time equivalent employees. New Dawn primarily services local markets and, therefore, is grounded locally in most of its functions. Labour, management, markets, and built capital are all situated within its local community (see Table 4.4).

TABLE 4.4   NDE Grounding Mechanisms

Grounding mechanism	New Dawn
Labour	One hundred percent localized; New Dawn does not undertake any business activity outside of the region.
Management	All management functions are similarly localized.
Markets	New Dawn serves local markets only. New Dawn has occasionally attempted to expand into export-based markets, but thus far has been unsuccessful.
Capital assets	All of New Dawn's physical assets are local.
Supply	As a predominantly service-oriented enterprise, New Dawn's supply chains are mostly local. Some supplies come off-island, but local suppliers are be given preferential treatment.
Knowledge	New Dawn has been and continues to remain connected to the local university. This connection often occurs through the governance structures, as university members often hold seats on the board, although there is no policy requiring this.
Investment and financing sources	New Dawn was originally financed through member loans. Current financing occurs through retained earnings and conventional debt. Debt is often held through the local credit union, but is also held by off-island institutions. New Dawn is beginning to expand its use of community-based financing through Nova Scotia's Community Economic Development Investment Fund (CCEDIF) mechanisms.
Ownership	Ownership in New Dawn is indirectly attributed to the community through the articles of incorporation that identify the organization as an enterprise operating in trust of the community. This is recognized as socialized equity on New Dawn's balance sheet.
Governance structures	New Dawn's governance structures are based in the community but occasionally include directors from off-island.
Profit distribution	All profits are reinvestment in the enterprise to pursue the purposes of the corporation.

New Dawn originated with the intention of stimulating local economic development. New Dawn formalizes its local rootedness and social purpose through its legal structure. Its articles of incorporation root ownership of the organization within Cape Breton. New Dawn accomplishes this by removing private ownership (there are no shares) and simultaneously linking the purpose of the organization to the "social, cultural and economic growth of Cape Breton" (articles of incorporation, article b). Generated surpluses, according to the articles of incorporation (article c), must be directed toward the purposes of the business and cannot be distributed for private gain. Thus, while much of the geography of New Dawn is local, it is a place-based business in that it formally roots its ownership and profit distribution in the local area. In effect, New Dawn is operated "in trust" of the local community (MacLeod 2002). Presumably, all other aspects of New Dawn's value chain

CASE STUDY   Just Us! Fair Trade Coffee

Fair trade is an interesting example of the arguments we make in this chapter. Fair trade systems are, at their roots, socially motivated geographical fixes to inequalities in global commodity chains. That is, they are intended to redistribute the values created within international trade to those who have historically had the least amount of negotiating power within the chain—the producers. Fair trade organizations understand the need for value creation but also seek to address fundamental inequalities wherein value is appropriated within the commodity chain. Fair trade, therefore, is place-based; its social purpose is to realize value for specific communities by paying premiums (fair prices) over the market (exploitive) rate to producers. However, the communities to which they are rooted are not always located in the same place as where the business is controlled. Fair trade processors and distributors based in the North are established for the benefit of producing communities in the South. That is, they are place-based, but the places in which they are based are distant. Just Us! Coffee Roasters Co-op is an example of such a fair trade place-based organization.

Based in Wolfville, Nova Scotia, Just Us! Coffee was started in 1995. Co-founder Jeff Moore was searching for information on fair trade development in Canada but was dismayed by the lack of information and support. Not finding any information in Canada, Moore travelled to Chiapas, Mexico to see a fair trade producer co-operative in action. Moore witnessed how fair trade networks were benefiting the communities in the region—communities that traditionally were exploited by both the Mexican state and global coffee companies. A local producer co-operative, Unión de La Selva, was interested in doing business in Canada (Moore 2006).

continued...

...continued

Moore returned to Canada with the conviction that fair trade benefited the producer communities. He also saw that they produced a quality product. In fact, the high-mountain land in Mexico into which native populations were displaced produced better quality, shade-grown coffee than traditional coffee production fields. The business began from an understanding of the impacts of fair trade on producer communities and an appreciation for the product quality. Moore explains:

> We had no capital, no business experience, and no customers—just a conviction that there should be a market for higher quality coffee that was produced in a socially and environmentally responsible way. (Moore 2006)

Just Us! is a place-based business that is motivated by the desire to bring economic justice to disempowered producers and their communities. This is reflected in the mission statement of Just Us!, which includes the words: "helping indigenous communities move beyond the poverty level" (Just Us! 2008). The social purpose is formalized in Just Us! Coffee's constitution, which states that the purpose of the co-operative is to "import and market fairly traded products" (Just Us! 2008). In practice, Just Us! Coffee's commitment to the producer communities is embedded in its supplier relationships and contacts. A key component of Just Us! Coffee's screening process is to ensure that the benefits of the business relationship are spread throughout the local community. Just Us! often participates in organizing local development initiatives with its suppliers; the relationship is not simply about supply. The supply contract then guarantees that the beans are organic and fair trade certified. By subscribing to fair trade principles and enshrining them within the business's constitution, Just Us! commits itself to operating for the benefit of its supply partners. The benefits of operating the business are purposefully rooted in the particular supplier communities with which Just Us! contracts. Thus, although the control and operations of the firm are located in Canada, the firm is rooted in particular communities in Mexico and South America from which it sources its coffee, tea, and chocolate.

could be moved outside the region. The formal rooting of ownership and surplus distribution identify New Dawn as a place-based enterprise.

Conclusion

In this chapter we have described place-based businesses as one innovative approach to the social economy. Place-based businesses are significant institutions in that they address the critiques of the social economy listed above. Those critiques included:

1. a focus on wealth redistribution over wealth creation;
2. an exaggerated emphasis on the local in conceptualizing both the causes and potential solutions to local depletion; and
3. a simplistic view of social exclusion that focuses on symptoms rather than causes.

As business firms that are not limited by mandates to meet social needs, place-based businesses are better able to focus on wealth creation. The inconsistent demands observed in traditional forms of social enterprises are not present in place-based business. Wealth creation is important if the social economy is to become a sustainable economic alternative. A social economy must be able to reproduce itself; wealth creation is key to such sustainability.

Effective wealth creation is linked to the remaining two critical issues: conceptualization of the role of geography and the complexity of social exclusion. Economic depletion occurs when effective circuits of capital are no longer grounded within a location (Hudson 2001). That is, economic depletion is the result of decreasing (economic) relationships (in both quantity and quality) between the local and the regional and global. Places that lack such relationships suffer from ensuing economic depletion and show symptoms of that depletion, including unemployment, poverty, substance abuse, and crime. The causes of economic depletion and social exclusion are very often one and the same; they are products of the unevenness of capitalist development. Place-based businesses, by grounding circuits of capital and wealth creation within the locality, are mechanisms that counteract forces of uneven development. They are place-driven organizations that seek to temper, arrest, and reverse processes of uneven development.

Given this analysis, wealth creation not only is important as a driver of the social economy but also leads to geographic connectivity. Wealth creation implies involvement in value chains that may extend beyond the community. Place-based businesses, at their most effective, link depleted communities to the rest of the world by engaging in and grounding value chains within the community. Thus, while place-based business may root business functions in a particular area, it would be counterproductive to forgo wealth-creating opportunities by insisting that all business functions be rooted in one area. Such a form would constrain a business's ability to achieve efficiencies and remain competitive in external markets and therefore constrain (perhaps critically) wealth creation. In other words, *it is possible to be too local.* There are many ways to root enterprise in place; successful roots, as demonstrated above, do not confine a firm to place, but instead meaningfully ground circuits of capital while engaging in external (global) value chains.

This is borne out by our examples. The MCC has been most successful in engaging global circuits of capital and has consequently had the largest impact on its community. In comparison to New Dawn and Just Us!, MCC operates on a vastly larger scale. As such, it is able to have a much larger impact on its community. The fair trade model exhibited by Just Us! manages global value chains at significant advantage to the local communities it is rooted in. New Dawn Enterprises Ltd., on the other hand, has remained so locally focused that its growth has been slow and prone to crisis. New Dawn's impact on the community has been modest in material terms, though it does have symbolic importance to the community.

In many ways, New Dawn has not had to deal with the same type of spatial decisions as has MCC. While New Dawn has remained focused on the local, MCC's commitment to growth has forced it to make specific decisions that affect its place-rootedness. For example, the decision to move production processes to low-cost global regions required a consideration of and a balance between wealth creation and local employment. Thus, MCC has had to make decisions regarding what elements or aspects of the organization would remain rooted in place and what elements would be allowed to be mobile. As a result, MCC has had to face the nature of its place-rootedness in a much deeper way than other place-based organizations such as New Dawn.

Wealth creation, when socialized, leads to less economic exclusion and poverty. The place-based businesses we outline above do not confront social exclusion directly. Their purposes are not to deal with the specific manifestations of exclusion that appear in their respective locales. Rather, they address social exclusion at its roots. If the causes of social exclusion are primarily economic in nature, then by combatting uneven development place-based business can arrest the creation of exclusion. The business form of organization is a poor form for dealing directly with social exclusion. The business form, however, is specifically organized for the purpose of organizing resources and creating wealth. To ask it to do anything else seems counterproductive. Business can be shaped in more socially beneficial ways. Profitability, when occurring in a place-based business, can benefit rather than marginalize a community. Focusing on wealth creation shifts the "social" component of the social economy debate from the "needs to be served" to "how profits are used." In so doing, it shifts the approach from one based on dealing with the symptoms of depletion to one based on addressing the causes of depletion.

Glossary

Depleted community   A place that is suffering from economic decline but to which its inhabitants remain attached. Depleted communities maintain high values as social places despite their low valuation as economic places.

Fordism   A system of social relations broadly used to distinguish a period of time between the Second World War and the mid-1970s. The period of Fordism was characterized by the mass-production assembly line developed by Henry Ford, for which the period was named, and by a general social contract in which workers were paid enough to consume the products of production and which resulted in the establishment of a social safety net funded by the state.

LETS (local economic trading systems)   Local systems of exchange in which members trade goods and services without using paper currency. LETS typically use a credit system so that direct barter is not necessary. LETS promote the exchange of self-produced goods and services.

Place-based businesses   Businesses rooted in specific geographic communities. Place-based business use formal or informal mechanisms to remain in place. By being locally rooted, place-based businesses are less mobile than conventional forms of business.

Reciprocity   Reciprocity refers to a mutual exchange of benefits. Economic actors may reciprocate (give back) when they see a mutual benefit. In the context of the social economy, consumers may opt to do business with a social enterprise rather than with competing providers because of the perceived social benefits of doing so (supporting local jobs, providing a social service, etc.).

Redistribution   Redistribution refers to the transfer of value from one place or group to another. Welfare systems are based on systems of redistribution in which value is transferred from those who have to those who lack.

Uneven development   The geographic and temporal unevenness of economic and social development. Uneven development is a process, often considered endemic within capitalism, in which the opposing forces of centralization and decentralization create socio-economic difference. Centralization occurs as capital accumulates and concentrates in particular places. Decentralization occurs as capital leaves particular places for new centres of accumulation. The outcome is a process of development and depletion.

Discussion Questions

1. What is unique about a place-based focus for the social economy?
2. What is the nature of the debate around the social economy in this chapter?
3. What is the difference between wealth creation and wealth distribution and why is it important for understanding the social economy?

Suggested Further Readings and Resources

Amin, A., A. Cameron, and R. Hudson. 2002. *Placing the social economy*. London: Routledge.

MacLeod, G. 1997. *From Mondragon to America: Experiments in Community Economic Development*. Sydney: University College of Cape Breton Press.

Mondragón Cooperative Corporation. Online at http://www.mcc.es/ing/index.asp.

New Dawn Enterprises. Online at http://www.newdawn.ca.

References

Amin, A. 2005. Local community on trial. *Economy and Society* 34 (4): 612–633.

Amin, A., A. Cameron, and R. Hudson. 2002. *Placing the social economy*. London: Routledge.

Amin, A., A. Cameron, and R. Hudson. 2003. The alterity of the social economy. *Alternative Economic Spaces*, eds. A. Leyshon, R. Lee, and C.C. Williams, 27–54. London: Sage.

Amin, A., and P. Cohendet. 2005. *Architectures of knowledge: Firms, capabilities and communities*. Oxford: Oxford University Press.

Blackburn, R., and M. Ram. 2006. Fix or fixation? The contributions and limitations of entrepreneurship and small firms to combating social exclusion. *Entrepreneurship and Regional Development* 18 (1): 73–89.

Defourny, J. 2001. From third sector to social enterprise. In *The emergence of social enterprise*, eds. C. Borzaga and J. Defourny, 1–28. London: Routledge.

Fontan, J.-M., and E. Shragge. 2000. Tendencies, tensions and visions in the social economy. In *Social economy: International debates and perspectives*, eds. E. Shragge and J.-M. Fontan, 1–15. Montreal: Black Rose.

Gide, C. 1912. *Les institutions de progrès social*. Paris: Librairie de la Société du Recueil Sirey.

Harvey, D. 1996. Justice, nature, and the geography of difference. Cambridge: Blackwell.

Hayton, K. 2000. Scottish community business: An idea that has had its day? *Policy and Politics* 28 (2): 193–206.

Hudson, R. 2001. *Producing places*. London: Guildford.

Johnstone, H., and D. Lionais. 2004. Depleted communities and community business entrepreneurship: Revaluing space through place. *Entrepreneurship and Regional Development* 16: 217–233.

Just Us! Coffee Roasters Co-operative. 2008. http://www.justuscoffee.com.

Laville, J.-L., and M. Nyssens. 2001. The social enterprise: Towards a theoretical socio-economic approach. In *The Emergence of Social Enterprise*, eds. C. Borzaga and J. Defourny, 312–332. London, Routledge.

Lee, R. and A. Leyshon. 2003. Conclusions: Re-making geographies and the construction of "spaces of hope." In *Alternative economic spaces*, eds. A. Leyshon, R. Lee, and C.C. Williams, 193–198. London: Sage.

Leyshon, A., and R. Lee. 2003. Introduction: Alternative economic spaces. In *Alternative economic spaces*, eds. A. Leyshon, R. Lee, and C.C. Williams, 1–26. London: Sage.

Leyshon, A., R. Lee, and C. Williams, eds. 2003. *Alternative economic spaces*. London: Sage.

Lionais, D. 2008. Entrepreneurship in depleted communities: High growth firms in declining regions. Paper presented to the Association of American Geographers conference, Boston, April 15 to 19.

MacLeod, G. 2002. The corporation as community trustee. In *Alliances, cooperative ventures and the role of government in the knowledge based economy: Policy issues for Canada and beyond*, ed. M. Nakumura. Vancouver: Centre for Japanese Research, University of British Columbia.

Massey, D. 1995. Spatial divisions of labour: Social structures and the geography of production. London: MacMillan.

Mondragón Cooperative Corporation (MCC). 2001. *The history of an experience.* Mondragón: Mondragón Cooperative Corporation.

Mondragón Cooperative Corporation (MCC). 2008. Mondragón Cooperative Corporation 2007 Annual Report. Mondragón: Mondragón Cooperative Corporation.

Moore, J. 2006. Just Us! How Canada's first fair trade coffee roaster was born. Éléments Online Environmental Magazine. http://www.elements.nb.ca/theme/food06/jeff/jeff.htm.

Moulaert, F., and J. Nussbaumer. 2005. Defining the social economy and its governance at the neighbourhood level: A methodological reflection. *Urban Studies* 42 (11): 2071–2088.

Moulaert, F., and O. Ailenei. 2005. Social economy, third sector and solidarity relations: A conceptual synthesis from history to present. *Urban Studies* 42 (11): 2037–2053.

Neamtam, N. 2005. The social economy: Finding a way between the market and the state. *Policy Options* (July–August): 71–76.

Ninacs, W.A. 2002. A review of the theory and practice of the social economy/ Économie sociale in Canada. SRDC Working Paper Series 02-02. Ottawa: Social Research and Demonstration Corporation.

Swyngedouw, E. 2005. Governance innovation and the citizen: The Janus face of governance-beyond-the-state. *Urban Studies* 42 (11): 1991–2006.

Zografos, C. 2007. Rurality discourses and the role of the social enterprise in regenerating rural Scotland. *Journal of Rural Studies* 23: 38–51.

CHAPTER FIVE

Educating for the Social Economy

JORGE SOUSA

Introduction

The role of formal education in preparing individuals to participate within the social economy has always been ambiguous. Currently, formal education institutions provide indirect training and support for the social economy through existing academic and vocational programs across disciplines; examples include departments of business, social work, and political science. There is a notable absence of opportunities through established educational programs for individuals to develop an understanding of and gain experience regarding the close relationship between values and practices characteristic of many initiatives connected to the social economy. As shown throughout this book (see especially the chapters by McMurtry, Vaillancourt, and Sumner and Mook), the social economy transcends notions of self-help and social services, and can be seen as a functioning alternative economy that intersects social values with economic practices. The unique nature of the social economy, therefore, deserves focused study within a formal academic setting. However, the opportunities to learn about the social economy as something more than social service provision and self-help has not been taken up as an issue either by the academic community or social economy actors themselves. The many examples of successful social enterprises and community economic development (CED) activities therefore warrants a closer exploration of the need to systematically address the barriers and biases against fostering learning opportunities, opportunities aimed at introducing individuals into the social economy in formal academic settings.

Recent efforts to integrate community-based learning opportunities into formal education programs has resulted in the integration of a pedagogical approach referred to as community service learning (CSL) into higher education institutions (Butin 2006; Parker-Gwin and Mabry 1998). CSL provides students with opportunities to experience the different facets of social economy organizations. In this chapter, I describe CSL as a partnership between social economy organizations and higher education institutions, including universities and colleges. The primary objective of these partnerships is to provide learning opportunities for individuals who are interested but unfamiliar with the fundamental characteristics and values of community-based and non-governmental organizations (NGOs). To that end, I conceptualize CSL as an opportunity to purposefully introduce students to the values and practices of the social economy. Using information from interviews of students and leaders from community-based organizations, I describe an effort to utilize CSL as an entry point for students into the non-profit sector of the social economy, as well as the opportunities for organizations to access specialized skills and mentor a new group of individuals by having students engage in learning placements in order to experience the vital work of social economy organizations.

There are five sections in this chapter. First, I situate the social economy as a key economic and social practice within Canada, the definition of which is highly contested by academics and practitioners (see McMurtry in this volume). Despite these disagreements, I argue that there is broad consensus among these actors that the social economy is composed of organizations that combine a social purpose with economic practices. In the second section, I describe the key features associated with community service learning, including the type of learning that is expected to occur within CSL. I conclude this section with a discussion of the relationship between CSL and the social economy. The third section outlines the research design used to collect the information for this study. In the fourth section, I share the outcome of the learning process using themes that were drawn from the experiences of both students and the participants from the community-based organizations. I conclude the chapter with a discussion of some lessons learned that can be applied to adopting the CSL approach in ways that can strengthen the social economy. While community service learning is in its infancy in Canada, and while both university and community actors do question its efficacy for a variety of reasons, there is much potential for students and faculty to gain important experience and exposure to a key structure within Canadian society—the social economy.

Understanding the Context of the Social Economy

There has been ongoing awareness concerning the weakening social fabric of modern society. This weakening has been seen in the forms of reduced social capital (Putnam 2000), an increasing gap across class and income indicators (Hulchanski 2001), and crises related to the provision of affordable housing (Hulchanski 2004). While these issues are not new, it is their pervasiveness that has raised alarms among social justice activists, academics, and practitioners. Many groups are calling for an improved economic and social ethic that places the needs of the many over the needs of the privileged. The social economy is seen, in different ways by different actors in government and within social justice movements, as a real alternative to both the directly state-controlled and private market sectors because of the social economy's successful track record of providing essential goods and services to individuals who are most vulnerable to the abuses and exclusions often inherent in these sectors (Shragge 2004). However, individuals are unaware of these successes because the outcomes are often focused on specific problems (for example, homelessness) and tend to be localized within disadvantaged community settings.

The definition of the social economy is highly contested within academic and practitioner communities (Sousa and Hamdon 2008). For instance, there is an ongoing tension as to which characteristics of some practices and organizations warrant inclusion as part of the social economy—such as private investment or political organizations. Moreover, some view the social economy as a bridging concept (Mook, Quarter, and Richmond 2007) as opposed to a viable alternative to the public and private sectors (Lewis 2007; Shragge 2004).

While there is a lack of consensus on a definition, there is widespread agreement that the social economy is a robust organizing framework that recognizes activities and initiatives that fall outside the sole purview of the public and the private sectors but that can be found at their intersection (Mook, Quarter, and Richmond 2007). According to Neamtan and Downing (2005), based on a "consensus among social actors in Quebec" the social economy encompasses a wide variety of activities (for example, community development and entrepreneurship) undertaken by individuals and organizations whose operations are based on the following principles:

1. A social economy organization serves its members or the community rather than simply to make profits.
2. It operates at arm's length from the state.

3. It promotes a democratic management process involving all users and/or workers through its statutes and the way it does business.
4. It defends the primacy of individuals and work over capital in the distribution of its surpluses and revenues.
5. Activities are based on the principles of participation and individual collective empowerment.

This basic agreement on activities leads to general acceptance that the social economy can be broadly conceived as encompassing a variety of organizations (for example, co-operative, mutual associations) that share the characteristic of mutuality for the purpose of meeting the social and economic needs of individuals and communities. These organizations are engaged in social processes and practices grounded in a sense of solidarity by emphasizing the social benefit of mutuality and collective action. Given these broad areas of agreement therefore, for the purposes of this study, the social economy is operationalized as

> encompassing the range of ways people exchange goods and services (often based on the principle of reciprocity) with each other and distribute profit as surpluses through various mechanisms, including: the family or household economy; local volunteer activities and opportunities; and the wide range of more formally structured organizations (such as charities or member based associations) that explicitly pursue social goals using business-oriented approaches. (Lewis 2007)

While there is agreement on some general features of the social economy, it is important to recognize that serious disagreements remain about the values which guide its activity. Organizations within the social economy vary in terms of purpose and objective, and cut across sectors, including non-profit and voluntary, co-operative business, non-market housing, and community-based social service ones (Sousa and Hamdon 2008). Some organizations operate as a business within the market, while others are oriented toward providing social services or advancing a cause. While different in form and values, these examples of organizations and activities share the characteristic of placing higher priority on mutuality and accountability, either to the public or to a defined membership (Mook, Quarter, and Richmond 2007). Furthermore, all social economy organizations have to differing degrees the clear purpose of bringing greater equity and fairness into our economic system. While many assail a capitalist system that makes it increasingly difficult for social economy organizations to thrive, there needs also to be positive support for the work of these organizations by providing a sound policy infrastructure as well as a new generation of individuals who can be leaders and participants within these organizations. This is where service learning for the social economy becomes important.

The presence of the social economy within Canadian society has become highly complex over recent years. Activities of different organizations are variant and often seem to operate as market agents, thereby making it very difficult to determine where and in what manner society is benefiting by the presence of a robust social economy. The social economy often has a dual nature, requiring both market and social skills. Consequently, the successful implementation and operation of these organizations requires skills and knowledge in areas of business financing and management, interpersonal communication, and community development in addition to the particular expertise required within their domain of operation (for example, social housing policy if a housing co-operative). Social economy organizations also rely on resources different from those of market-based organizations, such as sweat equity and social capital (see the Glossary). Furthermore, social economy organizations often require individuals to be aware of the need to combine a social mission within the market, which could be fostered by stressing the integral relationship between humanism and pragmatism in social-purpose businesses. Training people to be proficient in both areas of social economy activity requires a focused understanding within educational institutions from grade school to university of the unique and dual nature of these economic activities.

People are not aware of the need for a strong social economy because the issues that originally helped build it from the level of movement into a legitimate social structure are very different from the ones that pertain within the current economic climate. We have observed the rise of individualism on the social level and for-profit thinking and activity on the economic level, which has obscured the unique nature of the social economy in both (see McMurtry in this volume). As a result, we are seeing a decline in the number of organizations that make up the social economy— for example, a notable reduction in the absolute numbers of co-operatives and credit unions across Canada through mergers and demutualization (Sousa and Herman in press).

There are different ways in which individuals can be involved within the social economy. Involvement can be in the form of volunteering, patronizing a particular service, or donating money, the latter of which is referred to by Putnam (2000) as tertiary participation, a mode that is becoming an increasingly common form of participation. There is a widespread misconception that participating within the social economy primarily requires a commitment to volunteering. While in many cases a commitment to volunteering is vital, individuals are unaware that supporting the social economy can be done in many different ways. For instance, involvement can consist of becoming a member of an environmental organization or supporting a consumer co-operative rather than a corporate entity. In many instances, individuals unfamiliar with the concept unknowingly support the social economy through membership in an organization or supporting a local community initiative. In addition to this lack of recognition is the notion that some individuals may feel that they do not possess the skills and knowledge that would allow them to effectively participate in and benefit from the social economy. However, none of this highlights the key factor that demonstrates one's support for the social economy—whether she believes in or understands the social purpose associated with particular organizations. Therefore, a challenge for social economy organizations is providing individuals with opportunities to be engaged in a variety of ways while staying focused on educating participants about the social purpose of the organization.

It is my belief that CSL can be used as an entry point for introducing individuals to the social processes and values associated with the social economy by linking courses to the real-life contexts of many community-based organizations. The purpose of CSL is to have students participate in voluntary activities as part of a university or college course. The next section provides an introduction to service learning as well as some of the details associated with providing a successful program that provides students with an opportunity to be actively engaged in their learning. Through this type of learning, both the specific and complex skill set and the understanding of social values required by the social economy are developed by students and social economy organizations.

Describing Service Learning

The relationship between universities and community-based organizations has been fraught with challenges and tensions. The university is often perceived as a monolithic institution that is intimidating both because of its size and because of its role in constructing society and reproducing social structures that breed inequality. The university is often perceived as taking knowledge and value away from communities through research practices that lead to promotions within the institution and recognition for the researchers, regardless of the adverse impact on willing or unwilling participants. Consequently, there have been tense relations with community-based organizations, and these organizations question whether there is any benefit to be gained by working with universities. As a result of the criticisms of the university's often negative role, efforts to reduce the tensions have intensified across North America over the past 20 years. Many universities are exploring initiatives that promote active engagement with local community-based organizations, where each participant is seen as a partner in research and in learning (Arthur and Bailey 2000).

Community service learning (henceforth referred to as service learning) came about as a result of these efforts to improve relations between universities and community-based organizations across North America. The National Service Learning Clearinghouse (2005) defines community service learning as "a teaching and learning strategy that integrates meaningful community service with instruction and reflection to enrich the learning experience, teach civic responsibility, and strengthen communities." Service learning is built on communitarian notions of partnership, with the result that students can experience community contexts through active engagement rather than passive observation (Sherman 2008). The purpose of such engagement is to develop experiences that can either supplement or complement course content. Many postsecondary institutions apply the practice of service learning in order to achieve the goals of introducing students to the work of community-based organizations, providing them with the skills and knowledge that many of these organizations use on a daily basis (Sather, Carlson, and Weitz 2007). Service learning opportunities provide students with community experience and facilities the establishment of partnerships between universities and community-based organizations. As a result, service learning has taken on a greater role in pedagogy by integrating experiential learning through voluntary community service.

A key aspect of service learning is the combination of learning *and* service—that is, of learning through service. Current research has demonstrated different aspects associated with service learning practices. First, there exists a wide range of approaches to implementing service learning on the part of social economy organizations and universities both (Hondagneu-Sotelo and Raskoff 1994; Lamsam 1999). For instance, activities undertaken in service learning programs include research and data collection, front-line work, homework clubs, and community cleanup. The link to the social economy in practice is that these participatory activities demonstrate efforts to implement a particular social mission; students are engaged in activities that reveal how social issues can be addressed at the community level, and they are provided with the context for new experiences that they can reflect upon, which is a key element in adult learning theory (Imel 2000). The dynamic interplay between context and experience, which is understood through critical reflection activities, is important for students in order to help them not only reflect on their experiences, but also to see it as an important part of their educational development.

Universities, which when they operate as non-profits are social economy institutions within Canada, continue to accrue significant benefits through these partnerships, but there has been a notable gap in determining whether community social economy organizations are benefiting given their increase in work arising from the partnership; in fact, these organizations may allocate limited resources with little or no return. Furthermore, organizations are often resistant to student placements because participating in service learning activities places undue burdens on an already challenging workplace—and in addition links their work to the schedules of the academic institutions (Stoecker 2008). For instance, students may require special supervision above and beyond what the organization has the resource capacity to provide. Other organizations have found that these partnerships allow them to pursue their social mission with a new group of people who might otherwise not be aware of their work.

Service learning is intended to complement university or college course content by providing the real-life context for many of the issues and theories discussed or read about in class. For example, discussing in educational contexts notions of power reproduction (Apple 1995) or the importance of understanding cultural diversity (Nokes, Nickitas, Keida, and Neville 2005) can be challenging. However, addressing power imbalances and other inequalities are the raison d'être for many of these social economy organizations, as can be seen first-hand by students participating through service. The hope is that students will take this new knowledge and integrate it into their own practice. On the part of the social economy, the hope is also that these individuals will continue to participate in community-based activities or support social purpose businesses upon graduation.

Overview of the Research Design

In this section of the chapter I discuss the application of the above service learning framework within my own teaching where I attempt to introduce students to the social economy by participating in learning opportunities that focus on social justice and teacher identity. The present study took place over two years in an undergraduate course entitled Society and Education, a course that involved 40 students (15 in the first year and 25 in the second). A key facet of the course was the intention of including learning opportunities that focused on, complemented, and enhanced the teacher education program by introducing key social issues that students will be facing as teachers upon completion of their program—which reflects a deliberate effort to reinforce the significant role that experience and context have on Adult Learning (Imel 2000). Like many universities across the country, the University of Alberta in Edmonton supports service learning in ways that complement course content. As a researcher involved in community-based research, I saw this as an opportunity to investigate the type of learning that can be achieved as an outcome of the experience of being engaged with community-based organizations in the city of Edmonton.

In a teacher education program, the students are expected to declare a major that is based on their interests and expertise. In my course, the students' declared major included social studies, math, and the natural sciences. However, regardless of major, students were expected to complete a learning placement with a community-based organization. See the Appendix to this chapter for more detail about the course objectives as well as the expectations conveyed to the students about their participation in the placement.

From the outset, a concern for both myself and many individual students was whether there were placement opportunities available for all interested students. Therefore, the first step was to determine the level of interest on the part of community-based organizations for supporting this service learning initiative, an initiative that would allow students to link the course content to an organization's work in situ. A variety of organizations agreed to participate in this project, and all shared the common characteristic of using education and knowledge construction as the principal means to deliver their mandated activities. Table 5.1 provides a brief description of the type of organization, as well as the focus of their work.

A total of 15 organizations participated and were involved in all aspects of course design, including reviewing the course content in order to ensure

TABLE 5.1 Description of Organizations and Associated Tasks

Type of organization	Focus of work
• Community centre	• Youth programs
• Policy think tank	• Policy analysis
• Labour organization	• Education and awareness
• Student union	• Communication strategies
• Community-based	• Local/global education
• Faith-based	• Seniors program

that the individual tasks would fit within the scope of the course. Each organization was asked to develop tasks that would involve the students to different degrees within the organization and that would benefit the organization in some capacity. In these tasks, the student was expected to synthesize the course content and their placement experience in a reflective paper. The organizations were also provided the guarantee that a student would be working with them, which is often a challenge in instances where service learning is an optional component of a course rather than being mandatory as a student might choose to drop out during the process if their participation is voluntary. The following list breaks down the key elements in the development and implementation of the participatory learning component in the course.

- Meet with partners and share course objectives
- Community partners define particular tasks
- Develop course and integrate partners' tasks
- Introduce community learning placements into course
- Implement an assessment process that complements or supplements pedagogy (the method and practice of teaching)
- Purposeful reflection components, including relating course content to both experiences and skills learned
- Pre- and post-reflection meetings with all participants

With respect to the expectations placed on the individual organizations, they were to develop tasks that would directly benefit them in some immediate manner and to supervise the students. The supervision procedures varied across the organizations, and were primarily intended to ensure the students' completion of a particular task. Finally, the organizations were involved in evaluating the process of the completion of the task, but not on the students' academic performance. At the pre- and post-reflection meetings, all community partners had a chance to describe their tasks as well as share their experiences with the student placements. For the purposes of this study, all the original participating organizations were interviewed, as were ten students. For ethical considerations, a third party was involved in the information collection in order to reduce the potential for students to feel coerced into participating in this study, given that I was the instructor of the course. I assessed the information after I had submitted their final grade at the end of term. In the next section, I outline several themes arising out of the placement experience that are based on the experiences of the students and the placement supervisors.

Sharing the Outcomes of the Learning Placements

The information shared by the different participants in the interviews was quite broad and expressed a number of outcomes unanticipated by the study. Individual students were not sure what to expect by their involvement and how a volunteer task could be related to the course content. Consequently, connecting course content to the "real-life" contexts of the placements presented the largest challenge for the students; however, many students were pleased with the outcome nonetheless, as they started to see that being a teacher requires more consideration than that involved with simply being in the classroom. As stated by one student participant:

> I do not get a lot of practical knowledge from the education program, so such an experience was very valuable. And really just to make you an actual social citizen, so you can contribute to society, rather than just saying "I'm a teacher and I teach," and then I go home and that's it.

For the organizations that participated in this research, many recognized various benefits from having students participate in their organization. Some expressed enthusiasm regarding the inherent value of mentoring new groups of people who might never otherwise become aware of their individual organization's social objectives, such as creating a "strong, sustainable, prosperous, and inclusive society." According to one representative of a participating organization, she felt that through their involvement the students were able to further her organization's mission of engaging the public on education issues:

> We are supposed to be engaging Canadians in analysis and awareness building and also skills building to more actively address and be involved in global issues to more effectively critique and understand policies. And there's different ways of doing that, but I think by having [students] you have the opportunity to expose [them] to organizations they might not otherwise come in contact with and also engage [them] in some of the issues you're working on. So I think it definitely meets our mandate of our education [that is, our organization].

When asked why they were participating in this project given the time commitment expected of them, one representative of an organization responded that introducing students to a different reality was key to developing future leaders:

> Yeah, the future leaders are from the university. So it is of interest to us that these people are well-informed, not microscopic in their vision, and broad-

minded. The world is shrinking but many of our minds are shrinking as well. The world has become a small community because you can cross the world in less than 24 hours. But our minds have not kept pace with this. On the flipside, we would really have to be very specific of what we want. The downside of it for us is that we are such a small organization and I'm only part time and although they didn't complain about it they both mentioned that if they went to any other organization with full-time offices with several staff and somebody always there and you really get a feel for busy-ness and action, their experience would have been different.

For some organizations, a key motivator was accessing the specialized skills that students bring with them. One interviewee stated the following: "My original expectation was for students who would be able to grasp the importance and value of [organization name] to other U of A students like themselves, and be able to come up with original and creative ideas for engaging those students in our work." Another organization described its expectations with respect to a student's skills in the following manner:

> I think basic skills like research, like how to—if we said to them we need you to do outreach, they would have some basic understanding of how to call a school, like how to do public engagement, like speaking to people in a courteous manner. I think I had the expectation to—will they understand the culture of formal education and the steps and ways you can reach teachers better or reach principals at the schools better, like outreach. And I thought they would have some understanding or opinion on global issues. Maybe not really even a well-informed opinion or even the opposite opinion, but they'd have thought a little bit about global issues.

For another organization, there was a great desire for students to bring in softer skills that demonstrate an ability to understand people as subjects rather than objects:

> The most important skill, whether it be students or any volunteers, is communication and interpersonal skills. A non-judgmental attitude, an openness to trying new things, new ways, and an openness to learn from others, and I think that's the key, what I like about students. They seem to be in the learning mode and eager to learn. They're not here to be telling people to be saying this is the way you should be running your life. But they're there to be of assistance and to be learning at the same time so I think often people, if they come very … they're very willing to listen to people here, and I think that's important, to be a good listener.

However, the purpose of the placement was to also help students recognize the importance of being able to communicate effectively with challenging populations, as described in the next quotation:

> I think we help them build communication skills, and that's often what volunteers say: "I learn to relate to people who are totally different than me. I learn to recognize when someone is having mental health problems and the best thing I can do is listen or get out of the way."

Yet another organization felt that the placement task provided an opportunity for political socialization as opposed to just volunteering one's time: "Coming to understand how the organization is structured. How we do our advocacy work. Some of the critical issues that we're dealing with and how we partner and network with other organizations. There is some core basic learning that happens no matter how long it is." For many participating organizations the communication skills just mentioned above was an important component, but equally important was the benefit of having education students involved in their work:

> Because they're education students coming from the background that I have or the background that [the organization] is, is the idea that education can either be critical and about critical analysis and about interrupting all these oppressive structures. Part of our mission again is about addressing the root causes of poverty, so education is inherently involved in that. So I think it's a huge moment when you can actually expose students [to the belief] that education can be about transformation and about participation and about challenging oppressive structures.

While the quotation above recognizes what education students bring to the context, another organization was surprised at the lack of experience with our political system exhibited by many individuals:

> I guess I thought that more of the students would be politically aware and hopefully more engaged than they were ... I know lots of teachers, in retrospect, there shouldn't have been much surprise! The vast majority of teachers out there are woefully ignorant of social policy and what's going on in our society in a broad political and social economic level and I understand the dynamic of the job. They come up through middle-class backgrounds to a middle-class profession and they've never had the opportunity to be challenged and see what's happening until they actually go out and be teachers if they are placed in areas—well, no matter where they are in the city, they will always be confronting issues of students that have been sexually assaulted, their parents lost their job or on welfare or committed suicide. Every teacher

in their career will be facing that multiple times. What they never experience in their education programs and the reason I so support the education faculty pushing all of this [service learning], is the notion that through their profession or through their voluntary work, social change can happen and they as individuals can participate in that, because they've never had that ability to be exposed to those things in all the other courses that they do. So that's where, despite in terms of what we get out of it as an organization, that doesn't matter. We've planted some seeds I hope and who knows if anything will come of that in 5, 15, 20 years, but at least all the education students will have seen that our professional association is not just looking at grievances or disciplinary hearings.

Finally, while there was a general sense that the placements were useful for the organizations, some were not as enthusiastic as others about them, as stated by one person:

We are unsure of how successful this placement was with helping the students make the connection between their course materials and the placement. If we were provided with more direction of how we could incorporate course material, we would have ensured to make that connection during the placement.

Comment on the challenge of connecting the course content to the placement was also found among some of the students:

As I'm going through my portfolio [one of the course assignments], I'm finding it kind of hard to apply some of the class material to how my experience went. At the same time, I can see what the intention was. To some extent, it's not even really enough experience to really apply it. Because you show up, and our coordinators knew that we're only supposed to do 20 hours of work, which isn't a whole lot to establish a good feeling of what it is they do in the context of some of the theories covered in class.

However, in spite of the challenges, students did find the reflection component crucial for their development as teachers:

I definitely do like the reflection portion of it. Just looking back at it, it was a lot easier to connect the course material with it. In terms of starting to study now, with finals coming up, it's a lot easier to look back at the theories and understand them if you can apply them to something at the organization I worked with, even if I didn't actually do that with them. I'm not a big memory-cue kind of person, so those connections make studying a little easier. Some of the definitions, I'm not the most articulate person in the world—I had three classes this term that use terms like liberalism, neo-liberalism, colonialism, neo-colonialism, Marxism, neo-Marxism. I probably didn't know what any of them meant, wasn't able to define any of those until about three weeks into class. My first big revelation was "neo" actually just means new.

Another student responded with a statement that the reflective process requires time and patience in order to understand the relevance of service learning for their professional practice:

> And I want to bring up certain things that I've realized, like what the aims of service learning are. Because I think it's not immediately apparent to people what the aims of it are, and they're struggling with it, and it just seemed so obvious to me. And I definitely had the literature to help me out on it. I figured out that it was about professional and personal development. And the sort of "Aha moment" that people can have, the moment of actualization that will change them and their views on social justice, and the role of social justice, all these things.

Finally, when students were asked whether the experience will encourage future involvement with these organizations, there seemed to be a general concern that time and family commitments may make future participation challenging:

> It's funny, because I've been thinking about that for the last little bit. This sounds cheesy, but I say in my heart, yeah, for sure. Because it's crucial and I feel more optimistic about change than I have in a long time, and I think that there are things that are necessary for change, and I think that one of those things is being involved in your community, and with organizations like the [organization]. But that being said, I'm finishing school, and I'm looking for a job, and I have a family. So I'm thinking, how do you do this, how do you incorporate everything into your life? And I don't want to be just once a year. I really want it to be part of my life, I just don't know how to make it part of my life.

As revealed in the experiences expressed by both the students and members of the participating organizations, the outcome of the service learning experiences was the engendering of a sense that community-based organizations promote social change through active involvement. The characteristic of promoting social change is a key function for many social economy activities and initiatives (see McMurtry in this volume), which was consistent with the goals and objectives for all of the participating organizations. As stated in the introduction of this chapter, my study had the intention of describing how service learning can be an entry point into the social economy, an intention that was successfully achieved. The service learning assignment outlined in this chapter provided students with exposure to experiences and to contexts that they likely had taken for granted, if indeed they had ever given it thought at all. For instance, students were exposed to the value of informal exchanges within a community setting that required the use of sophisticated communication skills. Moreover, the students were introduced to voluntary and community-based organizations that they did not know existed. In fact, many of these same organizations are likely to be located within their future school community. However, formally introducing and connecting the social economy to the service learning activities was not attempted because it was beyond the scope of the course. In other words, introducing elements of the social economy is often done surreptitiously rather than explicitly, which can have the effect of minimizing its legitimacy.

Finally, most of the organizations involved in this research were unaware of the notion of the social economy, and those that were aware of it did not agree with being included as a part of it. In fact, many participants questioned both the efficacy of the social economy as an organizing framework—some expressed concern that being considered part of the social economy may in fact ghettoize them or can negatively impact their organization's work. While those concerns and issues are very real, it is time to move beyond concerns that divide and separate toward looking for common links.

Lessons Learned: Challenges and Rewards

The exploratory nature of this research demonstrates the need to continue efforts to fully recognize the complex and contested nature of the social economy by formally integrating key characteristics across higher education programs. As stated above, the students were exposed to the work of organizations that operate within a social economy framework. An important feature of this experience was that students were exposed to work that is done in a community setting and that often goes unrecognized or is misunderstood. The key issues that came out of this research exposes many challenges that proponents of the social economy will need to address if there is hope that service learning can support efforts to strengthen and further entrench the social economy within Canadian society.

First, there is a general sense that many of these organizations are benevolent entities. While the examples of organizations participating in this study may warrant that label, it is a generalization that needs to be critiqued.

The sense of benevolence is both appropriate and unfounded, which is illustrative of the contested nature of the social economy beyond its being an organizing framework. Many of the social processes found within social economy organizations can be found in less favourable contexts. For instance, the concept of reciprocity and mutuality is as likely to be found in a local chapter of a racist organization as it is in a local community centre. Even within progressively minded organizations there can be malevolent practices that the students came to realize needed to be challenged. Further reflection is required to recognize the importance of balancing social processes aimed at benevolence but that result in malevolence, a problem that can exist in both for-profit as well as non-profit entities.

A second lesson related to increasing efforts to link service learning to the social economy is the absence of a common understanding that demonstrates the social economy as a viable alternative to the public and private sectors. The organizations that participated in this research all expressed a commitment to social change and achieving social justice through education and non-formal learning and may not in fact represent the interests and breadth of the social economy. It would indeed be interesting to investigate the experiences of students participating in a social enterprise in addition to community-based non-profits.

A third challenge arising from this research is the recognition that those organizations that operate within the private market are as common in community settings as are community-based non-profits. Social enterprises straddle a tenuous line between promoting private wealth and the redistribution of wealth. In some instances, what identifies a social economy organization is a group's culture as much as its mission statement. For instance, should all enterprises that operate a for-profit business and are from groups that have been systematically oppressed for generations be included as part of the social economy? I am not advocating the inclusion or exclusion of particular organizations, but the infusion of private-sector practices into the social economy makes it more difficult to tease apart what makes the social economy distinct from the private and public sectors. (See McMurtry in this volume for further discussion of this problem.) A key issue that kept recurring throughout the discussions, which is the fourth lesson, is related to explaining the general purpose of the social economy when there is considerable overlap between it and the private and public sectors. Students generally understand why the idea of the social economy is conceptually useful; however, paradoxically, our understanding is based on approaches advanced by the public and private sectors, such as fiscal accountability and human resource management practised by large corporations.

Perhaps a more authentic way to make the best use of service learning as an entry point into the social economy is for universities to encourage the participation of innovative for-profit social enterprises rather than partnering with non-profit organizations.

In light of the various challenges described above, there are many areas of research that can demonstrate the usefulness of service learning as an approach for introducing students to the social economy. First, emerging research that investigates the linkage between learning processes and the social economy should be broadened. To date, the literature focuses on experiential learning rather than other forms of learning, including contexts. As shown in this study, and since the site was as important as the experience, greater efforts should be made to understand how adults learn in different social contexts. Individuals will come into the experience seeking to learn something new, but this seeking needs to be complemented by an enhancement of participants' understanding of their recognition of the context where the new learning is taking place.

An additional area for further research is the realm of assessment strategies, something that has not yet been emphasized in this chapter as an area of concern. There should be care and thoughtful consideration given to developing appropriate assessment strategies that account for the authentic experience of the learning process. Since service learning occurs in part within formal education settings, the experiences need to be evaluated in an appropriate manner. The goal of this project was to have students demonstrate a level of competency in the course content demonstrated through reflection on their placement experience; therefore, the evaluation strategies had to be closely tied into a student's experiences, an area that community-based organizations are not particularly familiar with. The challenge in this case was to ensure that the assessment strategy not only accounted for the formative aspect of the experience but also accounted for the ways in which students were able to demonstrate how their experiences both complement and enhance the course objectives. For this course, I applied authentic assessment (AA), which refers to assessing performance of particular real-life tasks that result in students developing and practising new skills or competencies outside of the formal classroom (Wiggins 1993). Accordingly, I felt that AA was the most effective measurement tool that could account for the real experience and impressions of the student experience.

As such, the issue of assessment in service learning is also a key area that needs to be addressed by curriculum developers. Many service learning projects can meet the needs of people in particular courses as long as the learning objectives are both clear and fair, but that means a highly tailored and often intensive mode of implementing service learning activities. If one is trying to identify and evaluate a change in students' knowledge, then the challenge is to capture that change within an evaluative framework. However, the challenge for the evaluator lies in the fact that individual students may not immediately demonstrate such a change until *after* they are outside of the purview of the course and its instructor—which is to say, that learning can be cumulative and often takes time, more time than is allowed for in a course term.

Conclusion

I conclude this chapter by encouraging the reader to view the experiences outlined here as a springboard for the exploration of the way in which one can support learning opportunities within their community. I feel that we need to foster a new discourse, one that focuses on learning through engagement rather than on engagement through learning. A guiding objective must be to strengthen social bonds rather than continue practices that dismantle them, and it is important to learn first-hand the nature of how social bonds are in fact constructed. I encourage the reader to get involved in this discourse in order to celebrate the efforts of individuals and organizations trying to make a change in the world by adopting practices intended to improve well-being and intended to reduce the gaps that permeate Canadian society. However, it is as important to critique as it is to celebrate. Can first-hand experience through service learning become an impetus for social change? My answer to this question is that it can.

Finally, I feel it is crucial that we build a common understanding of the social economy. All individuals can be involved in this discourse as long as the common thread is to build rather than solely deconstruct. Most of all, it is crucial to recognize that social economy organizations can be both sites of learning and sites of progressive social change.

Appendix: Description of Course and Placement Assignment

It is important to recognize a service learning component appropriate for all higher education courses. Considerations involved in whether to include a service learning component should involve the content and objectives of the course. In this appendix I describe the learning objectives of the course, Society and Education, that formed the context for this study. The course is an elective within the Education program. I also describe the purpose of the learning placements from a community organizing perspective. I conclude the appendix with a description of the assignment that the students completed.

Course Description and Content

The purpose of the course is to introduce students to the sociology of education by focusing on the reciprocal nature of the relationship between education and society. The course is intended to develop the pre-service teacher's capacity to critically analyze the impact that education and schooling has had on the development of contemporary Canadian society. To understand the relationship between society and education, students require a basic understanding of social theory, logical argument, and contemporary educational research if they are to become successful practitioners. Student teachers will come to understand that teaching is more than a set of technical skills but encompasses a form of politics to realize in practice competing definitions of what is right, good, and true.

In this type of course students are expected to assimilate a number of definitions and facts while critically evaluating the meaning of these facts. While that can be achievable, a key feature of the course was to integrate their lived experiences and learning from a community-based placement into the course content. The learning objectives associated with the course include:

- Have a clearer and a theoretically grounded understanding about the reciprocal relationship between society and education;
- Be familiar with a broad range of literatures that investigate educational and societal structures;
- Demonstrate an ability to critically analyze issues and practices associated with society and education;
- Develop a more sophisticated grasp of the limitations and possibilities you may face as teachers;
- Appreciate the diversity of voices and practices that inform educational systems; and
- Understand how education principles are practised and contested in diverse sites of learning.

Community-Based Learning Placement

A function of education is to produce and reproduce social processes. While many of these processes help make sense of a complex society, these practices are also considered to be a root cause of social inequality in Canada.

Community-based organizations and various interest groups have used education practices as a means to raise awareness and to rectify societal disparities. An implicit aspect of these experiences is for members of diverse communities to acquire new skills that require broadening common definitions of education and learning.

Community-based organizations can take different forms, but in all instances they apply principles of community organizing to support and undertake their mission of diminishing social inequality. At the heart of community organizing is an ability to understand social processes and to be engaged in community activities. In general, there are four features to community organizing:

- *Preparation*—recognize leaders, assess situations; decide on a mission
- *Mobilization*—seek and build a base of support; hold meeting; and develop organizational goals and objectives
- *Strengthening*—capacity development; building alliances and networking
- *Evaluation*—assess status of ongoing activities

In each of the four features there are different tasks associated that requires specific skills. For instance mobilizing can involve tasks such as: organizing a meeting(s) to discuss a group's vision or mission, or to reach consensus across groups of diverse voices. Accordingly, mobilizing requires a variety of skills, such as public speaking and an understanding of rules of order.

Purpose of Learning Placement

Throughout the learning placement the student worked with a community-based organization who applies community organizing practices as a way to counter increasing inequality. The project provided students with an opportunity to experience community-based education by working with a non-profit or grassroots association. The focus of the experience is to be exposed to and reflect on the different skills associated with task(s) related to community organizing. The student will begin to learn what skills are necessary to undertake tasks related to community organizing, such as chairing a meeting or front-line service delivery. The specific skills and areas of knowledge that the students were exposed to included:

- Fundraising and technical skills
- Organizational/managerial skills (for example, how to organize resources, or to be a leader)
- Increased knowledge (for example, from reviewing manuscripts, reading papers and books)

- Communication skills (for example, public speaking, writing, public relations, etc.)
- Interpersonal skills (for example, to understand people better, to deal with difficult situations, etc.)

Anticipated Benefits

The intention of the learning placement is to provide the students with an opportunity to enhance their formal education experience through the first-hand experience of the valuable that the non-profit sector makes for the greater good of society. The hope is that the students develop a teaching identity that is connected to social phenomena. The experience will provide some or all of the following professional benefits:

- enhancing their professional reputation;
- developing contacts that can lead to new work/research opportunities;
- learning new skills;
- strengthening existing skills;
- diversifying social interaction; and
- improving their well-being.

Although this project occurs over a very short and specific time period (20 hours), students were given the opportunity to be introduced to over-looked aspects of community organizing. Specific benefits included:

- exposure to the non-profit sector and to the basic skills related to community organizing;
- develop an understanding of the planning involved in community-based education initiatives; and
- gain an appreciation for the work and learning that occurs in community-based organizations as agents of social change.

The students were evaluated using a version of Authentic Assessment in the form of a learning portfolio that was submitted to the instructor on a monthly basis. The following is a breakdown of the individual elements of the learning portfolio:

1. Personal narrative (500 words)
   - Describe your learning development
2. Reflections on presentations, discussions and group work
   - One-minute papers (one for each week of class)
   - Group work—Tasks and outcome

3. Placement—each section is (400 to 500 words)
   - Rationale for selection
   - Description of organization: What do they do?
   - Reflect on your experiences (at least 3 of them @ 500 words each)
   - Artifacts: images, brochures, field notes
4. Synthesis—Class and placement (1000 words)
5. Next steps—Relate to first narrative (500 words)
6. References
7. Appendixes

The synthesis element was intended to give the student the opportunity to critically reflect on their placement experience in an essay format. A key part of the synthesis was to have the student discuss how your experience relates to course material—for example, lectures and readings—and explore whether their experiences support, contradict, or alter any of the various sociological theories and claims studied in class.

Glossary

Community economic development (CED)   The process by which people build organizations and partnerships that interconnect profitable business with other interests and values—like quality jobs, marketable skills, good health, affordable housing, equal opportunity, and ecological responsibility. Businesses become an integral part of a far greater agenda—a local movement to build (or rebuild) a community that is creative, inclusive, and sustainable in the near and distant future. (Canadian Centre for Community Renewal [CCCR] 2009.)

Community service learning   An educational approach that integrates service in the community with intentional learning activities. Within effective CSL efforts, members of both educational institutions and community organizations work together toward outcomes that are mutually beneficial. (Canadian Alliance for Community Service-Learning 2009.)

Social capital   Connections among individuals—social networks and the norms of reciprocity and trustworthiness that arise from them. (Putnam 2000.)

Social enterprises   Businesses that sell goods or provide services in the market for the purpose of creating a blended return on investment, both financial and social. Their profits are returned to the business or to a social purpose, rather than maximizing profits to shareholders. (BC Social Enterprise Summit 2008.)

Sweat equity   Used to describe the contribution made to an activity or a project by people who contribute their time and effort. The term can also be used to describe the value added to businesses or property by individuals who make an investment through voluntary time. In essence, the more voluntary labour applied implies the greater sweat equity stake a person has in the business or property, often resulting in the greater likelihood of an increase in value. (Hough 2003; Advani 2007.)

Discussion Questions

1. What is service learning and why is it important for the social economy?
2. How did the students in this chapter develop social economy skills that they otherwise would not develop from a "regular" learning experience?
3. What does university-directed service learning tell us about the need for co-operation among social economy organizations?

Suggested Further Readings

Deans, T. 2002. *Writing and community action: A service-learning rhetoric with readings.* London: Longman.

Eyler, J., and D. Giles Jr. 1999. *Where's the learning in service-learning?* Hoboken, NJ: Jossey-Bass.

Gelmon, S.B., B.A. Holland, A. Driscoll, A. Spring, and S. Kerrigan. 2006. *Assessing service-learning and civic engagement: Principles and techniques.* Boston: Campus Compact.

Kezar, A., A. Chambers, and J. Burkhardt, eds. 2005. *Higher education for the public good: Emerging voices from a national movement.* Hoboken, NJ: Jossey-Bass.

Merriam, S., R.S. Caffarella, and L.M. Baumgartner. 2006. *Learning in adulthood: A comprehensive guide.* Hoboken, NJ: Jossey-Bass.

Pearce, J. 2003. *Social enterprise in Anytown.* London: Calouste Gulbenkian Foundation.

Shragge, E., ed. 1997. *Community economic development: In search of empowerment.* Montreal: Black Rose.

Suggested Online Resources

The following resources provide an excellent entry into the growing field of community service learning. The sites include curriculum resources and tools as well as links to different institutions promoting community service learning.

Campus Compact: http://www.compact.org
Canadian Alliance for Community Service-Learning:
    http://www.communityservicelearning.ca
Educators for Community Engagement: http://www.e4ce.org
National Service-Learning Clearinghouse: http://www.servicelearning.org

References

Advani, A. 2007. What is sweat equity worth? *Entrepreneur* (July 31). http://www.entrepreneur.com/money/financing/startupfinancingcolumnistasheeshadvani/article182440.html.

Apple, M. 1995. *Education and power.* New York: Routledge.

Arthur, J., and R. Bailey. 2000. *Schools and community: The communitarian agenda in education.* London: Falmer Press.

BC Social Enterprise Summit. 2008. Creating a supportive environment for social enterprise in British Columbia. http://www.enterprisingnonprofits.ca/files/uploads/BC_Social_Enterprise_Policy_Framework-jan09.pdf.

Butin, D. 2006. The limits of service-learning in higher education. *Review of Higher Education* 29 (4): 473–498.

Canadian Alliance for Community Service-Learning. 2009. Homepage. http://www.communityservicelearning.ca/en/.

Canadian Centre for Community Renewal (CCCR). 2009. Homepage. http://www.cedworks.com.

Droppa, D. 2007. Social welfare policy and services: Service learning through social policy projects in human service organizations. In *Social work and service learning: Partnerships for social justice*, ed. M. Nadel, V. Majewski, and M. Sullivan-Cosetti, 61–75. Lanham, MA: Rowman and Littlefield.

Hondagneu-Sotelo, P., and S. Raskoff. 1994. Community service-learning: Promises and problems. *Teaching Sociology* 22: 248–254.

Hough, P. 2003. What is sweat equity? http://www.canadianworker.coop/english/5/index_e5351.html.

Hulchanski, D. 2001. *A tale of two Canadas: Homeowners getting richer, renters getting poorer.* Centre for Urban and Community Studies, Research Bulletin 2. Toronto: Centre for Urban and Community Studies, University of Toronto.

Hulchanski, D. 2004. What factors influence Canada's housing policies? The intergovernmental role of Canada's housing system. In *Canada: The state of the federation in 2004*, ed. R. Young and C. Luprecht, 221–247. Montreal: McGill-Queen's University Press.

Imel, S. 2000. *Contextual learning in adult education.* Practice Application Brief no. 12. ERIC Clearinghouse on Adult, Career, and Vocational Education.

Lamsam, G. 1999. Development of a service-learning program. *American Journal of Pharmacological Education* 63: 41–45.

Lewis, M. 2007. *Mapping the social economy in B.C. and Alberta: Towards a strategic approach.* BC-Alberta Social Economy Research Alliance (BALTA). http://hdl.handle.net/2149/1337.

Mook, L., J. Quarter, and B.J. Richmond. 2007. *What counts: Social accounting for nonprofits and cooperatives.* 2nd ed. London: Sigel.

National Service Learning Clearinghouse. 2005. *Service-learning is … .* http://servicelearning.org/what_is_service-learning/service-learning_is/index.php.

Neamtan, N., and R. Downing 2005. *Social economy and community economic development in Canada: Next steps for public policy.* Montreal: Chantier de l'économie sociale.

Nokes, K., D. Nickitas, R. Keida, and S. Neville. 2005. Does service-learning increase cultural competency, critical thinking, and civic engagement? *Journal of Nursing Education* 44 (2): 65–70.

Parker-Gwin, R., and J.B. Mabry. 1998. Service-learning as pedagogy and civic education: Comparing outcomes for three models. *Teaching Sociology* 26 (4): 276–291.

Putnam, R. 2000. *Bowling alone: The collapse and revival of American community.* New York: Simon and Schuster.

Sather, P., P. Carlson, and B. Weitz. 2007. Research: Infusing service learning into research, social policy, and community-based practice. In *Social work and service learning: Partnerships for social justice*, ed. M. Nadel, V. Majewski, and M. Sullivan-Cosetti, 93–105. Lanham, MA: Rowman and Littlefield.

Sherman, A. 2008. Creating the engaged student. *Academic Matters*: 21–23.

Shragge, E. 2004. Mainstreaming CED and the social economy. *Making Waves* 15 (3): 23–24.

Sousa, J., and E. Hamdon. 2008. Preliminary profile of the size and scope of the social economy in Alberta and British Columbia. BC-Alberta Research Alliance on the Social Economy (BALTA), Port Alberni, BC.

Sousa, J., and R. Herman. In press. *A co-operative dilemma: Converting organizational form.* Saskatoon: Centre for the Study of Co-operatives.

Stoecker, R. 2008. Challenging institutional barriers to community-based research. *Action Research* 6 (1): 49–67.

Wiggins, G. 1993. *Assessing student performance: Exploring the purpose and limits of testing.* San Francisco: Jossey-Bass.

CHAPTER SIX

Social Accounting for Sustainability in the Social Economy

LAURIE MOOK AND JENNIFER SUMNER

Introduction

At its core, the social economy is concerned with questions of sustainability—that is, how to protect people from the effects of neo-liberal restructuring, how to create meaningful employment, and how to build humane alternatives to the self-regulating market. As such, it aligns with the overall goal of sustainability, which is increased well-being (Sumner 2005). Well-being, in turn, opens up discussions of "the good life" and "the common good," which both tie back to the role of the social economy throughout history.

In an age characterized by a growing, interconnected set of crises—climate destabilization, chronic unemployment, the privatization of public resources, and an exponentially increasing gap between rich and poor—the links between the social economy and sustainability become more crucial. For those involved in the social economy, these crises provoke fundamental questions because of a basic commitment to social, economic, and environmental justice. How can we know whether we are heading toward sustainability or moving away from it? How can we measure our progress, or lack of it? How can we teach people to be more sustainable and avoid promoting unsustainable ways of life? How can we remind ourselves to continue in a positive direction and leave behind destructive forms of engagement? One way of answering these questions is through the process known as *social accounting*.

Social accounting is a systematic analysis of the effects of an organization on its communities of interest or stakeholders, with stakeholder input as part of the data that are analyzed for the accounting statement (Mook, Quarter, and Richmond 2007, xix). As a social construct, it can be moulded to account for sustainability both within and beyond a particular organization. If sustainability counts, as various global crises indicate, then social accounting can be a vital tool for promoting individual and collective well-being within the social economy.

Definition of Social Accounting

Social accounting is a systematic analysis of the effects of an organization on its communities of interest or stakeholders, with stakeholder input as part of the data that are analyzed for the accounting statement.

(Mook, Quarter, and Richmond 2007, xix)

This chapter will outline the meaning of sustainability before moving to a detailed description of the process of social accounting. After presenting a case example of social accounting, it will explore how social accounting can be used to analyze sustainability at the local level. Overall, the chapter will introduce readers to the concept of sustainability, familiarize them with the intricacies of social accounting, and encourage them to make direct connections between sustainability and the social economy through the tool of the expanded value added statement. In doing so, it will both broaden and deepen readers' understanding of the social economy in Canada.

Sustainability

The word "sustainability" is a relatively new term in the English language, first used in 1970s. During that decade, a number of events paved the way for its acceptance. In 1972, the United Nations Conference on the Human Environment (UNCHE; sometimes called the Stockholm Conference) launched the word. In addition, the OPEC oil crisis beginning in 1973 was causing people to begin debate over the future of natural resources. At the same time, the Club of Rome, an informal international organization made up of scientists, educators, economists, humanists, industrialists, and national and international civil servants, published *The Limits to Growth* (Meadows, Meadows, Randers, and Behrens 1972), which highlighted the dangers of exponential growth in a resource-limited world. These crises demanded a concept that could highlight the need for a systematic response—the concept of sustainability.

The watershed in the sustainability debates was undoubtedly the Report of the World Commission on Environment and Development (WCED) in 1987, commonly known as the Brundtland Report. Published as *Our Common Future* (WCED 1987), the report defined sustainable development as *development that meets the needs of the present without compromising the ability of future generations to meet their own.* Far from advocating any limits to growth, the report called for a new era of growth, a position that accounted for its overwhelming popularity among politicians, economists, and business elites. Although the report brought sustainability to international attention and made it a household word, the vagueness of its definition ensured that no drastic changes were needed in the ways people treated the environment or each other. Non-renewable resource extraction and the exploitation of labour could proceed without interruption.

During the next two decades, people began to grapple with what sustainability involved, with confusing results. While some came to see it as a goal or an objective, others saw it as a condition or a state we live in or aspire toward. It was narrowed down to a management practice and broadened out to a vision, an ethic, a principle, or even a religion. Some regarded it in terms of the natural sciences—as a form of symbiosis or a manifestation of the second law of thermodynamics—while others thought of it in terms of the social sciences—as a social construct or an emergent property of a soft system (that is, a human activity system, not a hard, mechanical system). It has also been considered as a catalyst for creative thinking and as a process involving ongoing development without end.

The confusion surrounding sustainability is also apparent in disagreements about the term's definition. To begin with, some argue that it simply cannot be defined or that the term has been so abused as to be meaningless, and, therefore, not worth defining. Others proceed to define it, but only negatively, elaborating on what sustainability is *not*. And those who actually define it positively cannot find much common ground. All in all, sustainability appears to be a confusing term that no one opposes but most cannot explain. Instead, many people have warm, fuzzy feelings about what it means, and they project those feelings onto the term. But without a clear definition of sustainability, it is difficult to know whether we are actually becoming more or less sustainable. This debate is crucial to the social economy because its ultimate aim is a more sustainable society, one that is socially responsible, economically fair, and environmentally viable. If this definition is confused and contested, on what basis can we work toward such a society?

This chapter argues that the key to understanding sustainability is through the idea of the civil commons. This is a relatively new term developed by philosopher John McMurtry to describe a long-standing way of doing things. The civil commons is "any co-operative human construct that protects and/or enables the universal access to life goods" (1999, 1). The civil commons is based on cooperation, not competition. It does not occur naturally, but is constructed by people, and thus centres on human agency. It protects through rules and regulations, and it enables through opening up possibilities and opportunities. It involves universal access, not access only for those who can afford it. And it is focused on providing life goods, such as clean air, unadulterated food, potable water, education, and health care, not destructive goods like junk food, violent entertainment, and weapons. In essence, the civil commons is

> society's organized and community-funded capacity of universally accessible resources to provide for the life preservation and growth of society's members and their environmental life-host. The civil commons is, in other words, what people ensure together as a society to protect and further life, as distinct from money aggregates. (McMurtry 1998, 24)

Examples of the civil commons are all around us, often associated with the social economy: public education, the Canadian health-care system, old-age pensions, libraries, the *Charter of Rights and Freedoms*, and the Kyoto Protocol. The social economy can, therefore, be considered as part of the civil commons because it is a cooperative human construct that protects and/or enables universal access to a range of life goods, such as food, housing, employment, and leisure opportunities. By filling life-good gaps or initiating alternative life-good provision, people involved in the social economy contribute constructively to their own well-being and to the well-being of others.

The civil commons forms the basis of both sustainability and the social economy because it is based on the principle of universal access to life goods, thus leading to increased human and environmental well-being. From this understanding, we can define sustainability as *a set of structures and processes that build and protect the civil commons* (Sumner 2005). The structures can be either formal or informal, as long as they build the civil commons. Formal structures include governments, as well as many social economy organizations such as non-governmental organizations (NGOs), clubs, associations, co-operatives, non-profit organizations, and corporations. Examples include FoodShare Toronto, GreenPeace, the Greenbelt Association, and Newman's Own. Informal structures centre on traditions and customs, such as mutual aid and neighbourliness. The processes involve forms of ongoing development, such as teaching, learning, researching, writing, collaborating, and decision making—as long as they build the civil commons. These structures and processes work together dynamically to build the cooperative human constructs that protect and/or enable universal access to life goods—the essence of sustainability.

Three Types of Sustainability

Sustainability is commonly divided into three types: social, economic, and environmental. Social sustainability involves a set of structures and processes that work together to build cooperative human constructs that protect and/or enable universal access to social life goods, such as laws ensuring old-age pensions and declarations of women's rights. Economic sustainability centres on human constructs that provide economic life goods, such as fair trade, minimum wage laws, and legislation guaranteeing the right to form unions. Environmental sustainability focuses on human constructs that provide environmental life goods, such as organic farming, clean water bylaws, and the creation of outdoor public spaces like provincial parks. While we can distinguish between types of sustainability, an organization would be considered more sustainable the more that it addresses all three sets of life goods.

If sustainability involves a set of structures and processes that build the civil commons, and the social economy is a subset of the civil commons, then sustainability can also be understood as involving a set of structures and processes that build the social economy. The structures would include the range of social economy organizations described by Jack Quarter— namely, co-operatives and credit unions, non-profits serving the public, and non-profit mutual associations (1992). What is important for sustainability within the social economy, however, is how it can be measured in a specific way—how one tells whether an organization is tending toward or drifting away from sustainability. This measuring involves a particular process known as social accounting.

Social Accounting

Accounting as a professional field has a lengthy history, dating back to at least the mid-19th century (Tinker 1985). However, the field of social accounting is more recent and surged during the early 1970s (Mathews 1997). It is also referred to as social and environmental accounting, sustainability accounting, social auditing, and full-cost accounting.

As with many terms, there are a variety of definitions of social accounting. Generally, they share two main features:

1. they expand the range of criteria that are taken into consideration when measuring performance by looking at the organization in relation to its surrounding environment, both social and natural; and
2. they emphasize a stakeholder approach.

Many definitions aim toward a more socially responsible, and more sustainable, organization and society. Non-profits, co-operatives, and social enterprises are natural choices for social accounting statements, because they define success in terms of more than just the economic bottom line.

BRIEFING   Social and Environmental Accounting Research

- Accounting plays a key role in defining organizations and, increasingly, in mediating the relationship between the organization, society, and the environment;
- As well as generating consequences which may be interpreted as largely "positive," accounting is also implicated in many of the "negative" aspects of organizational life. For example, environmental damage can be shown to be inevitable given current accounting orthodoxy;
- There is a false perception both within and outside the profession that accounting norms are somehow fixed, objective, and non-negotiable: that accounting simply describes the situation within organizations;
- Changes in accounting practice occur constantly because of, among other things, changes in the aims of the organizations concerned and in the law. Sustainable development is now providing major impetus in both these areas;
- Social and environmental accounting are therefore experiencing a (long overdue) resurgence as academics examine the consequences of current accounting practice and look for new ways of providing accounts of organizational life;
- This in turn has raised the awareness of non-accountants as to the critical importance that the accounting function does, and can, play in re-negotiating organizational relationships;
- Increasingly, sustainability is seen as the key issue and both social and environmental accounting are experiencing a new vitality in their attempts to help articulate sustainability at the organizational level.

Gray (1995, 1)

Additionally, co-operatives are guided by an explicit set of social principles, initially formulated in 1844 by the Rochdale Pioneers (the founders of the first modern co-operative in England). The principles have since been updated, most recently in 1995 in Manchester, England, by the International Co-operative Alliance (ICA), the umbrella body for co-operatives in 87 countries representing about 800 million members (International Co-operative Alliance 2008). These principles are:

1. open and voluntary membership (co-operatives are open to all persons willing to accept the responsibilities of membership and cannot engage in discrimination by gender or by social, racial, political, or religious criteria);
2. democratic control (co-operatives are democratic organizations controlled by their members according to the principle of one member, one vote);
3. member economic participation (members contribute equitably to financing the organization and are also the primary beneficiaries of the organization's services);
4. autonomy and independence (co-operatives are autonomous self-help organizations and must not jeopardize their independence through agreements with government or external lenders);
5. education, training, and information (co-operatives have an obligation to educate their members and employees about their organization);
6. co-operation among co-operatives (co-operatives are expected to work together, both to serve their members and to strengthen the co-operative movement); and
7. concern for the community (the obligation of co-operatives to work for sustainable development of their communities). (International Co-operative Alliance 2009)

Such commitment to social principles means that there is already a tradition in co-operatives in support of social accounting—they are its leading edge. Individual credit unions have developed social audits, and they are working together to develop protocols for future social audits (as with, for example, Alterna Credit Union, Heritage Credit Union, The Co-operative Bank, and VanCity).

An Integrated Approach to Social Accounting

A distinct characteristic of the predominant tradition in social accounting has been its separation from financial statements, which focus on economic issues. For most organizations, the social account is presented as a supplement to financial accounting and generally is treated as a less important piece of the picture. Ironically, this is true not only of profit-oriented businesses but also of social organizations. However, to segregate the social and environmental from the economic is artificial, a point also emphasized in the field of alternative economics (Daly and Cobb 1994; Ekins 1986; Mies 1986; Schumacher 1973; Waring 1996, 1999). One integrated approach to social accounting is the value added statement, which accounts for other forms of value that are added by organizations besides the purely economic.

The Importance of Value Added to Social Accounting

Value added is an accounting term that refers to the wealth created by transforming externally purchased goods and services into new goods and services through the application of labour and capital. The value added statement takes a different approach from other financial statements. As Burchell, Clubb, and Hopwood (1985, 388) state:

> Value added has the property of revealing (or representing) something about the social character of production, something which is occluded by traditional profit and loss accounting. Value added reveals that the wealth created in production is the consequence of the combined effort of a number of agents who together form the cooperating team.

In contrast to profit, which is interpreted as the wealth created for owners or shareholders, value added represents the wealth created for a larger group of stakeholders.

Income statements that analyze the return to shareholders may be logical for a private sector firm, but they are not an ideal fit for non-profits and co-operatives because the mission of such organizations is to fulfill a social purpose rather than to earn profits for shareholders. By comparison to an income statement, the value added statement assumes that an organization is based on a group of stakeholders whose combined efforts create additional value (Riahi-Belkaoui 1999). Indeed, value added is distributed in its entirety to the different stakeholders necessary to sustain an organization in accordance with its goals and values. Thus, the value added statement focuses attention on the wider implications of an organization's activities beyond the profits for its shareholders, or in the case of a social organization, beyond the surplus that it generates. Value added emphasizes that the organization also employs people, contributes to societal costs through taxes, rewards investors and creditors for risking their funds, and sets aside funds to ensure that it can continue functioning in the future. As such, the value added statement emphasizes well-being.

Table 6.1 illustrates a typical corporate value added statement. There are two parts to the statement: the value added that is created, and then its distribution to stakeholders. In the first part, the total of the firm's purchases of external goods and services was subtracted from its sales to arrive at the value added that is created. The second part shows how this value added is distributed to stakeholders.

Traditionally, this has only included financial information, leaving out social inputs such as volunteer or social labour and social and environmental outputs. However, there are two shortcomings to the typical value added statement: it does not take into consideration non-monetized inputs such as volunteer labour, and it does not take into consideration social and environmental impacts. In order to overcome the limitations of this typical approach, the expanded value added statement was developed to include social and environmental variables that are normally ignored and to attribute a financial value to these variables.

TABLE 6.1 Typical Corporate Value Added Statement (in thousands of Cdn$)

Sales		100,000
Less: Purchases of external goods and services		74,032
Value added		25,968
Distributed in the following way:		
To pay employees		
Wages, pensions, and benefits		15,308
To pay providers of capital		
Interest	2,513	
Dividends to shareholders	1,544	4,057
To pay government		
Taxes		1,596
Reinvestment in the business		
Amortization of capital assets	2,546	
Retained profits	2,461	5,007
Value added		25,968

Expanded Value Added Statement

The expanded value added statement brings together the concepts of value added accounting, critical accounting, sustainability, and social accounting (Figure 6.1). In this way, it combines financial information with quantified social and environmental data to make explicit the social, environmental, and economic impacts of an organization.

As an accounting statement, the expanded value added statement has a number of important features. First, it focuses on the wider implications of an organization's activities beyond profits/losses or surpluses/deficits. Second, it takes a critical accounting perspective by recognizing that accounting is not a neutral practice, and that accounting can be a driver of behaviour.

Third, the expanded value added statement is guided by the principles of sustainability in that the types of behaviour we want to promote are those that drive us toward building the civil commons. And finally, as a form of social accounting that integrates financial, social, and environmental information (as distinct from social accounting reports, which are supplemental to the financial report), it provides both methodologies for estimating a monetary value for non-monetary activities and examples of working models that synthesize economic, social, and environmental factors into one statement.

FIGURE 6.1   The Expanded Value Added Framework

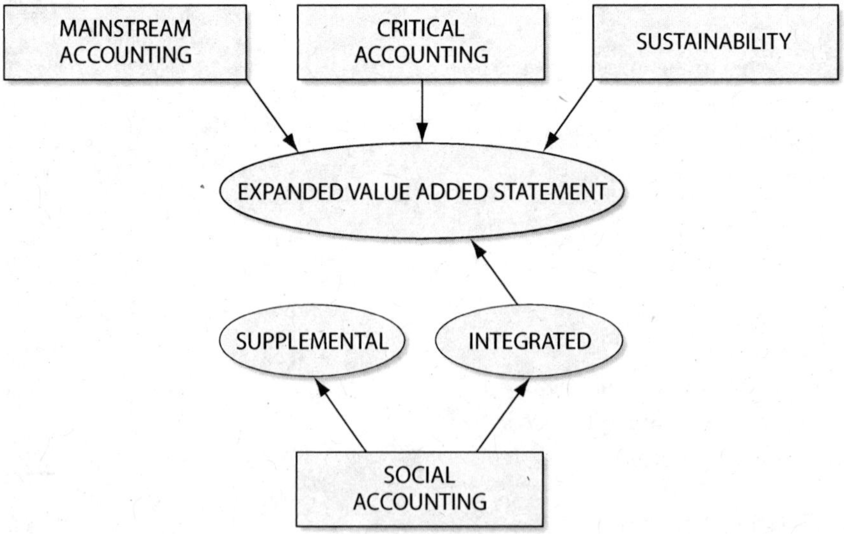

Viewing accounting as a mechanism to drive social change is not the typical way we are taught to think about accounting. Often, accounting is presented as an objective, neutral, value-free, and technical enterprise that simply attempts to capture a picture of reality. However, it can be argued that accounting, by the very act of "counting" certain things and excluding others (deemed as irrelevant to the enterprise of doing business), shapes a particular interpretation of social reality, which in turn has policy and decision-making implications (Hines 1988). For example, by focusing on the measurement of socially constructed categories such as profit, accountants deal with complex realities in a restricted way, treating the economy, community, and environment not only as separate entities but also as mutually exclusive ones. From this perspective, accountants are not just number crunchers but also active participants who construct a particular social reality (Morgan 1988).

The limitations of conventional accounting are particularly problematic for the subset of organizations that rely heavily on either grants or donations from such external sources as governments, individuals, corporations, and foundations. For organizations of this sort, conventional accounting documents their costs without assessing their benefits (Anthony and Young 1988; Henke 1989). Through the particular reality constructed by accountants, these organizations are portrayed as users of resources rather than as creators of value through their services to society. Their financial accounts are one-sided and lack information upon which to base decisions affecting the organizations and the communities they serve. Additional information is required to assess the impact of individual non-profit organizations as well as the sector as a whole.

If we are to drive behaviour toward building the civil commons, we need to make visible actions that build or reduce capacity to protect and enable an equitable quality of life rather than those that document an accumulation of wealth for a select few. Some examples might include actions taken toward the prevention of the destruction of the natural environment, the promotion of a healthy balance between work and life, and the provision of universal health care and education. Organizations may have direct control over these factors or indirect control where they can have potential influence. An example of direct control is the decision to buy energy-efficient compact fluorescent light bulbs to use in office spaces. Influencing the activities of customers or clients by working with them to reduce their environmental footprint is an example of indirect control.

In the expanded value added statement, these activities are made visible by highlighting how the economic, social, and environmental value added, created or destroyed by labour and capital through the organization is distributed to key stakeholder groups. Typical stakeholder groups are employees, volunteers, the community, the environment, public sector, providers of capital, and the organization itself. If we use the energy-efficient light bulb as an example, the higher initial cost of the bulb is more than outweighed by the long-term savings, reduction in energy use, and reduction in waste.

Valuing Non-Market Inputs and Outputs

If social accounting frameworks are going to assess properly the effects of an organization, it is necessary to measure inputs (such as volunteer labour) and outputs (such as climate change due to direct energy use) that normally would not be monetized. In the absence of established benchmarks or indicators for evaluating these outputs, innovation is required.

NON-MARKET INPUTS

Assessing the social effects of non-profits and co-operatives is of particular importance because such organizations are based on a social mission. However, these organizations often operate outside of the market, and thus traditional accounting does not capture these effects. For example, many social organizations depend on volunteers for social labour. Because no market transaction is involved, this component of the organization's labour force does not normally appear on its accounting statements. Yet for organizations in which most of the labour force is volunteer, this is a major oversight. Without their involvement, the level of service would be drastically curtailed; in some cases, the organization might not function at all.

Many organizations that estimate the value of volunteers use a replacement cost method and evaluate the cost of volunteers from the perspective of the organization, as if it had to pay the market rate for such a service. There are different ways of doing this. One method is to simply calculate a gross average based on the average hourly wage in a jurisdiction. For example, the Independent Sector—an advocacy organization for non-profits in the United States—suggests using the average hourly wage for non-agricultural workers published in the Economic Report of the President, plus 12 percent for fringe benefits (Independent Sector 2008). For Canada, Ross (1994) suggested a weighted average of hourly and salaried wages based on Statistics Canada data for employment earnings. He calculated both national and provincial averages.

Another method for applying replacement cost estimates to volunteers is to base the calculation on the type of service (Brudney 1990; Community

Literacy Ontario 1998; Gaskin 1999; Gaskin and Dobson 1997; Karn 1983). For example, Community Literacy Ontario uses an hourly rate for volunteer literacy workers based on a survey of the average annual salary of full-time support staff of 94 community organizations that supply training. The Volunteer Investment and Value Audit (VIVA), developed in the United Kingdom, uses market comparisons based on both the job titles and the component parts of the jobs (Gaskin 1999; Gaskin and Dobson 1997).

An estimate can also be based on the average wages paid within a certain industry sector, using the North American Industry Classification System (NAICS) jointly developed by the statistics agencies of Canada, the United States, and Mexico. This system classifies organizations such as businesses, government institutions, unions, and charitable and non-profit organizations according to economic activity. For example, NAICS subsector 624, social assistance, includes organizations engaged in a variety of services such as food and housing within the community and emergency and other forms of relief both to the individual and family. The NAICS classification combines all the tasks for a subsector such as social services (including executive and administrative ones) and puts forward an average wage rate for all levels of occupation in that category, making its subsequent use straightforward.

NON-MARKET OUTPUTS

Although establishing an appropriate value for volunteer labour is a major factor in creating a social accounting framework for social organizations, we also have to consider outputs that do not involve market transactions. In one of the earlier works in social accounting, Estes (1976) proposed a number of techniques.

1. Surrogate Valuation: "When a desired value cannot be directly determined, we may estimate instead the value of a surrogate—some item or phenomenon that is logically expected to involve approximately the same utility or sacrifice as the item in which we are interested" (Estes 1976, 110). Estes gave the example of estimating the value of building facilities loaned to civic groups and suggests as a surrogate the rent that would be paid for commercial facilities of a similar quality. Another example involves establishing a surrogate value for the personal growth and development of volunteers from participating in a non-profit organization's activities. In this case, the cost of a community college course in personal development could be the surrogate.

2. Survey Techniques: This procedure involves asking participants what a service is worth to them. To assist in establishing an accurate estimate,

Estes (1976) suggests using, as a prompt, a list of either prices or consumer items and asking the respondents to situate the service in relation to others on the list.

3. Restoration or Avoidance Cost: "Certain social costs may be valued by estimating the monetary outlay necessary to undo or prevent the damage" (Estes 1976, 115). It is possible to estimate the cost of restoring environmentally damaged land to either industrial or residential use. For example, in the event of a plant closure, many governments require a cleanup of the work site to residential standards, a liability that can be determined.

Each of these methods can be used in assigning a comparative market value to externalities. It is important to be very transparent about which method is being used, and the assumptions made in doing calculations. In some cases, your choice may be delineated by the availability of data, or the cost of collecting new data.

Case Example: The Expanded Value Added Statement

To illustrate the expanded value added statement approach, we present a simplified case example of a student housing co-operative, the Waterloo Co-operative Residence Inc. (WCRI). WCRI is the largest student housing co-operative in Canada, and the second largest in North America. It houses over 800 resident members, and has a paid staff of about 30.

WCRI provides housing in dormitories and apartments for students of two major universities. Its mission statement states that "WCRI aims to provide quality, affordable student housing, emphasizing member participation and superior service in the spirit of cooperation, while promoting pride, education, and diversity in a dynamic co-operative community" (WCRI n.d., 1). As a cooperative, WCRI is run by its members—current students as well as former residents. The governance of WCRI is based on democratic and cooperative principles. Each resident becomes a member of the co-operative and is entitled to one vote at annual general membership meetings held each October. The general membership elects ten directors for one-year terms, and directors may be re-elected. Members can remove a director for non-performance of duties, but this is an unusual circumstance. The co-operative's democratic approach to decision making distinguishes it from other university residences.

Each resident of WCRI is required to perform social labour—service to the organization that helps to reduce the housing charge. Common examples are food preparation, serving meals, dish and pot washing, common-space cleaning, snow shovelling, grounds maintenance, writing for the newsletter, participating in committees, and sitting on the board of directors. Residents may also become members of committees responsible for internal education, environmental education, and such practical issues as menu planning, conflict resolution, and special events. These member contributions are part of the value added of the organization and, therefore, are presented in the expanded value added statement.

Table 6.2, which presents the value added by WCRI, has three columns that refer to different sources of value added:

- Financial, which represents information from audited financial statements only and which is also referred to as a traditional value added statement;
- Social, which represents information about non-monetized inputs and outputs for which market comparisons are estimated;
- Combined, which represents the total of the financial and social columns.

In order to calculate the amount of value added, the first step is to assess the total outputs of the organization and assign a comparative market value to them. Total outputs are the results of an organization's activities toward accomplishing its mission—all of the services that it offers. Total outputs, as given in Table 6.2, are subdivided into primary, secondary, and tertiary, reflecting how directly the associated items are connected to fulfillment of the organization's mission (Richmond 1999). Primary outputs are the direct services of the organization—in the case of WCRI, the housing for students. The secondary and tertiary outputs are the indirect results of an organization's activities to fulfill its mission. Secondary outputs are indirect outputs that accrue to the organization's members or customers; tertiary outputs are indirect outputs that accrue to those other than the organization's members, customers, or clients.

For WCRI, a secondary output was its provision of skills development for its residents. This included leadership skills from participating in co-op management, skills in community and democratic decision-making processes, and other skills such as cleaning and cooking. An example of a tertiary output was the consultations with other co-operatives. This was classified as tertiary because, unlike the skills training of residents, it was not related directly to WCRI's primary service; rather, it was a service to other organizations or, arguably, to the co-operative movement. Not all organizations would have all three categories of outputs, but for WCRI this division seemed logical.

TABLE 6.2 Expanded Value Added Statement (Partial) for WCRI for the Year Ended April 30, 1999

Creation of Value Added		Financial	Social	Combined
Outputs	Primary	$3,964,031	$246,128	$4,210,159
	Secondary	65,192	424,808	490,000
	Tertiary		2,500	2,500
	Total	4,029,223	673,436	4,702,659
Purchases of external goods and services		1,538,561		1,538,561
	Value Added Created	**$2,490,662**	**$673,436**	**$3,164,098**

Distribution of Value Added		Financial	Social	Combined
Employees	Wages and benefits	$838,222		$838,222
Residents	Value from social labour		$244,128	244,128
	Skills development	65,192	424,808	490,000
	Property tax credit		141,800	141,800
		65,192	810,736	875,928
Society	Government: municipal property taxes	216,586		216,586
	Government: property tax credit		(141,800)	(141,800)
	Government: housing of war refugees		2,000	2,000
	Co-operative sector: consultations		2,500	2,500
		216,586	(137,300)	79,286
Capital	Loan interest	519,961		519,961
Organization	Amortization of capital assets	433,450		433,450
	Operating surplus	417,251		417,251
		850,701		850,701
	Value Added Distributed	**$2,490,662**	**$673,436**	**$3,164,098**

As described above, there are two sections to an expanded value added statement: the value added created and the distribution of value added. Whereas the former *measures* how much value added has been created, the distribution of value added *analyzes* how it was disseminated. For the statement of distribution, the value added created by the organization (as shown in the second half of Table 6.2) is distributed to the stakeholders in its entirety. Stakeholders are selected on the basis of their contribution to the viability of the organization and its values. For a value added statement, the stakeholders suggested by accounting regulatory bodies normally are employees, government, investors, and the organization itself. For purposes of the expanded value added statement of WCRI, one additional stakeholder was identified—residents—and one was modified—the stakeholder "government" was changed to the stakeholder "society" and expanded to include the non-profit co-operative sector.

As noted, the stakeholder-based approach of the expanded value added statement differentiates it from most other forms of financial statements that are oriented toward shareholders. The expanded value added statement not only is based on the assumption that a broad group of stakeholders contribute to an organization but also attempts to analyze how much value added each stakeholder receives from these combined efforts from year to year. Therefore, this form of financial statement acknowledges the importance of stakeholders, as so many organizations do in theory, and additionally attempts in a very practical manner to assign a portion of the value added to them.

Another way of looking at the significance of resident contributions is to examine the proportion that residents contribute to the human resources of the organization. Resident activities accounted for over 35 percent of WCRI's human resources (Figure 6.2). Based on the estimate of 30,516 resident hours, residents contributed the equivalent of 17 full-time equivalent (FTE) positions for the year. This means that WCRI had the equivalent of a total workforce FTE of 48, not just a paid staff FTE of 31. These figures are significant given consideration of issues related to managing the equivalent of an additional 17 FTE positions distributed over 800 residents.

FIGURE 6.2   Proportion of Total Activity Hours by Residents and Staff

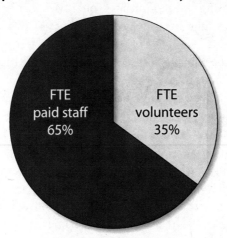

FTE
paid staff
65%

FTE
volunteers
35%

Thus, by synthesizing traditional financial data with social inputs, the expanded value added statement can be another mechanism for understanding the dynamics of an organization, one that shows great potential for enhancing the importance of social inputs and outputs. For WCRI, the expanded value added statement creates a greater awareness of:

- the collective effort needed to run the organization;
- the role of the organization in providing employment;
- the role of the organization in providing skills training;
- the impact of social labour and other contributions;
- the role of the organization in supporting the co-operative sector; and
- the role of the organization in contributing to society through taxes and donated services.

The strengths of social accounting lie in its ability to take a broader look at an organization and the role of stakeholders within it, and to put this in a larger social-economic perspective. For example, by including non-monetary social inputs, the expanded value added statement presents a more robust picture of an organization's economic and social impact. Through this approach, benefits that are unknown, undisclosed, or not measured are made explicit, allowing for different emphases in decision making. By combining financial and social variables, the expanded value added statement focuses attention on the interconnectedness and interdependence of the economy, community, and environment. The model particularly highlights the contribution of the organization to its wider community, something that is invaluable to non-profits and co-operatives, and a key feature of any social accounting model.

The challenges faced by social accounting are shared by other forms of alternative accounting and economics—quantifying and placing a value on goods and services that are usually thought of as "free." And yet, as the expanded value added statement for WCRI shows, free goods and services are used and produced in large measure by the organization and, therefore, need to be accounted for if the whole performance story of the organization is to be told. The expanded value added statement attempts to develop a methodology that supports the integration of financial information for which there are strict methods of accounting with non-financial or social information.

Another challenge faced by social accounting involves assessing not only value added but also value subtracted. This category might be pertinent to variables like the environment where citizens, through the taxes paid to government, have to bear the costs of externalities, such as cleaning up pollution. Such an approach might be threatening to large corporations, particularly those engaged in industrial production and resource extraction; however, it is important for accounting statements to illuminate rather than to obscure the full costs, and full benefits, of organizations.

Social Accounting for Sustainability

If sustainability involves a set of structures and processes that build the civil commons, and social accounting systematically analyzes the effects of an organization on its communities of interest or stakeholders, then social accounting for sustainability is a process that systematically analyzes whether or not an organization builds the civil commons and the resulting effects on its communities of interest or stakeholders. Social accounting for sustainability helps to render the costs of doing business more transparent and to make organizations more accountable in the broad sense of that term.

The overarching importance of social accounting for sustainability is not that it can be moulded to account for the smallest details, but that it can change unsustainable behaviours. As mentioned earlier, all forms of accounting can be drivers of behaviour, whether acknowledged or not. Traditional forms of accounting determine certain forms of behaviour that can be detrimental to sustainability. For example, it can reward the closing down of not-for-profit daycare centres or the shipping of hazardous waste to a developing country as cost-saving strategies. But in rendering invisible the effects of these actions on others, such as parents and poor countries, traditional accounting promotes unsustainability by breaking down the civil commons. In this way, traditional forms of accounting can move us away from sustainability, not toward it. Social accounting for sustainability, on the other hand, openly acknowledges that accounting drives behaviour, and uses this fact to work toward greater sustainability by accounting for what builds the civil commons and what does not.

Meaningful employment provides an illustration of the importance of social accounting for sustainability. If we were accounting for sustainability, not financial returns to shareholders, then we would analyze meaningful employment in terms of the effects of an organization on its employees. For example, are they able to form unions, to be paid fair wages, to enjoy ample health benefits, to benefit from unemployment insurance, and to access onsite not-for-profit daycare or eldercare? We would also analyze whether the organization engaged in employee education, encouraged communication with other social economy organizations, provided paid time off for community projects, and guaranteed wellness days. In this way, social accounting for sustainability can both measure and reward behaviour that moves toward building the civil commons while punishing behaviour that moves toward destroying it. This form of accounting makes visible and valuable the economic, social, and environmental aspects of the civil commons, thus elevating these in the regard of the general public.

Conclusion

The strength of social economy organizations lies in the dominance of social interests over economic ones. J.J. McMurtry argues that these social interests make the lives of their memberships better than they were prior to participation by providing alternative modes of economic life-good delivery (however small). In this way, the social economy can be understood "not just as a reaction to the current hegemony of market relationships, but as a historically deep-seated and powerful alternative to them" (2004, 876). By providing life goods, the social economy is inextricably part of the civil commons, and, as such, contributes to the ongoing creation of a sustainable present and a more sustainable future.

Quarter's work reinforces the importance of the social economy as an alternative to the current global market economy when he reminds us that "the term 'social economy' is not simply descriptive but also prescriptive. It implies a vision of social transformation" (1992, x). As such, the social economy provides a link between what is happening today and what is possible tomorrow. By highlighting concern for social interests, it models the transformation to a more sustainable society. Social accounting for sustainability can help to guide and monitor this transformation. It not only measures current achievements in this area, but also normalizes them. And through its ability to drive behaviour, social accounting for sustainability can bring us closer to the vision of a more sustainable society.

Overall, social accounting for sustainability can be seen as a tool for connecting sustainability and the social economy, for valorizing the civil commons, for encouraging sustainability, and for contributing to increased human and environmental well-being. It can model sustainable behaviour, reward movement toward sustainability, and discourage movement toward unsustainability. Social accounting for sustainability is aimed at creating common wealth for social economy communities of interest and stakeholders, not private wealth for individual shareholders. In this way, social accounting for sustainability can ultimately be understood as accounting as if sustainability mattered—as if economic, social, and environmental sustainability were the reasons for, not the casualties of, doing business. In this way, we can understand social accounting as a key tool for measuring the social economy in practice and for moving behaviours toward sustainability.

Glossary

Civil commons   Any cooperative human construct that protects and/or enables the universal access to life goods.

Expanded value added statement   An accounting statement based on the value added statement, but expanded to include a measurement of social and environmental information.

Externalities   Factors not included in traditional forms of accounting that affect human well-being; the (usually) unintended consequences of doing business. Negative externalities include pollution.

Non-profit mutual association   A social economy organization that serves a defined membership by satisfying a mutual interest.

Non-profit serving the public   A social economy organization that provides humanitarian and social services.

Profit   Wealth created for owners or shareholders.

Social accounting   A systematic analysis of the effects of an organization on its communities of interest or stakeholders, with stakeholder input as part of the data that are analyzed for the accounting statement.

Sustainability   A set of structures and processes that build the civil commons.

Value added   Wealth created by transforming externally purchased goods and services with labour and capital into new goods and services; wealth created for a large group of stakeholders.

Discussion Questions

1. What are the definitions of sustainability and social accounting used in this chapter?
2. How does social accounting provide an understanding of "value added" for the social economy?
3. How is the civil commons different from and similar to the social economy?

Suggested Further Readings and Resources

Mook, L., J. Quarter, and B.J. Richmond. 2007. *What counts: Social accounting for nonprofits and cooperatives.* 2nd ed. London: Sigel Press.

Sumner, J. 2005. *Sustainability and the civil commons: Rural communities in the age of globalization.* Toronto: University of Toronto Press.

The Social Economy Centre website: http://www.socialeconomy.utoronto.ca.

Unerman, J., J. Bebbington, and B. O'Dwyer. 2007. *Sustainability accounting and accountability.* London: Routledge.

References

Anthony, R.N., and D.W. Young. 1988. *Management control in nonprofit organizations.* 2nd ed. Burr Ridge, IL: Irwin.

Brudney, J. 1990. *Fostering volunteer programs in the public sector.* San Francisco: Jossey-Bass.

Burchell, S., C. Clubb, and A.G. Hopwood. 1985. Accounting in its social context: Towards a history of value added in the United Kingdom. *Accounting, Organizations and Society* 10 (4): 381–413.

Community Literacy of Ontario (CLO). 1998. *The economic value of volunteers in community literacy agencies in Ontario.* Barrie, ON: Community Literacy of Ontario.

Daly, H., and J. Cobb Jr. 1994. *For the common good: Redirecting the economy toward community, the environment, and a sustainable future.* 2nd ed. Boston: Beacon.

Ekins, P., ed. 1986. *The living economy: A new economics in the making.* London: Routledge and Kegan Paul.

Estes, R. 1976. *Corporate social accounting.* New York: John Wiley.

Gaskin, K. 1999. Valuing volunteers in Europe: A comparative study of the volunteer investment and value audit. *Voluntary Action: The Journal of Active Volunteering Research* 2 (1): 35–48.

Gaskin, K., and B. Dobson. 1997. The economic equation of volunteering. http://www.jrf.org.uk/knowledge/findings/socialpolicy/SP110.asp.

Gray, R. 1995. Briefing: Social and environmental accounting research. http://www.st-andrews.ac.uk/~csearweb/intromaterials/esrc.html.

Henke, E.O. 1989. *Accounting for nonprofit organizations.* 2nd ed. Boston: PWS-Kent.

Hines, R.D. 1988. Financial accounting: In communicating reality, we construct reality. *Accounting, Organizations and Society* 13 (3): 251–261.

Independent Sector (IS). 2008. Value of volunteer time. http://www.independentsector.org/programs/research/volunteer_time.html.

International Co-operative Alliance (ICA). 2008. Home page. http://www.ica.coop.

International Co-operative Alliance (ICA). 2009. ICA rules: Article 6. Geneva: ICA. http://www.ica.coop/ica/rules.html.

Karn, G.N. 1983. Money talks: A guide to establishing the true dollar value of volunteer time, Part 1. *Journal of Volunteer Administration* 1 (Winter): 1–19.

Mathews, M.R. 1997. Twenty-five years of social and environmental accounting research: Is there a silver jubilee to celebrate? *Accounting, Auditing & Accountability Journal* 10 (4): 481–531.

McMurtry, J. 1998. *Unequal freedoms: The global market as an ethical system.* Toronto: Garamond.

McMurtry, J. 1999. The lifeground, the civil commons and global development. Paper presented at the Annual Meeting of the Canadian Association for Studies in International Development (CASID), Congress of the Social Sciences and Humanities, Sherbrooke, Quebec, June 7.

McMurtry, J.J. 2004. Social economy as political practice. *International Journal of Social Economics* 31 (9–10): 868–878.

Meadows, D.H, D.L. Meadows, J. Randers, and W.W. Behrens III. 1972. *The limits to growth: A report for The Club of Rome's project on the predicament of mankind.* New York: Universe.

Mies, M. 1986. *Patriarchy and accumulation on a world scale: Women in the international division of labour.* London: Zed Books.

Mook, L. 2007. Social and environmental accounting: The expanded value added statement. PhD diss., University of Toronto.

Mook, L., J. Quarter, and B.J. Richmond. 2007. *What counts: Social accounting for nonprofits and cooperatives.* 2nd ed. London: Sigel Press.

Morgan, G. 1988. Accounting as reality construction: Towards a new epistemology for accounting practice. *Accounting, Organizations and Society* 13 (5): 477–485.

Quarter, J. 1992. *Canada's social economy: Co-operatives, non-profits, and other community enterprises.* Toronto: James Lorimer.

Riahi-Belkaoui, A. 1999. *Value added reporting and research: State of the art.* Westport, CT: Quorum.

Richmond, B.J. 1999. Counting on each other: A social audit model to assess the impact of nonprofit organizations. PhD diss., University of Toronto.

Ross, D. 1994. How to estimate the economic contribution of volunteer work. Ottawa: Department of Canadian Heritage.

Schumacher, E.F. 1973. *Small is beautiful.* New York: Harper and Row.

Sumner, J. 2005. *Sustainability and the civil commons: Rural communities in the age of globalization.* Toronto: University of Toronto Press.

Tinker, T. 1985. *Paper prophets: A social critique of accounting.* New York: Praeger.

Waring, M. 1996. *Three masquerades: Essays on equality, work and human rights.* Toronto: University of Toronto Press.

Waring, M. 1999. *Counting for nothing: What men value and what women are worth.* Toronto: University of Toronto Press.

Waterloo Co-operative Residence Inc. (WCRI). n.d. WCRI mission statement. Waterloo, ON: WCRI. Photocopy.

WCED (World Commission on Environment and Development). 1987. *Our common future.* New York: Oxford University Press.

CHAPTER SEVEN

Aboriginal Perspectives on the Social Economy

WANDA WUTTUNEE

Introduction

This chapter begins with a profile of Aboriginal peoples today, followed by an examination of several definitions of social economy and social enterprise that will form part of the framework for an analysis of Aboriginal perspectives on this topic. The relevance of these concepts to the Aboriginal experience of development will also be considered. The idea of "community capitalism," a term used by some Aboriginal peoples to describe their approach to development—an approach that includes consideration of profit making and community well-being—will be considered in the context of three case studies and compared to the concept of social economy and social enterprise for its relevance to these communities. Ultimately the question for Aboriginal peoples is which of these three concepts most nearly fits their experience and desires.

Community capitalism and the long history of Aboriginal approaches to development are undertakings that are holistic in nature and as such are precursors to social economy as it is understood today. With its focus on community, community capitalism as a concept and practice fills the gaps left in society after application of private and public sector development approaches. Capitalism is

the economic system based on private property and private enterprise. Under this system all, or a major proportion, of economic activity is undertaken by private profit-seeking individuals or organizations, and land and other

material means of production are largely privately owned. (Black, Hashimzade, and Myles 2009)

As such, community capitalism is to be seen as aligned with the premises
that underlie both the social economy and social enterprise (see McMurtry
in this volume). The focus on capitalism remains because, while there may
well be some other methods of economic development in the future, alternatives to capitalism (namely the form of socialist command economies)
have historically proven to be immensely problematic, and free market
capitalism remains dominant. Aboriginal communities may make the
choice to engage in capitalistic activities or not, but what is crucial is that
when they do so they strive to do so on their own terms and for the benefit
of their societies. Adding the concept of "community" to "capitalism"
acknowledges these efforts in the world of capitalism.

This raises the question of the social economy. The Aboriginal community, just as in the academic one, is grappling with the issue of understanding what the social economy is (or is not), but for the former community,
the questions are of a different nature: Is the concept of social economy a
reformulation of the continuing push by the federal government to force
development on Aboriginal communities—that is, a form of development
that can turn out to be inappropriate to Aboriginal reality? Does the definition of social economy include and value activities initiated and led by
Aboriginal communities, or will these communities' activities continue to
be marginalized, resulting in the marginalization of the communities themselves? What is the process whereby Aboriginal communities are engaged
in addressing and answering these questions and thereby informing the
discussion with Aboriginal concerns, insights, and knowledge? Finally, and
following upon the previous issue, what do Aboriginal communities have
to contribute to the dialogue? These are some of the questions that will be
examined in this chapter. The discussion is important because Canada is
both ethnically multicultural and academically interdisciplinary and these
different communities, conceptual and cultural, read broad policy initiatives in different ways. Furthermore, given this diversity, every portion of
Canada's population is integral to a healthy Canadian economy and needs
to feel free to engage in the issues that will promote development for the
benefit of all its members.

In sum, this chapter highlights Aboriginal experiences with private sector
and public sector development methods while outlining the complemen-
tary place that social economy holds as a helpful hybrid of the two. Like all
Canadians, Aboriginal people choose the vehicles that make the most sense

for the pursuit of their development goals and will contemplate any available option to achieve such ends. It is this rather open-ended relationship to the concepts and practices of the social economy, practices exemplified in important ways in the case studies presented here, that becomes important in the dialogue between Aboriginal communities and others conceptualizing and practising this kind of community-focused economic activity.

The First Peoples in Contemporary Canada

To understand the challenges faced in conceptualizing the social economy from a First Peoples' perspective, one first needs to understand the dynamic and diverse Aboriginal communities that exist in Canada. Demographics demonstrate that economic development challenges confront the population of First Peoples across this country. Canada's First Peoples growing share of the Canadian population rose to 3.8 percent of the total population as enumerated in the 2006 census, up from 3.3 percent in 2001 and 2.8 percent in 1996 (Statistics Canada 2006). Aboriginal people make up the largest share of the population in the territories and in the prairie provinces; for example, the 24,920 Aboriginal people living in Nunavut represent 85 percent of the territory's total population, which is the highest percentage of Aboriginal to non-Aboriginals in the country. The percentage of Aboriginal people in relation to the total population decreases in moving west across the other territories; Aboriginal people represent 50 percent of the population of the Northwest Territories and 25 percent in the Yukon Territory. The prairie provinces have significant Aboriginal representation, with 15 percent of the population in Manitoba and Saskatchewan and with 6 percent in Alberta (Statistics Canada 2006).

While most Aboriginal people live in Canada's west and north, the fastest increase in the last decade occurred east of Manitoba. Between 1996 and 2006, the Aboriginal population increased 95 percent in Nova Scotia, 67 percent in New Brunswick, 65 percent in Newfoundland and Labrador, 53 percent in Quebec, and 68 percent in Ontario. Among western regions having a significant proportion of Aboriginal people in the population, the largest increase was observed in Manitoba, at 36 percent. The Aboriginal population in Saskatchewan increased 28 percent, and in the Yukon Territory, 23 percent (Statistics Canada 2006). When considering the development issues confronting Aboriginal populations in Canada, these geographic particularities need to be kept in mind.

Another important demographic fact for development is that across the country, the Aboriginal population is predominantly young, which has consequences for the future labour force. Children and youth aged 24 and under make up 48 percent—almost half—of all Aboriginal people, in comparison to 31 percent among the non-Aboriginal population. According to population projections released by Statistics Canada in 2005, Aboriginal people will account for a growing share of the young adult population of Canada over the next decade. This is a particularly important trend given the geographical locations of these populations in the west of the country. Thus, it is projected that by 2017 Aboriginal people aged 20 to 29 will likely make up 30 percent of those in their twenties in Saskatchewan; 24 percent in Manitoba; 40 percent in the Yukon Territory; and 58 percent in the Northwest Territories. Already, more than 80 percent of Nunavut's population aged 20 to 29 is Aboriginal, and the proportion is expected to grow (Statistics Canada 2005).

A third significant feature of the Canadian Aboriginal population for those concerned with community development is that it is becoming increasingly urban. In 2006, 54 percent lived in an urban centre, both large and small, an increase from 50 percent in 1996. It is important to remember that there are different components to the total Aboriginal populations that have unevenly moved to the urban centres. Historically, a large share of First Nations (non-Inuit, members of traditional nations) people lived on reserves, a fact that continues today. As a result, this population, while demographically the largest proportion of the Aboriginal population in Canada, does not dominate the urban population. Thus in 2006, First Nations people comprised up to 50 percent of the urban aboriginal population, while 43 percent were Métis (mixed First Nation and European heritage); the share of the Métis population in urban centres has grown considerably since 1996, when they accounted for 35 percent of all urban Aboriginal people (as a general rule, Métis are not entitled to reserves lands—more on this below). Relatively few Inuit live in southern urban centres. Despite this trend toward urbanization, the Aboriginal population in Canada is still strongly rural. In 2006, 59 percent of the urban Aboriginal population lived in large cities compared with 80 percent of non-Aboriginal people. The remaining 41 percent of the urban Aboriginal population lived in small urban centres (Statistics Canada 2006).

Understanding the profile of Aboriginal people in contemporary Canada requires recognition of 2001 census data, which reported that more than half (53 percent) of the 505,000 First Nations people with legal Indian status lived on reserves at that time. Legal Indian status is defined under the federal government's *Indian Act* and as such has a legislated meaning that is beyond the control of Aboriginal bands (the latter being a legal entity separate from federal, provincial, and municipal government). Some Indians are recognized as community members on their reserves but may not meet the *Indian Act* requirements for status, and so they are called non-status Indians. Because reserves are set aside for First Nations people, very few Métis or Inuit live on reserve lands; for example, only 3 percent of Canada's 292,310 Métis live on reserves. Nearly seven in ten live in cities: four in ten in large cities, three in ten in smaller cities. Created under the *Indian Act*, Indian reserves are "Lands owned by the Crown, and held in trust for the use and benefit of an Indian Band, for which they were set apart. The legal title to Indian reserve land is vested in the federal government" (First Nations and Metis Relations n.d.). Indian and Northern Affairs Canada holds the responsibility for the administration of these lands.

A fourth issue that Aboriginal communities face in terms of developing the social economy is a history of racism and marginalization. Some of the many challenges that Aboriginal leaders must address include damage to members of their communities from experiences in residential schools, high suicide rates, low education completion rates, and high incidences of diabetes and other health challenges among the population, as well as high rates of incarceration of many of its community members. In terms of the social economy, these issues need to be addressed not simply as a problem or deficit, but rather as a challenge to be recognized and mitigated because they affect the capacity to create healthy communities. To this end, a language must be adopted that acknowledges the increased political savvy, improved legal rights, slowly improving social conditions, and other positive initiatives and indicators in Aboriginal Canada that are taking place. Aboriginal scholar David Newhouse addresses this issue when he wrote (2004, 40–41) that he

> spent a decade working for Indian Affairs and saw the language of deficit there. In their view, we were incapable of doing things. I think we need to challenge that by saying we are reconceptualizing, saying that what we are doing is thinking through and experimenting, and we're trying to sort things out for ourselves. This is the way economies develop. They develop by people sitting down and thinking about concrete problems, proposing solutions, trying them, and thinking about them, finding what does work and what doesn't and then thinking about a new set of problems. That has been the process for economic development in the West and we say that we are doing that as well and take ourselves out of the cycle of the problem. That places the onus upon us to find solutions but not solutions that are disconnected from our own ideas about society and social order and economies.

This raises the issue that not only are those interested in social economy development of Aboriginal communities confronted with the idea of "deficit," they are also confronted by a negative perception of these communities by other Canadians. Often, these stereotypes about Aboriginal peoples originate in a lack of understanding of history. As a result of this, Canadians often think of victims or of societal burdens when contemplating the place of Aboriginal peoples in Canada. It is very difficult if not impossible to then grasp the positive contributions of Aboriginal peoples to Canadian society and thus develop a more accurate picture of their place in Canada. Newhouse, Voyageur, and Beavon, the authors of the book *Hidden in Plain Sight: Contributions of Aboriginal Peoples to Canadian Identity and Culture* (2005), confront this issue directly; in their introduction, they state (x–xii):

> It is our hope that this book will add a new dimension to the picture of Aboriginal peoples, one that shows them to be industrious, meritorious and accomplished. We want to create a place of respect and dignity for Aboriginal Peoples of Canada. ... Concentration on the negative produces a distorted view in which Indians are portrayed as a people unable to do things for themselves. ... Canada is diminished by the seemingly permanent burden represented by this view.

This book treats topics as diverse as treaties, arts and media, literature, culture and identity, justice, sports, and the military, with a second and third volume planned to cover more aspects of Aboriginal contribution to Canada. Such a positive view of the social and economic contributions of Aboriginal Canadians is a necessary component of developing these communities and one that is crucial if these communities are to see themselves in a concept such as social economy or community capitalism. Having outlined four key issues for the development of First Nations communities in Canada, we now turn to the definitions of social economy and social enterprise that form the basis for further analysis of the relevance that these concepts have for the Canadian Aboriginal experience and how these are perceived from the perspective of Aboriginal communities.

Working Definitions for Social Economy Terms

Many authors note the lack of consensus concerning precise definitions of social economy and social enterprise (see McMurtry in this volume). The common thread of these definitions, the importance and impact of community and social concerns in economic sectors, highlights the underrepresented contributions that many organizations make to the dominant economy. In general this thread is important for current practices of Aboriginal development because these practices cross both the private and public sectors. The relevance of the concept of the social economy for Aboriginal development will be examined further in the next section.

According to "Linking, Learning, Leveraging: Social Enterprises, Knowledgeable Economies, and Sustainable Communities" (Waygood et al. 2007), a large social science research project based at the Centre for the Study of Co-operatives at the University of Saskatchewan:

> Social-economy enterprises direct organizational and community resources to the pursuit of social and community goals, providing flexible and sustainable tools to assist communities to achieve their own objectives in the areas of job creation and skills development, the environment, social support networks, economic growth, and neighbourhood revitalization. Today's social economy has developed primarily in two areas: "as a strategy to combat poverty and social and occupational exclusion—initiatives in response to urgent social needs and critical social situations; and in the creation of new wealth—initiatives in response not only to needs but to opportunities in which neither the market nor the state are effectively engaged" ... . (Waygood et al. 2007, 3)

The social economy deals with the gaps in the economy between the private and public sectors that result in exclusion of the marginalized groups in society. It also identifies the contributors who may be for-profit and not-for-profit, that generate net income that benefit communities, thus demonstrating different priorities from those held in the private and public sectors (Waygood et al. 2007, 3):

> Social-economy enterprises frequently grow out of broad-based community development strategies that involve a range of local partners—citizens, government, voluntary sector, learning institutions, and business ... .

The second quotation highlights social and community goals at the heart of social economy. These goals are of critical importance to understanding the links between the social economy and social enterprises as both embrace these social and community goals but with the latter accomplishing them through the profit motive. The difference between these concepts is not structural. In fact, these types of socially focused economic activity often share organizational forms with organizations in the social economy. A social enterprise may therefore "take the organizational form of a for profit business, a cooperative, a partnership, a sole proprietorship or it could be a revenue generating arm of a non-profit organization" (Wuttunee et al.

2008, 1). The difference between social enterprise and other revenue-generating organizations focused on social or community benefit is their dedication to the market economy and the retention of a profit (Wuttunee et al. 2008, 3):

> Social Enterprises are active participants in the market economy, offering goods or services with the intention of earning profits (or surpluses). Social enterprise places strong emphasis on social and environmental objectives in addition to the financial objectives. This is commonly referred to as the blended return or double bottom line, and triple bottom line where environmental objectives are included. The enterprise will have a clear plan for the application of profits or surpluses towards social or environmental objectives.

Further, in this view, while "a Social Enterprise is essentially a business that is dedicated to a social and/or environmental mission, that is, the 'blended mission enterprise,'" it "is subject to the same risks that for profit enterprises face, along with some additional ones that are attached to the social mission" (Wuttunee et al. 2008). Social enterprises can become even riskier undertakings than small business start-ups because they attempt to balance market and social goal demands. Social goals have costs associated with them that negatively affect the social enterprise's market competitiveness. While social goals are laudable and to be encouraged, the inherent disadvantages created by this perspective cannot be ignored (Gould 2006, 12–13).

The focus of the concepts of social economy and social enterprise have been outlined and contrasted. This chapter will now turn to examining how useful these concepts are as starting points for understanding the development issues outlined above from an Aboriginal perspective.

Relevance to the Aboriginal Development Experience

Aboriginal-owned enterprises operate in every sector of the Canadian economy. The question is, does the social economy help us understand and encourage these initiatives or is the social economy irrelevant for conceptualizing and meeting the needs of the Aboriginal community? Most important, does the focus on profit and market activity outlined by the concept of social enterprise lead to better development results for Aboriginal communities, as compared to the more socially and community-focused concept of the social economy? To answer these questions, we must examine the types of enterprises that currently exist from a First Nations perspective.

Private Sector

In a study of the private sector activity of Aboriginal entrepreneurs, it was determined that there were more than 20,000 Aboriginal-owned businesses in Canada (Aboriginal Business Canada 2002). Another study determined that Aboriginal business is wide ranging, from primary industries to manufacturing and services: "Today Aboriginal entrepreneurs are in virtually every facet of the Canadian economy—including software design, manufacturing, tourism, the arts, health care, engineering and management consulting" (Aboriginal Business Canada 2001, L-2).

Aboriginal entrepreneurs conduct business in their own communities whether they are in rural, remote, and urban locations—each of which presents unique challenges. For example, on-reserve Aboriginal businesses operate within a legal framework that makes accessing financing a challenge (a problem unique to these communities, although all social economy organizations experience some form of financial limitations). Under the *Indian Act*, no individual can pledge on-reserve assets—particularly real property—in return for debt financing or even capital in general. While it is possible to create corporate entities to work around this problem, it has been a barrier to on-reserve financing and almost certainly has affected the growth of on-reserve businesses (Aboriginal Business Canada 2002).

While Aboriginal organizational structures for accomplishing development differ across the country, a given community will often be affiliated with a regional tribal council; in turn, such councils at times are affiliated to a grand council. At any given level, there might also be a development corporation associated with these councils that focus on economic development for a particular community or region. It is important to understand what the goals of these organizations are in order to see where they stand in relation to the social economy. One example is the Prince Albert Development Corporation (PADC), which is primarily associated with the Prince Albert Grand Council although it has a limited partnership with 12 surrounding tribal councils in northern Saskatchewan. The mission of PADC is to "own and operate profitable business enterprises that create employment opportunities for First Nations people, generate earnings for reinvestment in new business enterprises and support First Nations' quest for economic self-sufficiency" (PADC n.d.).

These goals support the creation and sustainability of healthy economic communities and are at the heart of mission statements for development supported by many Aboriginal leaders. Partnerships with other businesses are a very successful strategy to achieve a healthy economy for some Aboriginal communities. For example, Lac La Ronge, one of the Prince Albert Grand Council's member communities, in 1981 formed Kitsaki Management Limited Partnership (originally Kitsaki Development Corporation) to accommodate community business investments that focus on economic development. It now has more than 20 partnership investments grossing more than $70 million for the benefit of its 8,000 community members through employment opportunities, a portfolio of solid business investments, and disbursements to support the wild rice industry, the covering of treaty land entitlement program expenses, and support of the band's charity fund (Kitsaki Management Limited Partnership 2009). This is an example of the importance of private capitalist enterprise in an Aboriginal community development context. The fact that the community owns this organization is important, but so too is the fact that the KDC is run as a private corporation. The value difference between social enterprise and social economy is around this issue of profit and relationship to the market.

This division, however, does not have to be confrontational. In exploring social economy and social enterprise concepts within an Aboriginal context, an important consideration is to examine business values and any symmetry that might exist between these concepts and such values. In other words, in trying to understand what aspects of social economy mesh with an Aboriginal world view, the commitments of the organization and its values provide key insights. Central to these communities is the issue of economic development. Box 7.1 outlines Kitsaki's perspectives on how community values and economic activity can be combined. Kitsaki's commitments focus on profitability, meeting its peoples' needs in the economic arena, and acknowledging the role of culture and traditional knowledge as "value-added." It also acknowledges a commitment to the environment. These community values are the cornerstone of the idea of community capitalism, but are also consistent with the idea of social enterprise and social economy. The fact that they are embedded in "market" or capitalist activity, however, is what is at issue.

Aboriginal businesses in most cases choose to operate in the mainstream Canadian business environment while some may remain small and focused only on meeting the needs of their communities. The challenge is whether or not Aboriginal world views and values can be incorporated into a successful strategy for doing business that meets community goals. Kitsaki has chosen a balanced or blended approach between business and community values. The key principles outlined in Box 7.1 represent the critical values that Kitsaki has brought into the business world. But it is clear that Kitsaki's values also conform to capitalist ones.

BOX 7.1 Kitsaki's Key Commitments and Principles (abridged)

Kitsaki's Key Commitments

We shall encourage and support education and training for people to prepare themselves for employment and economic opportunities.

We shall maintain a diverse group of profitable enterprises, allowing Kitsaki the flexibility to adapt to evolving markets.

We shall maximize Aboriginal employment in Kitsaki and Band enterprises through a "training-oriented" work environment.

We shall develop the resources of the Lac La Ronge Indian Band's Traditional Lands according to the principles of Sustainability, Environmental Protection, Multiple Use of Resources, Preservation of Traditional Activities, and Public Participation and Consultation.

We shall maintain and support Traditional Aboriginal Knowledge that provides value-added advantages to the Kitsaki group of businesses.

Kitsaki's Key Principles

Respect—We respect all cultures, traditions, values, and beliefs.

Profitability—We shall maintain profitable businesses to achieve our goals.

Sustainability—To responsibly manage Traditional Lands and Resources as a heritage for future generations.

Accountability—We are responsible for our business decisions.

Integrity—We are open, honest, and transparent.

Responsibility—We balance politics with good corporate governance.

While Kitsaki's blended approach has developed over many years, the fact is that it is not always easy to develop or maintain such an approach. At this point, it is appropriate to acknowledge that this tension between capitalism and community exists and is recognized by Aboriginal scholars and some Aboriginal entrepreneurs alike. For example, Newhouse (2001) urges Aboriginal people to consider the impact and cost of whole-heartedly embracing capitalism. In many ways, his warning implicitly supports the ideals of social enterprise for application by Aboriginal peoples. Newhouse argues that the guiding principles for traditional Aboriginal life were harmony, balance, and reciprocity (81). As communities rush toward economic self-sufficiency, Newhouse argues for the inevitability of economic change that will fundamentally affect Aboriginal world views, values, and perspectives.

The idea that we as Aboriginals can somehow participate in capitalism without being changed by it is in my own view wrongheaded. We already participate in the central institutions of capitalism within our own communities—private property, a desire to accumulate wealth and to use that wealth to create more, production for the market, institutions of credit and debt, policy frameworks at the band level to encourage for-profit businesses—and for the most part members of our communities have come to believe that progress is measured in material terms. As Newhouse suggests, Aboriginal people are becoming increasingly entrenched in modern society. The issue of maintaining our cultural integrity is consequently becoming more insistent and urgent. This issue is complexified by the issues mentioned above—from the urbanization of our culture to the demographic changes we are experiencing. Considering these issues is particularly crucial for understanding the ways in which Aboriginal communities can develop. Given the urgency of these issues, the question is not so much how communities develop, although this is important, but rather that they *do* develop. If social enterprises meet the needs of communities economically while balancing cultural values, then they will be considered by our communities.

In the final analysis, the focus of social enterprise is on profit and benefit to the community. It is therefore possible for Aboriginal business leaders to look to this component of the "third sector" for guidance and direction when dealing with tension between capitalism (profit) and the community (social benefit). This is a two-way street, however, as Aboriginal communities have been dealing with this tension for centuries. Aboriginal enterprises have been taking a blended approach to development for many years and it is possible that sharing their wisdom with non-Aboriginals in order to alter conceptions of the nature of the relationship between capitalism and community within social enterprise theory and practice would be of mutual benefit.

The language of capitalists is land, labour, and capital (as Newhouse 2001 notes). And this language is increasingly moving into the heart of the cultural agenda of Aboriginal peoples. However, there are new spaces of resistance to capitalism that are emerging in many communities. New approaches—such as lending circles, cultural adaptations such as the involvement of elders in decision-making, and the use of small-scale enterprises instead of large-scale enterprises—have been or are being developed. These, however, are in my view mere adaptations or variations on a theme of community economic development (CED); the central tenets of community and economic empowerment are still there. We can, however, given the dominance of the market economic form, only ameliorate the worst effects of capitalism through these activities. Doing so will take much determined effort and the development of cultural and social institutions that remind us of Aboriginal values of harmony, balance, and reciprocity (Newhouse 2001, 81–82). Overall, Aboriginals are not opting out of a capitalist approach to development; rather, they are determining how best to achieve their goals with the tools at hand. What is clear is that development must be nurtured through self-governance over political and economic resources in order for development to be meaningfully achieved.

A key means by which self-governance over economic resources and Aboriginal values can be realized within the social economy is for-profit co-operatives. This form of economic organization offers communities some autonomy over their development and allows for community values to be realized. By focusing on creating a surplus, but leaving that surplus in community control, for-profit co-operatives take a piece of capitalism (profit) and cordon it off under community control.

There are more than 133 Aboriginal-owned co-operatives in Canada (Hammond Ketilson and MacPherson 2002). Of those, 31 are independent Inuit and Dene businesses operating in northern communities and employing over 800 people in total. Their operations are varied and include retail outlets, hotels, cable operations, construction, outfitting, and arts and crafts production. They generated a total of $146 million in revenue in 2007 and provided patronage refunds of $5.8 million in the same year (Arctic Co-operatives Limited n.d. a). Among their values are "self-help, self-responsibility, democracy, equality, equity and solidarity." In the tradition of their founders, co-operative members believe in the ethical values of honesty, openness, social responsibility, and caring for others (Arctic Co-operatives Limited n.d. b). The connection to this form of organization can be seen in the fact that Aboriginal people are more likely to be members of co-operatives as compared to the general Canadian population. Co-operatives make valuable contributions to community infrastructure at all levels—"Putting their money where their nation is," like the Anishnabe Credit Union (Hammond Ketilson and MacPherson 2002).

Part of the affinity between Aboriginal communities and co-operatives is the fact that co-op members practise the seven principles of co-operation, principles that Bill Lyall, the chairman of Arctic Co-operatives Limited (ACL), says Aboriginals have practised for generations. "Despite all of our natural obstacles," says Lyall, "we have worked together with one voice, and have built a very impressive network of community-owned and controlled enterprises. They have become a model for Aboriginal development in

Canada," and these are working co-operatively toward "the goal of prosperity for our wonderful country, and in particular Canada's Arctic" (Arctic Co-operatives Limited and Arctic Co-operative Development Fund 2005, 3). There is a strong compatibility between the co-operative as a tool and Aboriginal needs—membership needs drive the co-op. The correlation between the goals of Aboriginal people in general and co-operative principles can be seen in the list below (Hammond Ketilson and MacPherson 2002):

- The principles of democratic member control and member education easily translate to the Aboriginal traditions of community consultation and consensus-building.
- Member economic participation in co-ops is similar to the community economic focus of Aboriginal experience and lead to a sense of ownership and personal commitment and participation over time.
- Concern for community as a principle fits well with the idea of self-determination and cultural preservation.
- Co-operation among co-operatives is a principle that is reflected in the co-ordination between organizations to develop Aboriginal communities.

Healthy co-operatives contribute to long-term social and economic health in their communities because they are deeply rooted in them and cannot be bought or sold without member agreement. Developing skills, opportunities, and personal networks of support over time results in economic security, personal empowerment, and community stability. Co-operatives have been especially well used by Aboriginal people as a way to meet community needs. Community boards train local co-op members to take on leadership roles (more than half of the Nunavut Legislature, for example, received valuable leadership training in their local co-operative) and these boards deal with the needs of their community in ways that are in sync with important community values. Co-op businesses provide employment and training opportunities, especially for the youth of their communities, an important consideration given the growing youth demographic identified above.

Finally, the needs of small, isolated communities (geographical marginalization is, as mentioned above, a key issue for Aboriginal populations in Canada) are met in a context of support through the activities of the apex organization—for example, Arctic Co-operatives Limited and its resources. This organization faces business, logistical, and other challenges such as meeting member needs for fresh produce when and where shipping goods is expensive and time-consuming, training board members who may be totally unfamiliar with how to contribute to the co-op, or establishing a credit policy despite community opposition (with an effort to work things out together with a view to the future). Where a co-op goes into bankruptcy, ACL will work with them to continue their operation where other business owners might give up. The last quote of Bill Lyall sums up the importance of this model of enterprise, a model that fits very neatly into social economy theory. The co-operative is focused on community well-being as a priority, and distributes what surplus it has to facilitate this well-being. The reason for this commitment and applicability to Aboriginal communities is rooted in the co-operative commitment to principles and values.

Public and Civil Society Sectors

To understand Aboriginal relationship to the public and civil society sectors in Canada, it is important to recall the long and painful history that marks the relationship. For hundreds of years, Aboriginal peoples have experienced abuse of power on the part of the state and its agents and agencies. The indifference of Canadian society to these abuses has led to suspicion and distrust toward the state and Canadian society more generally, including the civil society sector. First Peoples are often suspicious of government programs, but while the government may be a threat in many ways, changing the relationship can be difficult, as patterns of interaction have been deeply rooted on both sides. The Royal Commission on Aboriginal Peoples (RCAP) (1996a) noted several of the key abuses of power that interfere with positive relations between Aboriginal peoples and Canadian society.

First, the commission acknowledges the damage perpetrated under the *Indian Act*. Passed in 1876 under Parliament's constitutional authority over "Indians, and Lands reserved for the Indians," the legislation intruded massively on the lives and cultures of status Indian peoples. Though amended repeatedly, the Act's fundamental provisions have scarcely changed. These provisions give the state powers that range from defining how one is born or naturalized into "Indian" status to administering the estate of an Indian person after death. According to Patricia Monture (2002),

> the Indian Act has imposed a regime of colonial rules on the lives of registered Indians since it was introduced in 1876. Through exclusion, the lives of mixed-bloods and others who are not qualified for registration under the Act have also been affected. The Act regulated the lives of status Indians by making them wards of the Crown, establishing a relationship of dependency which denied registered Indians many benefits of citizenship. The original Act also imposed rules for community administration that displaced traditional systems of governance.

> Conceived under the nineteenth century's assumptions about inferiority and incapacity and an assimilationist approach to the "Indian question," the *Indian Act* produced gross disparities in legal rights. It subjected status Indians to prohibitions and penalties that would have been ruled illegal and unconstitutional if applied to other Canadians.

The Act has handicapped Aboriginals' ability to move forward, especially those Aboriginal communities that are rapidly advancing in today's economy. For example, chiefs and councils are limited in their ability to pass bylaws on reserves that could make investment by outside partners attractive. Further, as mentioned above, land and buildings on reserve are not generally available for use as collateral for loans to enable development. Aboriginal entrepreneurs are unable to access this and other sources of start-up funds that are typically accessed by most new businesses in Canada.

The residential school policy also had far reaching impacts. "Of all the nineteenth-century policies formulated to respond to the Indian question, none was more obviously the creature of that era's paternalistic attitudes and its stern assimilative determination than residential school education" (RCAP 1996a). Through the policy, "the schools would remove Aboriginal children from their families and cultures and expose them continuously to more 'civilizing' influences" supposedly prevalent in the dominant European, Christian society, with such "influence" demonstrated through the care of strangers. Only in recent times have Canadians become aware of the damage this policy has inflicted upon thousands of Aboriginal adults and several generations of their families.

Relocation of Aboriginal communities through unilateral acts by the government was a widespread practice that crippled numerous communities both economically and socially. "The rationales varied: the need to disperse Aboriginal people back to the land or to alleviate population or economic scarcity problems; the desire to centralize or to facilitate less expensive program delivery; and the intention to proceed with natural resource and other forms of economic development" (RCAP 1996a). Aboriginal peoples were seen as incapable of making their own choices and were ultimately "moveable" despite the human cost: "Many thousands of people were moved, their economic self-sufficiency was often weakened or destroyed, and their adverse health conditions were made worse. Aboriginal political leadership and structures collapsed in the inevitable malaise, not of their own making, that followed" (RCAP 1996a). Relocation of communities resulted in aggravated conditions for Aboriginal peoples that had to be overcome, conditions that included physical, mental, emotional, and spiritual challenges. The fact that Aboriginal communities have survived this sustained and multifaceted attack on their well-being speaks to their tenacity as well as their remarkable focus on positive development while dealing with past struggles that still impact their communities today. Obviously, healthy adults are needed to properly achieve prosperous and healthy communities, and for Aboriginal peoples their resilience has been and is now severely tested through their past and present experiences despite the recent expansion of population mentioned above.

Finally, as more Aboriginal people migrate to urban centres, many challenges are encountered, including the challenge of maintaining their cultural identity *as* Aboriginal people. "Some become trapped between two worlds—unable to find a place in either their Aboriginal culture or the culture of the dominant society. Others find ways to bridge the gap, to remain firmly grounded in traditional values while living and working in an urban milieu" (RCAP 1996b). They face systemic racism and unemployment, which underlines the inability of government capacity to deal with Aboriginal peoples living outside Aboriginal communities. Government policy, which was originally developed primarily to deal with Aboriginal people living in Aboriginal communities (that is, on reserves), has not kept pace with changing conditions. Policy has developed in a piecemeal, uncoordinated fashion, leaving gaps and disputes over jurisdiction and responsibility. Urban Aboriginal people have been caught in these gaps socially and culturally in a toxic combination, with many suffering extreme poverty.

Aboriginal peoples living in urban settings do not give up being Aboriginal. This is evident in the report of the Royal Commission on Aboriginal Peoples (1996b), which was basing its observations on depositions given by Aboriginal peoples:

> Aboriginal people want urban institutions that reflect Aboriginal values. As we have seen, this often means creating or strengthening Aboriginal-controlled institutions. Urban Aboriginal people also want to be able to practise their culture and traditions in the urban setting. And like Aboriginal people everywhere, urban Aboriginal people are seeking self-determination.

Social economy organizations have stepped in to deal with these gaps, and their efforts, as will be shown below, have been quite effective. While gaps still remain, efforts are being made to address them. The key is that given the mistrust that Aboriginal people have for the public and civil society sectors as a result of the above history and issues, the social economy has emerged as an effective tool of community development. It allows for a variety of forms while maintaining control in the hands of Aboriginal communities, and even allows for the flow of government money to these communities while maintaining some community voice. Canadian government public sector activity varies between First Nations, Métis, and Inuit communities. Where economic activity is possible, a given community usually has some type of community-owned economic development arm. These organizations are usually incorporated and are at arm's length from Aboriginal or non-Aboriginal government in their governance. (Note, however, that this form of community development corporation is not as well developed in the east of the country, because the members of the nations of the Iroquois Confederacy have historically relied on economic development through the practice of individual business people). For example, the Prince Albert Grand Council in Saskatchewan has created a development corporation that makes band-owned investments. The profits are reinvested in their corporation, and employment opportunities for band members are generated and support self-sufficiency (PADC n.d.). And while there are fewer of this kind of corporation in the east, when they do emerge they are often successful. The 2007–8 annual report of the Kitigan Zibi Anishinabeg First Nation (Kitigan Zibi Anishinabeg First Nation 2008), located in Quebec, presents an active council supporting education, training, capital improvements, and other similar activities that benefit the community through an economic fund. Training for entrepreneurs is also provided by the band.

Other communities have made similar choices for developing community-focused economic activity—the social economy. If businesses are run by the community, such as a band-owned company or are non-profit, and if they have social and profit goals, then they fit into this "public sector" category. I place development corporations in the private sector on the basis that they are usually set up as for-profit operations with boards of directors. Other analysts, however, might place development corporations in social economy sector because of the blended mission (both community benefit and market activity), or they may place them within a broad definition of social enterprise, but for now I would like to keep the division between public and private because it highlights the differing focus on values and relationship to the capitalist market between them. In studying the social economy, it is important to realize that there is no clear dividing line because, in practice, the boundaries between private, public, and the third sectors blur (Quarter 2006)—they are all interdependent (see Figure 7.1).

In summary, the public sector has particular relevance and significance for Aboriginal communities engaged in economic development in both its social economy and government form. The public sector, however, presents unique challenges that are complicated by a general lack of trust in the ability

FIGURE 7.1   The Social Economy: A Schema

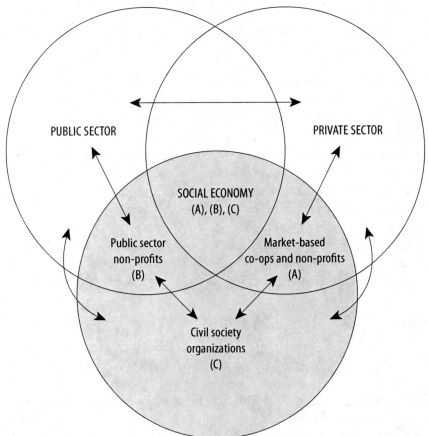

of the various levels of government to meet the people's needs fairly and with integrity. Communities can point to a long history in which there are examples of poor decisions that did not protect their rights. The result is that the building of trust such that good decisions can be made is problematic and very challenging. Within the current legislative and bureaucratic regime, Aboriginal communities have no choice but to meet these challenges directly through their own enterprises and institutions.

Quarter's analysis (2006) makes space for diverse institutions within the social economy, a space that can embrace elements of private, public, and civil society organizations. Within the Aboriginal community, there are many Aboriginal-controlled family, health, and education non-profit organizations that focus on social goals that, using this definition, would be part of the social economy. The difference lies, as Corbiere, Johnston, and Reyes (2007) point out, in the fact that social economy activity on reserve can never fully be "neither state nor private" because such activity requires the approval of the band council through resolutions. No such requirement to consult "municipal government" is present off reserve. Therefore, there is automatically a strong relationship with the public-sector government (the chief and council) on reserve that is contrary to the experience of off-reserve enterprises. This relationship is further complicated when a band member raises an issue about the social enterprise and its operations with a chief and council rather than directly with the social enterprise itself. Chief and council are then obligated to resolve the issue, and this may involve issues of governance wherein chief and council owe a duty to the community. The result of this structure is that there can be interference with the way the social enterprise operates and with control removed from the enterprise's own board and decision-making structures. This problem led Corbiere, Johnston, and Reyes (2007) to conclude that the definition of social economy does not include the reality of Aboriginal social enterprises. This issue will be considered again in the final section. The next section considers how Aboriginal peoples approach development through several case study examples.

Community Capitalism with Case Study Insights

The tensions, gaps, abuses, and challenges outlined in the preceding sections are being met by First Nations communities with creativity grounded in Aboriginal values and world views. The attempts to develop economically within a context requiring the prioritization of key community values is here outlined through three case studies. This section juxtaposes the mainstream approach to development and emphasis on the bottom-line with an approach that aligns much more naturally with a social economy approach that includes community. But the focus of this social economy is not so much "neither state or private," but rather community development and community wealth creation within challenging circumstances created by both the state and the private sector.

In trying to understand the process of wealth creation, I asked Prince Albert Development Corporation president Ted DeJong how the balance between traditional values and the very different values of capitalism can successfully co-exist within their organization. His reply was "community capitalism." He went on to explain that, within their operation, this means that the best business skills are embraced during their assessments of their investment opportunities and in the running of their development corporation. The process did not stop at return on investment, however, which is where most business analysis ends. Instead, the final and critical focus was on determining whether the investment had a "fit with the community" and met the community's objectives. This means that the 12 bands that are owners of the development corporation are integral to the entire operation and have to be consulted along the way (Loizedes and Wuttunee 2005, 2).

How do entrepreneurs fit into this scenario? According to DeJong, entrepreneurial activity is supported by the Prince Albert Grand Council, and consequently there is an active and healthy community of business owners in their region. As a result of this healthy economic community, these business owners are planning on teaming up and bidding on contracts. When one organization or individual is eliminated in the bidding process for a contract, it is not unusual to see that individual or organization brought in as a partner in a later stage. The building of strong connections between businesses by these owners is consistent with personal and general business principles of success and is part of their blended approach that incorporates profit and community.

In order to examine the concept of community capitalism as a unique articulation of the social economy in greater detail, three case studies will be analyzed. First, Goodfish Lake, a small northern First Nations community in Alberta, determined a method for working with their neighbours by identifying needs and meeting those needs, resulting in training and employment opportunities for their band members. Second, Donna Cona Inc. is making inroads in the software technology industry as an Aboriginal-owned business catering to the Aboriginal sector. President John Bernard uses partnerships as a main vehicle for meeting company goals. Finally, Louise Champagne is proud of her worker co-op Neechi Foods, a co-operative that operates in a challenging environment within a community that has changing needs.

Case Study 1: Goodfish Lake Development Corporation

A small northern Albertan First Nation called Goodfish Lake was experiencing out-migration of the men who were leaving to work at the nearby Fort McMurray oil sands project operated by Syncrude. The community was heavily reliant on agricultural activities, but their leader Chief Bull saw the need for change. The community formed Goodfish Lake Development Corporation (GLDC) in 1978 as a response. Its goals were to develop economic opportunities that would benefit the community and provide employment to band members. In speaking to their band members and Syncrude, the band determined that Syncrude needed a dry cleaning plant for their workers and it proceeded to develop one. After a while, it become clear that the tattered work clothes presented another opportunity, and several years later the Goodfish Lake Sewing and Garment Manufacturing Company was established. A supportive partnership was formed with Syncrude, which agreed to use the band's companies (Sisco and Nelson 2008, 6). A rental service was added later to the dry cleaning division for small companies who need equipment, including clothing, but who prefer to rent rather than purchase.

Training and mentoring programs are integral to the success of these businesses. Trainees work with skilled fellow workers, and this allows local community members to fill more than 80 percent of the positions. Skills are critical to the success of the businesses, and profits are generated in order to continue to provide these employment opportunities. The community understands that hiring decisions focus on skills and that people from outside of the community must sometimes necessarily fill positions. With most of the men of their community working in Fort McMurray, women hold the majority of positions in the dry cleaning plant and the sewing and garment company (Sisco and Nelson 2008, 7).

Band-owned businesses that operate under the control of the community are expected to respond to both the needs of the band (often community) and business—needs that sometimes conflict. As a band-owned enterprise, GLDC has a responsibility to the social well-being of community members. Therefore, it has a mandate to create wealth and employment for the community. However, as a business, GLDC must ensure that its bottom line looks good. After all, if the corporation is not generating profits, it cannot create jobs and invest in the community (Sisco and Nelson 2008, 8).

George Halfe, CEO of the development corporation for more than 20 years, has built a reputation for consultation with his staff, knowing community needs, and building key partnerships for the benefit of the corporation. He has promoted an ownership perspective among his company employees. In addition to consultation, another way he has instilled this perspective is by promoting wellness. His program for work flexibility works well with the female staff because most have families and their scheduling needs are now more easily met (Sisco and Nelson 2008, 9).

The bottom line is not the most important business goal for GLDC. The company gauges its success, to a large degree, based on the economic and social welfare of the community. For GLDC, this in turn is based on its primary goal of providing local employment opportunities to community members. Currently, the corporation employs 100 people among its four businesses—eighty-eight of these individuals are First Nations people. GLDC also redistributes profits back into the community through social events and functions. GLDC is not only concerned with building internal capacity—it also promotes local economic development through knowledge transfer. This ensures that employees who leave the company to pursue other business or employment opportunities build capacity in the community (Sisco and Nelson 2008, 10).

Goodfish Lake Development Corporation has made a meaningful difference in the health of the community of Goodfish Lake. The vision of community leaders and the ability to act on opportunities successfully have made the difference in this dynamic community. The community's recent history could have been a more dismal one; it is a history in many ways similar to the many other communities that suffer from dysfunction in both their leadership and among their community members with the resulting unhealthy communities.

In determining how best to describe this community's experience in the context of community capitalism and the link, if any, to social economy, it becomes important to consider a critical question of how similar the objectives are for both of these concepts. Putting people first and placing profit an important second is commonly referred to as a blended approach. The difference between the two approaches lies more in how each is accepted and understood by a community. Community capitalism is demonstrated for Goodfish Lake through the fact that they run a profitable business but do so while keeping with community values and needs. It is important to recognize, however, that the Goodfish Lake community has not self-consciously labelled their approach either community capitalism or social economy. Both have the possibility of having the community identify with these. In other words, researchers may label an activity as clearly an example of social economy while a community member would not recognize that term and may have a term for that activity that is more culturally relevant. Applying these concepts is an evolving process that will continue to unfold as research continues and more thought is given to these processes. Again what matters most for Aboriginal communities are the results of this activity, not the conceptual framework. This poses a problem that researchers and academics have to consider in their frameworks.

Case Study 2: Donna Cona Inc.

The next case study focuses on the experiences of an Aboriginal entrepreneur in an urban setting, in contrast to the small and remote setting of the previous case. Donna Cona Inc. offers information technology and business services, serving the off-reserve Aboriginal markets in Winnipeg, Vancouver, and Ottawa. The decision by president and chief executive officer John

Bernard to locate off reserve was a deliberate strategy to access larger opportunities—opportunities larger than would be available if his business had been restricted to a reserve location. Bernard's father had owned a business on their reserve. It closed when a larger band-owned business competitor opened that could undercut prices (Sisco and Nelson 2008). His message—"Go where the market is!"—encourages Aboriginal entrepreneurs to venture off reserve if necessary (Sisco and Nelson 2008, 17).

Given that the reserve's economy is underdeveloped, criticism can be directed at the broader entrepreneurial strategy used by Bernard in terms of its off-reserve emphasis. His response to such criticism is that with the possibility of larger profits comes the opportunity to give back to the wider Aboriginal community.

For example, in 2006, Donna Cona (in coalition with EnCana, Ironhorse Oil and Gas, Grand River Enterprises, and Louisburg Pipelines) donated $58,000 at the Assembly of First Nations Christmas party toward the Make Poverty History for First Nations: The First Nations Plan for Creating Opportunity campaign (Sisco and Nelson 2008, 17). The company also promotes educational initiatives for Aboriginal people. Donna Cona started a scholarship fund for Aboriginal students enrolled in the computer sciences program at Trent University. The business also supports TeknoWave, a program dedicated to providing educational opportunities for Aboriginal people (Sisco and Nelson 2008, 18).

Among the challenges facing Aboriginal entrepreneurs are preconceptions about the types of businesses Aboriginal people are able to do well. Bernard works to have a track record that speaks for itself and that builds believers in the quality of his company's services. Bernard has said that one mistake Aboriginal entrepreneurs commonly make is that they allow their cultural identities to overshadow their identities as business persons. He added that Aboriginal business owners must overcome the challenges that negative stereotypes present by "showing up to work as a business person first." Regardless of one's cultural background, good business practice must be a priority in the workplace (Sisco and Nelson 2008, 18). This attitude may personify a capitalist business person or a community member taking up his community's call for the need for successful entrepreneurship. The questions that arise are whether the ethnicity of a business owner carries weight in determining what type of enterprise should be engaged in, how this way of doing business off reserve meets or compromises community goals, and finally, who is the final judge of the appropriate sector for an enterprise as private or civil society. Should opinions of the business owner, the community, or a third party (such as a researcher) carry weight—and if so, how much? Is the labelling exercise an academic one, a meaningful distinction, or are the players even ready to engage the issue? These questions are raised here because this case study lends itself to them specifically, but they apply in different ways to the other case studies.

Attracting well-trained Aboriginal staff is difficult. Half of Bernard's 42 employees are Aboriginal, and in order to increase the Aboriginal proportion he encourages Aboriginal youth by offering internships in his company. To attract and keep his staff, Bernard is competitive through redistribution of 18 percent of pre-tax company profits to his employees. Bernard uses partnerships to best advantage in building the capacity and marketability of his company. As such, Donna Cona partners with Aboriginal and non-Aboriginal information technology (IT) service companies, one-person consulting firms, and large, multinational companies (MNCs) such as IBM and CGI. The company also has product partnerships with Micro, Storagetek, Veritas, and Nortel, and has previously partnered with Sun Microsystems and Hughes Satellite Corporation (Sisco and Nelson 2008, 18). Bernard's long-term goal is to be the largest Aboriginal-owned firm in Canada. His goals still include gifting to the community from the profits of his company. This case study shows how the community is broadly defined even though members may live outside of their reserve communities.

The critical question in terms of this case study is whether or not this is the most efficient way to give back to community. While this question is culturally sensitive (why should other communities "tell" Aboriginal communities what is more efficient given the long history of racism), it *is* culturally appropriate to let the reader have a role in the analysis, because learning takes place in different ways for each of us and we have insights into questions that may change over time as our experiences change. The answer to this question is not easy. Much of the approach in this case study is closely aligned with success within a mainstream economy. The difference is that Bernard's "gift" to the community of a portion of his profits is in keeping with his personal and community values. Noting this difference acknowledges the role that Aboriginal entrepreneurs play in a context of social responsibility. They may not embrace the concept of community as a first priority, but it clearly *is* a priority and is engaged through blended goals of profit and community betterment. Aboriginal entrepreneurs are a growing set of contributors to economic diversity and opportunity. Is it enough to take these acts beyond simply charity in order to exemplify close ties to community values commonly manifested by mainstream businesses as acts of social responsibility? The conceptual divisions blur, just as in the model of the social economy that Quarter (2006) shares with us.

Case Study 3: Neechi Foods

Neechi Foods, a for-profit worker co-op based in the inner city of Winnipeg, was founded in 1989. Louise Champagne has been involved from the beginning, first as a support person and then as manager and president. She is proud to walk into Neechi Foods, a local grocery story serving the inner city residents, and be greeted by Aboriginal staff (Findlay and Wuttunee 2007, 14). In the beginning, St. Boniface Co-op, true to the principle of co-operation among co-operatives, sold products to Neechi and stored them until they could be put onto the shelves. The original store owner and a senior staff person provided expertise in its first year of operation. Many young people have been involved as volunteers over the years and have experienced first-hand the ethic promoted by Neechi—an ethic that balances commercial viability with social responsibility. In particular, the Neechi workers define their CED contributions according to the principles (Findlay and Wuttunee 2007, 14) listed in Box 7.2.

Each of the terms within the statement of principles was defined by the Neechi workers, and each principle has a focus on community need. For example, public health was defined as including physical and mental health, healthier community residents, more effective schooling, and a more productive workforce, while physical environment was defined with a focus on a healthy, safe, and attractive neighbourhood combined with ecological

---

BOX 7.2 Neechi Workers Define CED Contributions

- Use of locally produced goods and services
- Production of goods and services for local use
- Local reinvestment of profits
- Long-term employment of local residents
- Local skill development
- Local decision making
- Public health
- Physical environment
- Neighbourhood stability
- Human dignity
- Support for other CED initiatives

sensitivity. Human dignity was understood in terms of self-respect, community spirit, gender equality, respect for seniors and children, and finally social dignity regardless of physical, intellectual, or psychological differences or national or ethnic background, colour, or creed (Findlay and Wuttunee 2007, 14). This is a wonderful example of a community building its values into its economic activities—the essence of the social economy.

People are the crux of Neechi's story. There is a core of workers who remain with Neechi, but Champagne notes that being ready to deal with each person as an individual and thus his or her situation is a critical part of the way Neechi chooses to operate. People are often empowered by their experience in the co-op and move on to other employment; such moves are seen as a success in terms of Neechi's goal to support their community (Findlay and Wuttunee 2007, 15). The challenge of balancing social goals—the quality of social relationships with business profitability—is delicate but one Neechi regularly engages in as it works to encourage consensus and also people's support of the business. This balance is made harder by the fact that Neechi Foods is also dealing with the fallout from the oppression that its workers and customers have experienced as Aboriginal people. They act out this oppression on each other in order to work out the distress that has built up, with the potential result that people do not get along and projects are destroyed. Champagne sees part of the answer in an alternative economy that nurtures Aboriginal people as individuals—which means the distress people feel has to be taken on and confronted directly, and not ignored.

Neechi Foods provides an excellent example of a successful for-profit co-op. Community support has allowed Neechi Foods to survive as it practises employee empowerment, nurturing leadership, the building of consensus, and the fostering of a healthy, resilient community in the workplace and in the inner city. Neechi has had an impact on both the residents of Winnipeg (both Aboriginal and other residents), as well on as the workers who have found employment there. This broad-based impact on both the economy and society as well as cultural empowerment make Neechi Foods an excellent example of social economy in an Aboriginal context. This transforms the community from one where oppression has sapped the energy of Aboriginals to one where economic and social community leadership is nurtured in everyone. As Champagne (in Findlay and Wuttunee 2007, 15) argues:

> Every human being is capable of leadership. Big things get in our way and prevent us demonstrating our leadership so we have to know how to help each other. Helping is leadership. Getting healthy is leadership. Groups of

people are targeted for destruction by statistics that support expectations that I will, for example, smoke, be diabetic, and die young. I take leadership over my health and fight those statistics.

These case studies add depth to an understanding of the link between Aboriginal people, community capitalism, social enterprises, and the social economy, as well as raising important issues worth investigating. Goodfish Lake and Neechi Foods very clearly acknowledge the dual goals of social responsibility to both their bottom lines and the health of their communities. Values of respect and reciprocity are embedded in the way they conduct their business. Donna Cona also demonstrates these values while maintaining its drive for profitability, with profits then shared with employees and the broader community. These organizations provide an important contribution to the discussion, but by no means are the case studies presented here a comprehensive sample or a complete representation of the experiences of Aboriginal peoples. What they do show is how what matters for Aboriginal communities is that when development happens, it must be both economic and social and needs to occur within the control of those communities— not under the direct control of the state or under the motivation of only making profit.

Reflections

A number of questions have been raised by the observations contained within this chapter. They form the framework for this final section. I will deal with each in turn.

Appropriateness of the Concept of Social Economy for Aboriginal Communities

In the words of Inuk leader Bill Lyall of Arctic Co-operatives Limited, Aboriginal development activity for the benefit of the community has been going on for generations. According to the history laid out by the Royal Commission on Aboriginal Peoples, the holistic economic attitudes demonstrated by Aboriginal peoples—a world view that encompasses mind, body, and spirit and that includes a time frame of seven generations for critical decisions—brings this point clearly home. Aboriginal peoples have been practising key elements of social economy (such as economic activity in the service of community, social goals rather than profit driving economic decisions, and democratic decision making) from time immemorial (see McMurtry in this volume for further elaboration of these points).

The economic relations imbedded in traditional cultures emphasized conservation of renewable resources, limiting harvesting on the basis of need, and redistributing resources equitably within the community, normally through family networks. Because families and clans owned rights to resources through their use, and because everyone was connected in a family, no one was destitute and no one lacked meaningful work. Even on the Pacific coast, where a wealth of resources was available and accumulation of surplus was a feature of the culture, the obligation to show generosity dictated that surpluses were accumulated in order to be given away (RCAP 1996a, 658). See Box 7.3.

Aboriginal contributions to the practice of the social economy should be acknowledged and honoured by Canadian society, a society that so often speaks about the deficits of Aboriginal economic and social systems, as noted by Newhouse. In *Hidden in Plain Sight: Contributions of Aboriginal Peoples to Canadian Identity and Culture*, Newhouse, Voyageur and Beavon (2005) draw attention to the contributions made by Aboriginal peoples in all walks of life to Canadian society and economy, contributions that are all but invisible to the average Canadian. Aboriginal leaders are recognizing—indeed, have long recognized—the need for stories to be passed on to their children, stories that celebrate our culture and our strengths as befits healthy communities. The stories of pain, suffering, and dysfunction had their time and that is over. The story of the genesis of social economy in the history of Aboriginal people's in Canada and indeed around the world would be a timely story to replace the negative ones mentioned above.

Inclusive or Exclusive Nature of the Social Economy

The insights into Kitsaki, Goodfish Lake, Donna Cona and Neechi Foods make it clear that these are organizations fit both the definitions of social economy and social enterprise. In particular, holistic development goals, which include profit as well as social and community impacts, go to the heart of the definitions of social enterprise and social economy and guide these four endeavours. The question for Aboriginal peoples is how well these organizations deliver both—with the understanding that profit is made to distribute in some way back to the community.

Academic discourse is by its nature a quest for understanding, with space made for including differing experiences within this understanding. This is occurring as Aboriginal scholars examine the place of and for Aboriginal peoples in the social economy discourse. I am engaging in this discussion, for example, when I note above that the chief and council, representing the

BOX 7.3   The Potlatch

According to the 'Namgis, a west coast tribe ('Namgis First Nation n.d.),

> the potlatch revolves around the act of giving gifts, which was central to almost all aspects of social, political and economic life. By giving, the members of a 'na'mima, meaning "one kind"—an extended family-unit, demonstrated their obligations and gratitude to the plants, animals, birds and fish in return for giving themselves up for human use. Potlatches and feasts are also where marriages and births are announced and celebrated and where deaths are mourned. By giving at these ceremonies the members of the 'na'mima also demonstrate their rights to certain ranks and accompanying privileges and property.
>
> Under the authority and direction of their Chief, the members of a 'na'mima have rights to hunting and trapping grounds, fishing stations and plant gathering sites—the traditional territory. This territory was given to the 'na'mimas' founding ancestor at the beginning of time. At potlatches, which were hosted in a Chiefs' Big House, guests witnessed the inheritance of, and validated claims to, certain ranks and their accompanying privileges and property. Historically, therefore, potlatches were central to the system of governance.

In 1884, there was a prohibition against potlatches. The intention of the ban was to further "civilize" the people through assimilation (the goal of "Indian" policy), a policy that would be advanced by abolition of what a BC official referred to at the time as an evil that lay "like a huge incubus upon all philanthropic, administrative or missionary effort for the improvement of the Indians" (RCAP 1996a). Speaking at the Royal Commission on Aboriginal Peoples round table on justice, BC Provincial Court judge Alfred Scow (who was the first Aboriginal to be called to the bar in British Columbia) supported the conclusion that official harassment of the potlatch and other traditional ceremonies was harmful to the traditions of his people, the Kwicksutaineuk of Vancouver Island.

According to Chief Alfred Scow, Kwicksutaineuk First Nation,

> the Indian Act did a very destructive thing in outlawing the ceremonials. This provision of the Indian Act was in place for close to 75 years and what that did was it prevented the passing down of our oral history. It prevented the passing down of our values. It meant an interruption of the respected forms of government that we used to have, and we did have forms of government be they oral and not in writing before any of the Europeans came to this country. We had a system that worked for us. We respected each other. We had ways of dealing with disputes. We did not have institutions like the courts that we are talking about now. We did not have the massive bureaucracies that are in place today that we have to go through in order to get some kind of recognition and some kind of resolution. (RCAP 1996a)

public sector, are intimately drawn into any social enterprises operating on the reserve through their own membership in this community. It is their own members who may question a decision made by their own social enterprise and, rather than bringing it to the leaders of the social enterprise, the members can take the issue to their chief and council who then have an obligation to answer the members' concern. The method used by chief and council to resolve an issue may interfere with the arm's-length activities of the social enterprise. This then means that the social enterprise has both private and public sector aspects. Where does such a situation fit in the dialogue of social enterprise and social economy when both are usually defined as the absence of control or dominance by the logics of either sector?

Corbiere, Johnston, and Reyes (2007) note that the blurring of the public and private sectors does not sit well with scholars who deny the call for an expansion of the definition of social economy to accommodate these seemingly unique activities that bring both direct private and public sector logics into the equation. I argue that the model put forth by Quarter (2006) does enable the blurring of definitional boundaries of the social economy and therefore allows for inclusion of the above scenario in the social economy framework. In particular, the dynamic nature of his model as previously discussed means that boundaries are flexible; this can mean that in some concrete cases (such as with a non-profit on reserve having a relationship with chief and council), the case may go beyond the characteristics of most recognized structures of the social economy. As described above in the case of Donna Cona and as indicated by Corbiere et al.'s comments, if a model regarding social economy is going to work for Aboriginal communities, then allowing for flexibility in defining relationships will more accurately reflect Aboriginal enterprises and their relationships to the other players— including the private, public, and civil society sectors. The definition must fit historical and cultural reality, not the other way around. Put another way, this is to argue that definitions must arise out of a people's historical and cultural experience and be reflective of their knowledge.

Process for Continuing the Dialogue

Corbiere, Johnston, and Reyes (2007) note that the question of whether or not Aboriginal communities are interested in engaging in the dialogue concerning their connection or lack of connection to the social economy is one that needs to be asked directly without presumption. I agree with this position, and if there is a positive response to the issue of dialogue on the part of some Aboriginal peoples, then interested Aboriginal and non-Aboriginal scholars should be invited to continue the investigation. The quality of the connection needs to be examined for the benefit of First Nations, Inuit, and Métis peoples, but such examination needs to occur with their consent and with a commitment to give them full voice in the process. Practitioners and other interested community stakeholders, such as elders, youth, and women, have a role to play in this dialogue. We need to ensure that the work is not theorized by scholars to the point that it becomes meaningless to the Aboriginal communities who are in the end the supposed beneficiaries of this economic activity.

In order to be successful, this dialogue would need to be led by either an Aboriginal researcher or a researcher with strong ties to a given community, or both. This recommendation addresses the issue of trust, the trust that must be established for a successful dialogue. The question of the way in which the community engages in development would need to be thoroughly examined by all community members. The presumption must be that the social economy label is a term that comes from *outside* a given community—and as such may or may not fit with the terminology used by that community for naming its experience, even though many aspects of what is labelled by the concept describes centuries-old Aboriginal practice. This process of engagement and the results thereof would be of equal interest to both parties, because the dialogue marks a theoretical and practical approach to meeting the needs of marginalized populations.

Aboriginal Contribution to the Dialogue

Newhouse (2004) called for a development that encourages and supports links to Aboriginal ideas of economy and social order. In other words, he raises his voice against an unthinking engagement with capitalism, a form of engagement that would come with great social costs for both Aboriginal communities and individuals. The gift that Aboriginal people bring is the rich history of living the precepts of social economy. We have seen this above in the cross-generation links among the Dene and Inuit, links that exemplify some of the basic values of co-operatives.

Community capitalism is an idea that links the business community to social and cultural communities and indeed ethical economic practice. This idea is addressed in many popular texts—for example, in Benioff and Southwick's *Compassionate Capitalism: How Corporations Can Make Doing Good an Integral Part of Doing Well* (2004) and also in the wide variety of literature on corporate social responsibility (CSR). In important ways these organizations are "doing" the social economy as outlined in Quarter's model. Community capitalism is part of the positive language that Newhouse for one is seeking—a language that avoids casting Native communities as being in deficit. Kitsaki, Goodfish Lake, Donna Cona, and Neechi each support communities through their blended development activities, the hybrid of profit and community benefit; however, they themselves define that community. Neechi finds its community scattered in the urban setting within an inner-city core. Donna Cona deliberately chooses a broad community to support while including its employees in generous bonus schemes and a redistribution of wealth.

Newhouse adds insight into understanding an Aboriginal perspective of community by exploring the Aboriginal imagination for the possibilities that allow for strong communities beyond the reality of everyday challenges. With imagination "comes a world that we want to exist. ... It is the link between what is and what could be" (Newhouse 2003, 3). He notes (11) that the community at the heart of modern Aboriginal society is an

> "imagined" community; it exists as a metaphysical ideal that we carry around with us. ... This "imagined aboriginal community" creates and supports aboriginal individuals and informs the notion of self. We are not individual isolated selves in a manner similar to the western ideal; our selves are community selves. ... The modern Canadian sense of self, as an isolated individual, collides with the traditional sense of the connected self resulting in a continual tension between community and individual, between social order and social chaos.

It is in investigating this Aboriginal imagination that the priorities and thus the "packaging" and ultimate success of economic development goals become clearer. The ideas of community capitalism, social enterprise, and, most important, social economy are areas ripe for further investigation in what can potentially prove to be a mutually fruitful discussion of balancing social and profitability goals within a cultural context that is centuries old. Taking this investigation into key challenges facing the contemporary world—mitigating the impact of capitalism on Aboriginal communities as well as on others—is a necessary next step in the development of the concept of the social economy. By beginning the journey down this path, Aboriginal peoples can join in a discourse of equality and reciprocity with other cultures around the world. This would be a journey that would fit well within our traditions and values.

Glossary

Capitalism   An economic system based on private property and private enterprise. Under this system, all or a major proportion of economic activity is undertaken by private, profit-seeking individuals or organizations, and land and other material means of production are largely privately owned (Black, Hashimzade, and Myles 2009).

Community capitalism   In its simplest form, any investment made by an Aboriginal community that must pass regular financial tests and, more importantly, must complement community values and goals.

Indian Act   Passed in 1876 under Parliament's constitutional authority for "Indians, and Lands reserved for the Indians," the legislation intruded massively on the lives and cultures of status Indian people. Though amended repeatedly, the Act's fundamental provisions have scarcely changed. They give the state powers that range from defining how one is born or naturalized into "Indian" status to administering the estate of an Aboriginal person after death.

Potlatch   Historically, potlatches were central to the system of governance among northwest coast Aboriginal peoples. The potlatch revolves around the act of giving gifts, gifting being a reciprocal activity that was central to almost all aspects of social, political, and economic life (see Box 7.3 for more detail).

Social economy   Social economy has developed primarily in two areas: first, as a strategy to combat poverty and social and occupational exclusion— initiatives in response to urgent social needs and critical social situations; and second, in the creation of new wealth—initiatives in response not only to needs but also to opportunities in which neither the market nor the state are effectively engaged (see McMurtry in this volume for more detail).

Social enterprise   May take the organizational form of a for-profit business, a co-operative, a partnership, a sole proprietorship, or a revenue-generating arm of a non-profit organization. Social enterprise places strong emphasis on social objectives in addition to financial ones. This is commonly referred to as the blended return or double bottom line, and as the triple bottom line when environmental objectives are included. A social enterprise will have a clear plan for the application of profits or surpluses toward social or environmental objectives.

Discussion Questions

1. What are the differences between capitalism, community capitalism, and the social economy?
2. How is the Aboriginal experience of the social economy affected by the history of colonialism in Canada?
3. What are the similarities and differences between the Aboriginal, English, and Quebecois experiences of social economy?

Suggested Further Readings and Resources

Findlay, I., and W. Wuttunee. 2007. *Aboriginal women's community economic development: Indicators of success: Measuring and promoting success.* Montreal: Institute for Research on Public Policy. http://www.irpp.org.

Newhouse, D. 1999. The development of the Aboriginal economy over the next twenty years. *Journal of Aboriginal Economic Development* 1 (1): 68–79.

Royal Commission on Aboriginal Peoples (RCAP). 1996. *Report of the Royal Commission on Aboriginal Peoples.* http://www.collectionscanada.gc.ca/webarchives/20071115053257/www.ainc-inac.gc.ca/ch/rcap/sg/sgmm_e.html.

Salée, D., with D. Newhouse and C. Lévesque. 2006. Quality of life of Aboriginal people in Canada: An analysis of current research. *IRPP Choices* 2 (6). Montreal: Institute for Research on Public Policy. http://www.irpp.org/fasttrak/index.htm.

References

Aboriginal Business Canada. 2001. *Aboriginal entrepreneurs in Canada: Prospects and progress.* http://strategis.ic.gc.ca/pics/ab/440_ref_rep001_e.pdf.

Aboriginal Business Canada. 2002. *SME financing in Canada, 2002—Part II: B—Demographic factors.* http://strategis.ic.gc.ca/epic/site/sme_fdi-prf_pme.nsf/en/00652e.html#64.

Arctic Co-operatives Limited (ACL). n.d.a. Home. http://www.arcticco-op.com.

Arctic Co-operatives Limited (ACL). n.d.b. About co-ops: Statement on co-op identity/principles. http://www.arcticco-op.com/about_co-ops-statement.htm.

Arctic Co-operatives Limited/Arctic Co-operative Development Fund (ACL/ACDF). 2005. *Annual report.* Winnipeg: ACL/ACDF.

Benioff, M., and K. Southwick. 2004. *Compassionate capitalism: How corporations can make doing good an integral part of doing well.* New Jersey: Career.

Black, J., N. Hashimzade, and G. Myles, eds. 2009. *Oxford dictionary of economics.* 3rd ed. Oxford: Oxford University Press.

Corbiere, A., R. Johnston, and J. Reyes. 2007. *An Aboriginal perspective on the social economy.* Webcast presentation, March 28. Social Economy Centre. Toronto: Ontario Institute for Studies in Education, University of Toronto. http://142.150.98.64/SEC/20070328-120554-1/rnh.htm.

Findlay, I.M., and W. Wuttunee. 2007. Aboriginal women's community economic development: Measuring and promoting success. *IRPP Choices* 13 (4). Montreal: Institute for Research on Public Policy. http://www.irpp.org/fasttrak/index.htm.

First Nations and Metis Relations, Government of Saskatchewan. n.d. Glossary. http://www.fnmr.gov.sk.ca/community/glossary.

Gould, S. 2006. Social enterprise and business structures in Canada. Fraser Valley Centre for Social Enterprise, February. http://www.fvcse.stirsite.com/f/SEandBusinessStructures.doc.

Hammond Ketilson, L., and I. MacPherson. 2002. Aboriginal co-operatives in Canada: a sustainable development strategy whose time has come. *Journal of Aboriginal Economic Development* 3 (1): 5–15.

Kitigan Zibi Anishinabeg. 2008. *The Kitigan Zibi Anishinabeg financial statements, March 31, 2008.* Kitigan Zibi, QC: Kitigan Zibi Anishinabeg First Nation. http://www.kza.qc.ca/assets/aar/KZ_AuditReport2007_2008.pdf.

Kitsaki Management Limited Partnership. 2009. Vision, mission and principles. http://www.kitsaki.com/vision.html.

Lévesque, B., and M. Mendell. 2004. *The social economy: Diverse approaches and practices—Proposal for a new CURA on the social economy.* Working document for SSHRC president.

Loizedes, S., and W. Wuttunee. 2005. *Creating wealth and employment in Aboriginal communities.* Ottawa: Conference Board of Canada.

Monture, P. 2002. Why we must end colonialism: Tinkering with the Indian Act won't solve our problems. *Herizons.* http://www.accessmylibrary.com/coms2/summary_0286-70941_ITM.

'Namgis First Nation. n.d. Potlatch. http://www.namgis.bc.ca/culture/Pages/Potlatch.aspx.

Newhouse, D. 2001. Resistance is futile: Aboriginal peoples meet the Borg of capitalism. *Journal of Aboriginal Economic Development* 2 (1): 75–82.

Newhouse, D. 2003. Imagining new worlds: The Aboriginal imagination. Unpublished. Peterborough, ON: Trent University.

Newhouse, D. 2004. The challenges of Aboriginal economic development in the shadow of the borg. *Journal of Economic Development* 4 (1): 34–42.

Newhouse, D., C. Voyageur, and D. Beavon. 2005. *Hidden in plain sight: Contributions of Aboriginal peoples to Canadian identity and culture.* Toronto: University of Toronto Press.

Prince Albert Development Corporation (PADC). n.d. The Prince Albert Development Corporation. http://www.citylightsnews.com/padc.

Quarter, J. 2006. Engaging and empowering: A national event for co-operatives and credit unions. 2006 annual general meeting and national congress, Canadian Co-operative Association. http://www.coopscanada.coop/assets/files/files/Misc/A_Quarter.ppt.

Royal Commission on Aboriginal Peoples. 1996a. False assumptions and a failed relationship. Part 2 of *Looking forward, looking back. Report of the Royal Commission on Aboriginal Peoples*, vol. 1. Ottawa: Indian and Northern Affairs Canada. http://www.collectionscanada.gc.ca/webarchives/20071211055417/www.ainc-inac.gc.ca/ch/rcap/sg/sg21_e.html.

Royal Commission on Aboriginal Peoples. 1996b. Urban perspectives. Chapter 7 of *Perspectives and realities. Report of the Royal Commission on Aboriginal Peoples*, vol. 4. Ottawa. Indian and Northern Affairs Canada. http://www.collectionscanada.gc.ca/webarchives/20071124124814/www.ainc-inac.gc.ca/ch/rcap/sg/sjm7_e.html.

Sisco, A., and R. Nelson. 2008. *From vision to venture: An account of five successful Aboriginal businesses*. Ottawa: Conference Board of Canada.

Statistics Canada. 2005. *Projections of the Aboriginal populations, Canada, provinces and territories*. Catalogue no. 91-547-XWE. Ottawa: Statistics Canada. http://www.statcan.ca/bsolc/english/bsolc?catno=91-547-X.

Statistics Canada. 2006. *Aboriginal peoples in Canada in 2006: Inuit, Métis and First Nations, 2006 census: Findings*. Catalogue no. 97-558-XWE2006001. Ottawa: Statistics Canada. http://www12.statcan.ca/English/census06/analysis/aboriginal/index.cfm.

Waygood, K., et al. 2007. Linking, learning, leveraging: Social enterprises, knowledgeable economies, and sustainable communities. Summary of proposed research. Centre for the Study of Co-operatives at the University of Saskatchewan. http://usaskstudies.coop/socialeconomy/files/Projectsummary_long.pdf.

Wuttunee, W., M. Chicilo, R. Rothney, and L. Gray. 2008. Financing social enterprise: An enterprise perspective. Working paper. Institute for the Study of Co-operatives. Saskatoon: University of Saskatchewan.

CHAPTER EIGHT

Building Bridges with Government: The Social Economy in Practice

DENYSE GUY AND JEN HENEBERRY

Introduction

During the years between 2004 and 2008, the community development sector in Ontario has spent much time defining the social economy in an attempt to determine who "belongs" to the sector and who needs to be at the table to participate in discussions related to it. A broad group of interested people has been moving this agenda forward over this same period in an attempt to shape a social economy network in Ontario. This process is not unique to Ontario, rather it is part of a growing worldwide social economy movement that is mobilizing and trying to define itself; the movement is also trying to be an active agent in shaping a world that would have a triple bottom line of sustainable development. This notion of sustainability takes into full account environmental and social impacts of economic activity while not compromising the ability of future generations to meet their own environmental, social, and economic needs (World Commission on Environment and Development 1987) (see also Mook and Sumner in this volume). This chapter is a critical analysis of this social economy movement in Ontario, and specifically of the social economy consortium, from the perspective of practitioners who have been involved in this process of creating this movement and consortium.

In the past few years, many meetings have been organized to shape the future of the social economy in Ontario. The primary challenge with these has been that most of the efforts have gone toward organizational development, with relatively few measurable outcomes or results being achieved. Practitioners refer to this as the "storming" stage of group development (see Box 8.1), which ideally is meant to facilitate decision making within the group and to identify the key ideas that would end up being part of the vision for the group. It is not uncommon for a group to get "stuck" in the storming phase, where ideas continue to clash and group members are unable to learn how to effectively interact with each other. Although it is important to give this phase the time required to give the group the space to reflect, share, and strategize, it becomes a challenge for building a "movement" if the team members do not move past this phase. Other jurisdictions in Canada and around the world have successfully moved beyond this stage—notably in Quebec (see Vaillancourt in this volume). We argue here that it is time for the social economy movement in Ontario to get beyond the storming phase and move fairly rapidly to the "performing" stage if the goals of this movement are to be achieved.

Before we begin, however, we should be clear on what we mean by a movement. In *Blessed Unrest*, Paul Hawken (2007) defines a movement in a way that is different from conventional wisdom. He and others have mapped out two million organizations worldwide that are working toward

---

BOX 8.1   Forming–Storming–Norming–Performing

"Forming–storming–norming–performing" is a commonly used model for group development meant to describe the necessary and inevitable phases that a group goes through in order to grow. Not all groups get through all four stages, and groups can move back and forth through the stages.

Forming The group first gets together and learns about the opportunities and challenges.

Storming Different ideas start to compete for dominance, and conflicting ideas clash.

Norming Rules and behaviour norms get established and team members learn to work with each other.

Performing The group functions effectively as a team and avoids inappropriate conflict.

There are often additional stages that describe group abandonment or dissolution.

Source: Tuckman (1965).

ecological sustainability and social justice. He states: "By any conventional definition, this vast collection of committed individuals does not constitute a movement. Movements have leaders and ideologies" (2). He further notes that it is possible to build a movement out of ideas, not necessarily fully formed ideologies, and that even without traditional centralized leadership, a movement can exist: "the movement can't be divided because it is so atomized—a collection of small pieces, loosely joined. It forms, dissipates and then re-gathers quickly, without central leadership, command, or control" (12). Hawken's explanations reflect the requirements of the time and process needed to develop a movement, and the Ontario Social Economy Consortium (OSEC) provides an example of this evolution, although the latter was not without its challenges. The major challenge confronting the Ontario Social Economy Consortium is how the process can be moved forward once a common understanding of the social economy, which has been the focus of activities so far, has been achieved.

The consortium's definitional discussion builds upon a more strategic conversation—a conversation that focuses on designing a policy framework that can be implemented across the province. This is similar to what has happened in other regions such as British Columbia and Manitoba, but especially Quebec, and in other regions in Latin America and Europe.[1] The current interest in the social economy in Ontario, however, has evolved within a climate of changing funding sources, both government and foundation-based, that has led to challenges in capacity building for organizations within the social economy. Instead of providing opportunities for the social economy to thrive as a sector in a way that can meet social needs, the climate of cutbacks and funding constraints within Ontario has created further social problems that have grown in intensity and has reached into the rest of Canada (which has shared federal funding cuts) and indeed is shared with other countries around the world. For example, one of six Ontario children lives in poverty, the number of food banks operating in the province has increased, and new immigrants to Canada face unemployment rates significantly higher than those of other segments of the Canadian population (Ontario Association of Food Banks 2003; Canadian Broadcasting Corporation 2007). All of this highlights the importance of the social economy movement understanding itself *as a movement* with a role to play in making these issues of social need clear to the governments and citizens of the day, regardless of these governments' political agendas and partisan viewpoints. Despite the significant barriers faced by the movement, it has been successful recently in creating an appetite among government, academics, and social economy stakeholders to build stronger collaborations and to find common ground in the pursuit of defining and building the social economy. In this context, we need to question whether the social economy can actually be considered a movement growing in awareness of itself and in influence, and, if it is, how it can move forward with a conceptual and practical framework that will support its growth and development in the long-term.

From a Practitioner's Viewpoint

As mentioned above, this chapter takes a practitioner's perspective—a viewpoint that has evolved through years of experience in community development, including work with not-for-profits (NFPs), co-operatives, mutual associations, and social enterprises. It will share facts, challenges, and passing or missed opportunities from our experiences of being involved in trying to build the social economy movement. Upon reflection, the most important discovery by practitioners has been that, to date, *collaboration* has been key to the movement's development and will be key to the future success of a strong social economy network in Ontario. Collaboration certainly resonates as one of the most popular buzzwords at municipal, provincial, and federal levels of government, and even though it is tempting to dismiss it as such, it is core to public–private partnerships (PPPs, or P3s). By public–private partnerships we mean collaboration between a number of different social economy organizations, government, and the private sector, a combination that offers the best hope of building an inclusive and effective social economy network because it utilizes assets from a number of different economic sectors and therefore has the potential to be more efficient for each partner. Collaboration would also ensure that there is a more holistic approach, from buy-in from all major community stakeholders to addressing community-wide problems. However, the reality of collaborative working relationships is that they demand hard work, planning, and human and financial resources. Making this level of commitment in 2009 is a huge challenge for many of the third-sector organizations being asked to contribute to this process (the third sector being the one comprising the many different organizations that are part of neither the private nor the public sector). Given this challenge, we will now turn to some of the details of the enormous amount of time and effort devoted already by the third sector to developing the social economy in Ontario during the past four years and analyze how well the social economy is positioned for future development. This description and analysis will provide insight into grassroots organizing within the social economy during its infancy in Ontario, an infancy marked by a dramatically shifting political, economic, and policy framework at the national and provincial levels.

Historical Building Blocks: Social Economy in Ontario

The social economy movement in Ontario as it stands today did not emerge out of thin air, but was the result of collaborations on numerous other projects on many different levels. For example, many of the organizations involved in the social economy movement work currently being undertaken in Ontario were originally involved in a federal initiative related to that government's interest and support of the social economy. It is useful to examine the development of the federal project in Ontario as a history lesson that in many ways set the groundwork for the current work of the social economy in Ontario. A review of the federal process is important because it ties together the original players who later came together to start the Ontario Social Economy Consortium, and it outlines the start of the process to define the social economy and the needed tools and policy framework. This was the first attempt to create a cohesive social economy group within Ontario and forms the basis of the current movement work.

The Government of Canada Embraces the Social Economy

Back in 2004, at the national level, there was a renewed political interest in supporting the third sector. This was in direct response to the shrinking government resources available for social services, similar to the situation that was occurring in Ontario during the same period. The result of these policies was, predictably, a corresponding increase in the need for those social services. Although Canada and Ontario were experiencing good economic growth and stability, social and community challenges were increasing as the number of food banks and homeless people were on the rise (Goldberg and Green 2009). As a result of this political interest, the federal Throne Speech in 2004 identified the social economy as a new priority; a priority that was realized in the 2004 federal budget with a national, Cdn$132 million initiative to support the growth of the social economy. Industry Canada was designated as the arm responsible for delivering the new funding that was going to strengthen the social economy: the community economic development (CED), not-for-profit, and co-operative sectors in Ontario. These funds would consist of both short-term and long-term tools and supporting programs that would facilitate the development of new organizations and support the growth of existing organizations (Department of Finance 2004). The vision was to strengthen the capacity of the social economy and thereby increase its ability to provide essential social services and reduce social and environmental ills as well as the need for government to provide those services.

Paul Martin, the prime minister responsible for the 2004 federal budget, had a deep appreciation of community economic development and had become an advocate of building the social economy in Canada. There were critics who felt that Martin lacked both a clear vision as well as a commitment to action toward the development of national policies to realize the social economy in Canada. However, his commitment was clear and could be seen in his relationships with CED actors such as Nancy Neamtan who worked with le Chantier de l'économie sociale (Social Economy Task Force) in Montreal (see Box 8.2). Martin was impressed with the work Nancy Neamtan was doing, work that influenced his views and helped him to understand the potential role of government in building the social economy. Martin believed that his Liberal government's role was to define, develop, and strengthen the social economy: "The social economy is relevant to the Government of Canada from a variety of policy perspectives. It creates wealth by providing goods and services, as well as addresses issues of social concern" (Industry Canada 2004). The federal government, following

BOX 8.2   Le Chantier de l'économie sociale

The main mission of Le Chantier (literally, the "builder"—that is, of the social economy) is to promote the social economy as an integral part of the socio-economic structure of Quebec and, in so doing, to recognize the diversity of Quebec's economy.

Le Chantier works to promote and support the emergence, development, and consolidation of businesses and organizations of social economy in a range of sectors of the economy. These provide an original response to the needs of their community and create sustainable jobs.

The mandates of Le Chantier are:

- promotion of the social economy;

- representation at the national and international levels;

- support for consolidation, testing, and development of new sectors and projects; and

- consultation with the various organizations of the social economy.

Martin's lead, then developed a working definition of the social economy through Industry Canada (2004):

> The social economy is "economic" in that it involved the production of goods or services and their sale in the market economy. It is also "social" in that its main objective is to meet the needs of the community, including disadvantaged or vulnerable members, and because of the values (democratic process, collective empowerment, etc.) on which its governance and operation are based.

This recognition in a formal definition was seen by many as a commitment on the part of the government to foster the development of this sector by creating conditions favourable to its growth. This was an especially hopeful sign given the fact that many organizations were struggling with shrinking financial and human resources after the years of cutbacks mentioned above. With an influx of capacity building and financing funds, there would be less emphasis on the operations of the delivery organizations, and focus could be shifted back from fundraising to doing the work that is necessary for the end users, resulting in a more sustainable sector.

HOW GOVERNMENT SUPPORT MANIFESTED ITSELF

As a part of the developing commitment on the part of the federal government to support the social economy, Industry Canada identified three phases of work. These ranged from an immediate release of funds to build the social economy sector through to medium-term efforts that would ensure that existing support systems for businesses were made available and applicable to social economy enterprises. The identified long-term solution was to develop a more robust political and policy framework to maintain and grow the social economy sector. The first phase was termed by Industry Canada the Social Economy Program for Ontario (SEPO). A request for proposals (RFP) was issued for a pilot program that would be administered by the Federal Economic Development Initiative of Northern Ontario (FedNor) of Industry Canada. The program had two components:

1. A capacity-building initiative with a $5.95 million budget over two years; FedNor would have been responsible for administering the program north of Muskoka (in northern Ontario) and would have retained $1.5 million for this purpose, while a third party would bid for a contract to manage southern Ontario, with a budget of $4,165,000.
2. A patient capital demonstration fund (funds invested with an eye to both environmental and economic sustainability) to facilitate access to financing

for the social economy across Ontario was established with a $33 million budget over five years. This patient capital fund would have been managed by a non-government agent, and would have offered loans to social enterprises for starting up, expanding, or consolidating their operations. It was designed in a way that would ideally leverage additional funding and create a larger self-sustaining fund.

This was a new approach for the federal government because it recognized the economic contributions that could be made by the social economy and saw that government needed to strongly support the sector with both short-term and long-term measures to capture the benefits of this activity. To understand what supports were needed, the government also recognized that it must work with partners within the sector in order to build these needed supports, as had been done in Quebec (see Vaillancourt in this volume).

GOVERNMENT INITIATIVE

Ontario social economy actors become involved in the federal government's process through a meeting that was held on January 26, 2005. A special invitation was issued to key Ontario social economy stakeholders to attend the "Industry Canada/FedNor Social Economy Roundtable." Approximately 150 people turned up for this one-day consultation between government and the sector. Such consultation was a relatively new practice for government, because public policy and programs had historically been developed and then brought to the public for comment. This new initiative was designed to facilitate input toward the development of a federal policy framework that would further set the stage for a national program on the social economy—the three phases mentioned above. However, despite their good intentions, the government did not effectively facilitate involvement from the organizations that they asked to attend. For example, organizations that wished to have a presence at this meeting were required to have their representatives sign a multi-page contract containing a number of requirements and restrictions—even the expense forms were cumbersomely long and complicated. This is a prime example of the challenges posed by the current culture of government in terms of building collaboration between government and stakeholders. Although the government indicates a willingness to work together and gather input through appropriate channels, they alienate practitioners through their highly bureaucratic mode of operation. Many of the organizations that were asked to participate in this meeting were grassroots volunteer organizations that did not have the time or organizational capacity to jump through the hoops that the government was developing just to attend a meeting.

Call to Action

A month after this first FedNor meeting, a smaller group of 15 sectoral leaders called an inaugural meeting of OSEC in order to develop a vision and submit a proposal to Industry Canada in response to their request for proposal to manage the capacity building funds and the patient capital fund mentioned above. It was an eclectic and passionate group, composed of members based in various institutions of the broad CED sector. They discussed collective capacity, abilities, and values as well as outlined the existing relationships within the growing network in Ontario. This was viewed as an innovative process bringing together networks, financial institutions, and, importantly, both the anglophone and francophone communities within Ontario.

Over the followup meetings, the groups membership shifted from time to time but the key participants from a number of sectors remained and ultimately signed the RFP that went to Industry Canada/FedNor (see Table 8.1). This group represented a good cross-section of those traditionally considered to be working in the social economy (NFPs, social enterprises, co-operatives, etc). However, it was not a completely inclusive group because key movement actors such as the women's, labour, environment, anti-poverty, and other movements were not represented. Right from the outset, then, the Ontario situation was distinct from that of the group working in Quebec at the same time (see Vaillancourt in this volume). These other sectors would have brought to the table a larger constituency base because they reflect a number of different ideological viewpoints. This is the characteristic of diversity that Hawken argues is necessary if a movement with broad appeal is to be formed. This limited appeal continues to be a challenge up to the present for this social economy configuration and, therefore, limits its capacity to build a social movement around this issue in Ontario.

It is important to note that although many of the organizations involved in the initiative work directly with the grassroots, they are not themselves grassroots groups. Further, they are not geographically diverse, and both these limitations remain a challenge for the organizations working on the social economy movement in Ontario. To the groups' credit, they recognized this as well as the fact that they did not have ideologically diverse viewpoints. However, they did realize at bottom that they were closer to an

TABLE 8.1   Background to the Industry Canada/FedNor RFP

Associations	Funders	Economic development agencies	Financial trade associations
These are organizations that represent particular sectors in the province and usually have grassroots organizations as a large part of their membership.	These are the primary support agencies for grassroots social economy organizations in Ontario or in particular geographic areas of the province.	These are more traditional economic development entities that support the growth and development of economic development.	These represent the financial institutions like credit unions and caisse populaires, which are both supporters of and members of the social economy.
• Ontario Co-operative Association (On Co-op) • Conseil de la coopération de l'Ontario (CCO) • Canadian CED Network—Ontario (CCEDNET) • Canadian Worker Co-operative Federation and Ontario Worker Co-operative Federation (CWCF and OWCF)	• Community Economic Development and Technical Assistance Program (CEDTAP) • United Way of Greater Toronto— Toronto Enterprise Fund	• Le réseau de développement économique et d'employabilité (RDÉE)	• L'Alliance des Caisses Populaires • Credit Union Central of Ontario (CUCO)

understanding of the requirements of grassroots organizations than the government, and further, the former recognized that consultation with the grassroots would be required. However, the lack of time and resources meant that it was difficult to seek out and include other sectors in a meaningful way.

Birth of the Consortium

The OSEC group felt that it was important to develop an effective and cohesive working relationship within the group to best be able to respond to the Industry Canada/FedNor RFP. Based on the experience with the federal representatives through 2005, the group felt that the process was likely to continue to be heavily bureaucratic and dominated by federal interests and agendas. Therefore, this group felt that a process parallel to the federal government one and focused on the development of a stakeholder-driven consortium was necessary to ensure protection of the broad interests of the social economy. This group would continue to attend the government roundtable meetings, but would develop a separate group with its own vision and ideas that would be better equipped to respond to the federal process. Each group shared whatever assets they were bringing to the consortium and thoughts about what role they would like to play regarding capacity building or financing. All felt this was a good way to share expectations and clarify intentions. An underlying principle that the group shared was that capacity building and financing must occur simultaneously for organizations in the social economy movement to be able to grow and be successful. Articulating these viewpoints and desired outcomes provided the base to build the beginnings of a true movement with goals and objectives that could then be part of the response to government. The organization needed a governance body, however, to lead it in achieving these goals.

THE OSEC STEERING COMMITTEE

A steering committee of OSEC was organized in response to the request of the government to further develop the proposal that would eventually go forward to receive funding. This steering committee was a subset of the 15 organizations that were in the larger consortium and would have the mandate to develop the program on behalf of the other participants. For the next few months, members of the steering committee with other groups were invited by Industry Canada/FedNor to work and to volunteer their insights to help shape the request for proposal for SEPO. Although the steering committee representatives were expected to bring forward the viewpoints of everyone involved, this was challenging for them because there had not yet been sufficient time devoted to the development of an overall strategy and vision for the OSEC. Despite this, the consultations between the steering committee and government representatives resulted in an RFP that included particular capacity-building programs and the outline of what the patient capital fund would do.

OSEC'S RESPONSE TO INDUSTRY CANADA

Once the RFP came out, the entire consortium met to determine how they were going to construct their proposal. All of the participants in OSEC had their own particular viewpoints about the best way to develop and manage the different components in the RFP and the most appropriate entities that should be involved. Since OSEC had not yet arrived at an overall strategy for the development of the social economy movement, at this point much of the discussion was in terms of deciding what the roles for each of the different sector and organizations were to be. The end result of these discussions was a proposal that included four capacity-building programming components: community development, sector development, technical assistance grants, and knowledge dissemination. All programming was to be delivered in both English and French. These decisions were to form the basis for the development of a larger movement in Ontario, with elements that had been widely agreed upon by all involved as important building blocks for the support of social economy organizations.

OSEC AND COMMUNITY DEVELOPMENT

OSEC's mission was to strengthen the capacity of local communities by making grants available for a community strategic planning process and for the building and/or strengthening of local networks of social economy organizations. The community planning process was intended to bring together stakeholders from the voluntary, public, and private sectors to identify leaders in social enterprise development. This would have resulted in strategic plans that could build the foundation for the further development of the social economy on a regional basis. It would have built a level of trust and sense of understanding between government and practitioners about the social economy. The OSEC was, therefore, a capacity-building structure to give voice to the community development sector through a consultative process and access to funding.

OSEC AND SECTOR BUILDING

OSEC was hoping to strengthen the social economy sector by unifying the various provincial networks (co-operatives, community economic development, social economy enterprises), convening regional and provincial forums, delivering regional and provincial learning events (including "train the trainer" sessions in local communities), creating an online social enterprise development curriculum and toolkit, and mapping the sector. Such mapping was important because it would help to identify additional partners and sectors to include in the building of a social economy movement. It would have also helped to provide the space to allow for the development of more effective relationships and collaborations, something difficult in the funding and operational climate for these organizations. The OSEC was facilitating recognition within the movement itself of the extent of social economy activity in Ontario, fostering collaboration through this awareness and educating social economy members to be more efficient actors through the "train the trainer" programs.

OSEC AND TECHNICAL ASSISTANCE

The OSEC's mandate was to support the increased capacity of individual social enterprises, including co-operatives, through a variety of technical assistance grant programs and through a coaching and mentoring program. Mature social enterprises would have access to grants, patient capital, and loans to develop and implement strategic plans for significant growth in the sector. Emerging social enterprises would have access to grants for feasibility studies, market research, business planning, organizational development, incorporation, board and management training, learning exchanges, integration of technology, and so on. These forms of technical assistance are key to supporting the growth of the sector at a grassroots level, and can provide a deeper understanding of systemic policy issues that are preventing growth and that need to be addressed through other means. By providing the actors at the grassroots level with technical assistance, the OSEC brings the skill level of the social economy sector to a higher level and, therefore, helps bring about awareness of a movement in Ontario.

OSEC AND KNOWLEDGE DISSEMINATION

OSEC was to help increase the knowledge base of the social economy sector in Ontario by documenting and disseminating best practices, capturing and telling stories, and establishing a database and referral system for coaches and mentors. New co-operatives and social enterprises were to receive direct coaching and mentoring to strengthen their organizations. This is another key component that would help build the burgeoning movement because it would share information between key partners and help develop working relationships between the partners.

IMPORTANCE OF THE FOUR AREAS OF FOCUS

The key to all of these program elements detailed above is that they were identified and developed by the sector for themselves. They identified well-defined goals for which they would be accountable to the grassroots and that would be reflective of the needs of the sector. This was truly an innovative "bottom-up" approach to development and to movement building, one that arose from several provincial-level organizations rather than being limited to just one or two regional or grassroots organizations. These key programmatic elements were built into the OSEC bid for the RFP, and also found ground and momentum in an Ontario context among practitioners. This is one key commonality between the outcomes of the Ontario process and the Quebec process—the programs that were successful in the bid process were those that were identified by the groups themselves.

Results

Largely as a result of the consultative process and four areas of focus, the Ontario Social Economy Consortium was successful in its application for the RFP on October 19, 2005. Negotiations with solicitors and staff at Fed-Nor occurred over the next several months and on January 10, 2006 a final meeting occurred between FedNor and OSEC representatives, at which time a clear understanding of roles, lines of authority, and budgets was finally agreed to. However, this understanding was not an easily determined outcome for the members of OSEC, as it also became clear how difficult it is for the government of Canada to work with a collaborative body such as OSEC. In significant ways, the problems of bureaucratic process that were experienced in the initial Industry Canada/FedNor Social Economy Round-table were repeated, as was the general lack of understanding of the unique make up and processes of the OSEC.

The government's requirement to identify a sole provider who would take the lead on administering the program (finally determined to be the Ontario Co-operative Association [On Co-op]) was a major challenge to the group as it required further understanding of roles, responsibilities, and authority that had not yet been determined. The group had spent the major-ity of its time up to that point collaboratively designing the program with the understanding that there would be multiple partners involved in mov-ing it forward. The government's requirement forced the group to adopt a more hierarchical organizational model contrary to their original vision. It also challenged their ability to continue to build the movement. Being asked to identify a lead organization in such a short period of time also strained the tenuous dynamic that had been developed thus far. Selecting a lead organization or spokesperson on the basis of bureaucratic logic was not the ideal way to select a partner, especially because it was done under time pressure. The defining factor for the choice of leader, therefore, became which organization had the capacity to take on the work at the time the bid was due rather than which organization would be best to take on the role based on the issue of the mandate and scope of OSEC. OSEC viewed this requirement as a matter of convenience for government; it had the unfor-tunate consequence of reinforcing government's unwillingness to deal with a multi-party group. The unique nature of the social economy was not clearly outlined for the government because of this acceptance of bureau-cratic logic, and making this clear therefore remains an issue today.

Further complicating things was a government announcement at this point in the process that they required all the deliverables and action plans to go through a separate bidding process subject to approval by a government advisory committee. After months of steering committee meetings with government concerning input into the RFP, followed by a thorough consultative process within the sector and further time spent developing a response, this new and unexpected additional process was seen by many social economy actors as a step backward. However, after all the work that had gone into creating the proposal, OSEC agreed to these terms in order to ensure that the funding would still be provided. Again, however, the unique nature and needs of the social economy as a sector were not clearly articulated in this process.

Just as things looked as if they were finally coming to fruition, on November 23, 2006 the federal Liberal minority government fell due to a non-confidence motion, and an election was called for January 23. This effectively stalled the project. Once the new Conservative government of Stephan Harper took power in January, the project remained stalled and was in danger of being cancelled completely. Perceiving this threat as a serious one, a lobby among all key organizations was initiated and took action for several months across the country in order to maintain momentum and ensure that the agreement that had been reached remained intact and that funding would flow. Letters were written and meetings were arranged, but to no avail; the funding never came through to Ontario or to the rest of Canada, with the exception of Quebec. This was obviously a huge achievement for Le Chantier (the body in Quebec led by Nancy Neamtan that received the funding) but was viewed by some as a federal government decision motivated solely by political considerations—keeping the powerful social economy movement in Quebec happy in order to attract votes for the Conservatives in the next election. For the Ontario partners, much work had been put into the OSEC project and many compromises made to meet government demands, but the outcome was that no funding and no resources were forthcoming to further help the development of the social economy movement in Ontario.

After the election dust settled, on September 21, 2006 On Co-op finally received a letter from Tony Clement, minister responsible for the Federal Economic Development Initiative for Northern Ontario (FedNor). The letter stated that "Canada's new government is committed to building a strong and united Canada, and is currently reviewing many of its programs and services." The terse nature of the letter indicated that even after months of lobbying, the funding for social economy capacity building and the capital demonstration fund would never be implemented under the current Conservative government. If the letter was not clear enough, it was followed by a "wave" of cancellation of programs that were attempting to build the social economy. The new federal government needed to get rid of any "superfluous" programs due to their ideologically driven "small government" position, but the cuts were justified to the public as a response to the perceptions of overspending and fraudulent undertakings on the part of the previous Liberal government. The language of fiscal accountability had been a key election platform issue for the Conservatives under the leadership of Stephen Harper. A lack of understanding of the third sector and its ability to contribute to Canadian community development alongside this ideological viewpoint meant that the social economy was not considered by the conservative government to be a way to achieve fiscal accountability or efficient service delivery and community economic development.

Lessons Learned

Once the above outlined process was over, there was a general feeling of exhaustion among all the social economy parties that had been involved. A huge amount of time and energy had been dedicated by a number of parties to the application and negotiation process, and the lobbying efforts to retain the contract after the fall of the government only added to the exhaustion felt by many. This did not mean that efforts to build a social economy movement ceased, however. After the final refusal letter had come from the federal government, the group began the process of debriefing. Out of this process there have been three key lessons learned, lessons that have been acknowledged by most of the partners working in the social economy movement. First, the group was not inclusive and was not representative of several major segments of the social economy. This remains a challenge for the current group, even though they are aware that they are not representative and they desire to become so. Second, the program design suffered from a lack of an overarching and connected vision and strategy. This was a result of the fact that it was a process that was relatively quickly put together in response to an outside call rather than a process that prioritized the needs identified from within the network. Third, government is not comfortable dealing with a multiple-organization consortium. There is a need for a movement to develop a voice that puts social economy issues on the policy agenda in ways that make sense to both practitioners and government.

Once this process outlined above finally ended in September 2006, the original members of OSEC for a time largely went their separate ways, and very little collective work related to the building of a social economy movement was undertaken. There were one or two instances where members of

OSEC came together to debrief about the outcomes of the entire process, and there were also other partnerships between some of the OSEC members that were developed in this time frame. However, for close to 18 months very little was done as a group to continue building the social economy movement.

The Ontario Experience Contrasted to Quebec

OSEC Versus Chantier

It is useful to compare and contrast the Ontario social economy movement's development to that of Le Chantier in Quebec. Le Chantier was ultimately successful in receiving money from the federal government as part of the RFP process, even though Ontario was not. Many critics have stated that this was solely due to the federal Conservative Party wishing to increase its standing in Quebec. However, even if this is solely the reason that Le Chantier was successful in their bid, it is still useful to compare the development of Le Chantier with that of the OSEC (see Table 8.2).

Where Did This Leave the Social Economy Movement in Ontario?

A new group composed of some of the initial participants in SEPO (On Co-op, CEDNET—Ontario Region, Le Réseau du développement économique et d'employabilité de l'Ontario [RDEE]) as well as others met in spring 2008 to discuss the need to regroup and continue work on the previously defined areas of mutual interest of the social economy. This new, larger group now included participants from the MaRS Centre, the Centre for Social Innovation, the Ontario Trillium Foundation, the Social Economy Centre—Southern Ontario Node, the Canadian Alternative Investment Co-operative (CAIC), and Alterna credit union. It rapidly became apparent that three areas of focus were important to the group:

1. defining and determining the relationships of structures within the social economy;
2. starting the advocacy work for a Social Enterprise Trust; and
3. examining how to grow membership within the network.

These foci were influenced by the previous work that had been done on the RFP in the federal SEPO process. In particular, the development of a Social Enterprise Trust and the identification of the need to broaden the membership were related very strongly to previous work that had been undertaken

TABLE 8.2 Comparison of OSEC and Le Chantier

	OSEC	Le Chantier
History	OSEC was started as a result of the RFP called by the government in 2005.	Le Chantier was started in 1997 and developed over time and was well in place by the time the RFP went out in 2005.
The players	Government: Industry Canada Contract for $33.6 million was for both a patient capital loan fund and capacity-building activities.	Government: Industry Canada Resulting in le Chantier de l'economie sociale Trust (Fiducie) as $52.8 million investment fund for the social economy.
Relationship with government	No working relationship with government or with each other as a whole group until the social economy tender from Industry Canada was presented.	Pre-existing relationship with provincial and federal governments, which began in 1996 at the Summit on Economy and Employment.
Policy framework and development	There was a lack of a policy framework for the development of the social economy within Ontario.	There were provincial policies to support CED and social economy rooted in the development of local development centres starting in 1997 (including mandates for collective entrepreneurship and involvement of civil society).
Definition of social economy enterprise and activities	Definition developed during the RFP process, but was not agreed upon beyond a superficial definition agreed to by the partners making the proposal. Lack of awareness of the definition and role of the social economy in the Ontario context.	Already developed definition, policy framework, and capacity requirements such as sectoral policies for social entrepreneurship: child care, home care, social housing, recycling, etc. Recognition of the social economy as an integral part of socio-economic infrastructure.

TABLE 8.2   Continued

	OSEC	Le Chantier
Partnership development	Limited partners in history working together with the exception of two or three limited partnerships of a subset of the OSEC participants. OSEC was mostly limited to a few provincial associations that supported social economy work. Very few connections outside of Ontario to other networks. Weak development.	Inclusive group including labour and environmental movements, fair trade organizations, chambers of commerce, private foundations, and community networks. Connecting to new emerging international networks with Latin America, Europe, and Africa. Strong partnerships that were over five years in the making at the time of the RFP.
Development of the program response	Program elements based on need and individual missions of the partners, but not rooted in a larger policy framework that would support the development of a robust social economy movement.	Holding of the November 2006 Summit on the Social and Solidarity Economy where 700 delegates met from every region and sector. This provided a clear analysis of strengths and challenges, with an evaluation of the past decade and consensus on actions for the next decade.
Financial understanding and tools	Limited understanding of financial requirements for social enterprises. The credit union sector in Ontario was much more fragmented than its counterpart in Quebec, and there was not the same support of co-ops and social enterprises.	New financial tools developed for collective enterprises (loan guarantees, RISQ, micro-credit, Fondaction, Investissement Québec, Fiducie du Chantier de l'economie sociale). There was also a strong history of financial support for the social economy due to the presence of the Desjardin credit union and government support of the co-operative and NFP sectors.
Level of represen-tative	Largely provincial organizations were leading the process with limited grassroots involvement.	Grassroots approach with regional infrastructure based on 16 (out of 17) Quebec regions to promote and develop collective entrepreneurship.

by some members. The need to define and determine the relationships and structures of the social economy was a relatively newer focus identified by this new group; however, an overall strategy related to movement building and the development of an overall policy framework was still missing, and it is only very recently that the group has started to address this strategic gap.

THE ISSUE OF STRUCTURE

Although there has been much discussion about whether or not the social economy network should incorporate, the general feeling is that the notion of a network works well, because it is a shared and transparent leadership approach. However, the challenge remains in the stewardship of the network when it comes to writing grant applications and administration or to managing the deliverables of the social economy network. There is still limited acknowledgment among the partners of the reality that the government wishes to deal with only one partner, and there has also been little movement toward the identification of one partner that would act as the steward and would help to guide the development of the network. One key outcome that has been developed is a mapping of the different organizations that should be included as part of the social economy movement and how they are all connected to each other, a project outlined as necessary in the original RFP. This has been developed as a Constellation Model by the Centre for Social Innovation in Toronto.

SOCIAL ENTERPRISE FUND

During the 18 months following the announcement terminating the Ontario social economy contract, there were several social financing activities and tools that had been introduced, and with the new group there is a now a concerted move to include these activities in the overall development of the social economy movement. The need for financing has always been a central need of social economy actors, and securing it is easier when there is collective action. In early 2007, several of the original social economy consortium partners mobilized to ask the provincial government to support the creation of a Social Enterprise Trust, which would have been very similar to the patient capital loan fund designed in response to the original federal proposal. The Enterprising Not-for-Profits fund was launched in the spring of 2008. This fund, based on a similar one in British Columbia, was largely supported by the credit union system and various foundations that provide small grants to support the development of social enterprises. This certainly helps out in the development of social enterprises, but it does not address the acute and long-term issues of financing social enterprises. To address this long-term sustainability gap, the 2008 budget of the province of Ontario announced an Ontario Social Venture Fund within the Ministry of Innovation. Some practitioners thought that this Social Venture Fund would replace the Social Economy Trust. However, the mandate is extremely limited, with government being interested primarily in for-profit social purpose businesses that are innovative and that are capturing new market opportunities while investing in communities. However, even though these provincial initiatives were all developed by different bodies and not part of an organized social economy movement, they are important financial and capacity-building tools that can assist in the development and growth of social economy organizations. They are still largely in their infancy, so it is important that the groups working to build the social economy movement are aware of these programs and include them in their planning. There is, however, always the danger that these programs could succumb to the bureaucratic logic that had undermined previous projects. This is why the social economy movement is so important as an observer of government activity and a political actor if necessary.

GROWING MEMBERSHIP

In order to have growing membership, a "brand" or identity for this group will be required so that a larger group of constituents can relate to and feel part of the network. The network will need to include individuals and organizations that work in key areas such as fair trade, environmental degradation, climate change, anti-poverty, peace, hunger, labour, resource management (water, forest, and animals), artistic development, and human rights. The current group's ability to identify and recruit additional organizations to assist in the building of a movement is very limited. One key reason is that the group has not yet been able to decide on an operational definition of social economy that can be used to brand and build a strategy for the movement. Another is that there is a lack of capacity on the part of the major organizations involved to support this work and so continue developing the social economy network.

The Current Period: The Social Economy Movement in Ontario

The development of the initial movement in Ontario was catalyzed by the federal government's RFP in 2005 that in turn brought together a group of people and organizations. Since then, the group has varied in size, and as of fall 2008 this group continues to meet regularly to try and move a social economy agenda forward. There are three main challenges facing this group: the lack of a cohesive definition for the term "social economy" (as noted above); an increasingly challenging funding and market environment for co-ops, social enterprises, and not-for-profits; and an inappropriate negotiation style with government. These challenges are not insurmountable, but they do reflect current real barriers to further development. We will deal with each of these in turn as they apply to the current state of the social economy in Ontario.

Lack of a Definition for Social Economy

The development of an inclusive understanding of social economy is of critical importance because it provides a common language and definition for the group to use. Although there are several basic definitions of the term "social economy" that are similar to each other (see the glossary for one frequently used definition), the current concern of practitioners to develop a definition is rooted in the desire for an operational definition that would more practically outline the types of organizations and activities that belong to the social economy. For the purposes of discussion, the social economy includes, at a minimum, not-for-profit organizations, voluntary groups, co-operatives, mutual associations, and social enterprises. However, merely defining social economy and the types of organizations that belong to the movement is insufficient in the long run because it is also necessary to develop an *operational* definition of what the term means such that additional groups can see how their activities and mission align with the concept. This operational definition would provide the space for these organizations to recognize themselves as members of the movement and allow them to effectively advocate on behalf of the social economy to government and the private sector. (See McMurtry in this volume for further discussion on the issue of definition for the social economy.) To date, the core group working on social economy initiatives has been unable to develop an agreed-upon definition at either the theoretical or operational levels. The debates are made more complex by the lack of full representation from the social economy sector in these discussions (mentioned above) and the desire to be as inclusive of everyone's concerns. This is ultimately not a very efficient process for creating a movement even if it meets Hawken's definition outlined in the introduction of this chapter. The most serious consequence of this debate has been that little of the practical, performance-based activity has been engaged in during this period.

A further issue is that the various proposed definitions did not meet each organizations' understanding of their activities—there is a lack of common terminology or language to describe social economy activity. Terms such as *social enterprise, social purpose business, civil society, third sector,* and *social financing* were all identified as different and even competing concepts that describe this new field of social economy. When people cannot even decide on what to call what they are doing, there is a problem. There was also additional tension in defining the social economy in financial terms, between measurements based on more traditional banking norms involving corporate structure and financial return in contrast to a more broadly defined concept of social return that involves measuring community benefit and social capital. (See Mook and Sumner in this volume for more on social accounting.) Underlying this financial measurement debate is the debate around the centrality of social purpose itself. The result of all of these tensions around self-conceptualization has led to difficulties in defining a cohesive group upon which to build a movement or even engage in practical activities.

A final challenge is that the lack of consistent and well-understood terminology related to the social economy means that the banking industry, including credit unions and caisse populaires, have not developed a paradigm or framework to effectively evaluate these types of organizations as economic organizations. Thus, the access to capital remains a challenge. Whether it is in banking or other sectors of the economy, the notion and definition(s) of the social economy are not well understood. The lack of definition and common vision for this group has therefore had real practical and strategic consequences. Despite this, interest in the social economy has not faded among practitioners. There is always the danger, however, that these definitional problems could become amplified and even fatal in the current challenging market and funding environments.

Challenging Market and Funding Conditions

The environment in which social economy organizations operate has become steadily more challenging over the last 10 to 15 years, primarily due to economic and financial drivers. This is a period bounded by two major recessions (1990 and the one beginning in 2008) and a sustained period of government withdrawal from social services funding. It is important to highlight this period as it is over this time frame that the concept of social economy emerges and the movement begins to articulate itself in Ontario. These policy and economic issues have been made more complex by the challenges posed by the development of social enterprises in Ontario (and even more broadly in Canada). In short, the funding climate for not-for-profit organizations as well as in the co-operative sector in Canada has changed significantly over this period. It is to this problem that we now turn.

CHANGING FUNDING ENVIRONMENT FOR NOT-FOR-PROFIT
ORGANIZATIONS

Since the early 1990s, most of the major funders in Canada began to move away from providing ongoing operational and administrative support for non-governmental organizations (NGOs) in general and not-for-profit organizations in particular. Instead, the trend became one of funding discrete projects, with a very small administrative component permitted for the organization to retain for the funding of the general operations of their organizations. Essentially, project-based funding meant that organizations were applying more frequently and for smaller pots of money for funding their work, without the funds needed to develop a stable operational base. It was difficult to develop or maintain stable sources of year-to-year funding for staff and operations. On a larger scale, this decreased stability and human resource capacity of organizations has created serious systemic challenges to this sector related to long-term strategic-planning partnerships and collaborative projects. Without stable funding, there can be no stable planning or organizational innovation in terms of service delivery or project funding, both in terms of individual organizations and for larger collaborative relationships. (See Box 8.3.)

In addition to these constraints imposed by the general funding environment, the funders themselves have shifted in terms of their areas of interest and their focus on transparency and effective outcomes. Funding is especially lacking for start-up and early phases of development, when groups

---

BOX 8.3   Grant Funding

Not-for-profit organizations, voluntary groups, co-ops,* and social enterprises all have different corporate structures, which reflect their different purposes and relation to the community. However, in terms of access to funding, these organizations have one commonality—by virtue of their not-for-profit tax status, they are eligible to receive grants from government and many other charitable sources, which are often a primary or sole source of revenue.

* Co-operatives can have either not-for-profit or for-profit status. Both types of co-ops have the same connection to the seven co-operative principles, and are member-owned.

often need a great deal of ongoing care and assistance. Funding can also be difficult to secure for established co-operatives and not-for-profit organizations that need large sums of funding for their operations or projects. Although there are a number of foundations and charitable granting agencies in Ontario,[2] their donation activity is often limited to qualified charitable organizations, a condition that excludes many co-operatives and NFP organizations lacking charitable status. We need, therefore, to examine the co-operative and social enterprise sectors separately to understand their specific funding challenges.

PRESSURE ON THE CO-OPERATIVE SYSTEM

Although several different types of co-operatives are able to access the same types of funding as NFPs (housing and child care being the two primary examples—see Box 8.4), co-operatives often tend to be excluded from this type of funding. This is a result of their character as "member-owned businesses," and therefore they

> ### BOX 8.4   Not-for-Profit Co-ops
>
> Housing co-operatives and child-care co-operatives make up the largest numbers of co-ops in Ontario, with over 550 housing co-ops (46 percent of all Ontario co-ops) and over 200 child-care co-ops (17 percent of all Ontario co-ops).

must rely on their ability to compete in the market in order to continue serving their members and community needs. Over the same period, the Ontario marketplace has become more and more competitive, with Ontario co-operatives having to differentiate themselves and maintain market share alongside increasingly desperate shareholder businesses as well as foreign companies or multinationals moving their businesses into communities. This has meant increasing pressure either to demutualize (to change the co-operative into a shareholder-based business) or to merge with other co-ops in order to increase size and market share. The co-op sector's reputation for longevity and success was dealt a blow during the mid-1990s with the bankruptcy and highly publicized financial woes of United Co-operatives of Ontario (UCO) (see Box 8.5). All of these factors put pressure on the community aspects of co-operatives and encouraged these consolidations and mergers in order to keep co-ops competitive in their communities.

During this same period, the credit union sector began seeing a large number of mergers, resulting in larger and larger financial co-operatives and fewer and fewer individual credit unions. Since 2000, the number of credit unions has dropped from over 900 to under 500,[3] a phenomenon due

---

BOX 8.5   United Co-operatives of Ontario

United Co-operatives of Ontario (UCO) was a second-level co-op that experienced financial difficulties in the early 1990s. At its peak, it had sales of approximately $500 million, had 49,000 agricultural members, and served a quarter of a billion people. GROWMARK, a US-based agricultural co-op, purchased UCO's assets and allowed UCO members to sell their shares back to UCO and then, in order to become members, purchase shares in GROWMARK. GROWMARK's revenue is currently higher than UCO's was, even though it represents fewer members (since many of its members are co-operatives rather than individual farm operations).

---

almost exclusively to mergers. Co-operatives are now competing with large foreign multinationals while trying to remain true to the co-operative principles and meet the needs of their members.

At the same time that the trend in the co-operative sector was toward mergers for the sake of efficiency and growth, the financial instruments that co-ops had at their disposal to fund their operations were not changing. Co-ops have many of the same options available to them as other shareholder businesses, but there are tax differences for co-operatives as well as differences in how co-ops can generate investment for their activities. These differences include a separate capitalization process for co-operatives whose limits and requirements have not changed since the mid-1990s. As co-operative businesses have tended to expand due to mergers and natural growth, the costs of doing business have also increased over time. However, because the limits and requirements for investment processes have not changed, co-ops have been put at a competitive disadvantage compared with their shareholder-based cousins.

As co-operatives get larger in order to operate under these pressures, their ability to retain a community character and contribute to the larger social economy movement is hampered. The co-operative principles are a key definition for co-operatives that can allow them to see their mission and mandate and connect them to a larger social economy movement (that is, the commitment to social values and community that are inherent in the seven co-operative principles are a key entry into self-identifying with the social economy movement). When looking at the pressures of globalization in a sector-by-sector perspective, the pressures to compete on a national or global scale are particularly evident in the agriculture and financial sectors, leading to a greater lack of attachment by these sectors to the social economy. If a co-op is less able to see how the seven principles are applicable to them (which many co-operatives and co-op developers report as a danger of growth), it can be hard to see how their co-operative is attached to the social economy movement. As with the funding challenges discussed in the previous section, when organizations and sectors are under pressure, it means that the human and financial resources available to help participate in movement building are scarcer. While co-operatives are a central component of the social economy, the funding pressures from government based on their general ignorance of the sector, combined with the market pressures from for-profit firms and globalization, have put stress on this relationship. Keeping the co-operative movement participating in the social economy through a focus on its values will be an important task for the future.

CHALLENGES WITH THE SOCIAL ENTERPRISE BUSINESS MODEL

The social enterprise business model is a relatively new one compared with the more traditional not-for-profit and co-operative ones, but the former is generally accepted as part of the social economy movement. With social enterprise the social mandate is the focus, and the business activities that they carry out are the means to the social end rather than being the end unto themselves, as with shareholder-based businesses. Although it is often assumed that social enterprises can and do include the co-operative business model, it is useful to examine the pressures and influences that shape social enterprises without particular attention paid to the corporate structure (that is, the difference between NFPs carrying out business activities and co-operatives). This is because the social enterprise business form is gaining in popularity in government circles around the globe as a vehicle for achieving a number of different public policy goals, and so it is worth looking at the challenges that have been identified for this entire sector as a whole.

There are five key challenge areas for the development of the social enterprise model that have had an affect on the growth of this sector and its ability to contribute to larger movement building activities. It is important to note the overlap that these challenges have with the social economy as a whole. The challenges for social enterprise are:

- lack of expertise, knowledge, and competencies among social enterprise managers;
- access to capital and investment;
- access to expanded market opportunities;
- support from an intermediary organization; and
- stronger links with research endeavours.

◯ Lack of Expertise, Knowledge, and Competencies Among
  Social Enterprise Managers

There is a lack of managers who have both business and social skills that support the social enterprise development path. Managers need learning opportunities to develop these types of skills, especially in business schools where many managers receive training and knowledge related to operating and managing business operations. There is a growing interest among young business professionals in expanding their knowledge of social enterprise, but there are few Canadian postsecondary institutions that have programs that foster these types of learning environments.

◯ Access to Capital and Investment

Social enterprises need access to long-term financing such as equity investment and patient capital to support their growth. Requirements for successful growth go beyond simple grant and loan financing. Financial institutions in Ontario have developed very few products to support the financing requirements of this type of enterprise. Leaders in the financial co-operative system are Vancity in Vancouver, Alterna Savings in Ontario, Assiniboine Credit Union in Winnipeg, and Desjardins in Quebec, and these have developed a wide range of products and support systems that account for social enterprise character as separate from business (Loewen, Reimer, and LePage 2008).

◯ Access to Expanded Market Opportunities

Social enterprises need to develop marketing and replicating schemes in order to have greater significance in the capitalist economy. Specifically, such schemes would help to grow business volume and thus would allow the possibility for gains to be made in terms of efficiency and profitability. Social enterprises need to better understand this system and be players in a changing supply-chain management model so that they move away from a "marginalized position." In particular, some key leaders in government have identified the procurement of goods and services from social enterprises as a growing potential market, and so it is important for social enterprises to understand how to take advantage of these processes and get access to this new market.

◯ Support from an Intermediary Organization

The sector needs to have geographically based and sector-specific organizations to provide supportive services to social enterprises such as the provision of business planning, policy design, advocacy, information sharing, and communication.

○ Stronger Links with Research Endeavours

Research is needed to support and illustrate how social enterprises contribute to the economy by creating employment and building social value. This research would encourage more awareness and understanding of the social returns of these types of enterprises.

While the idea and terminology of social enterprise continues to be an interest of government, it is important that these challenges are addressed by the larger work of the social economy movement and its member organizations. This would offer an important opportunity to have the entire social economy movement brought forward to government as a public policy solution or partner.

IMPACTS OF THESE FUNDING CONSTRAINTS

There are many similarities in the outcomes for NFPs (both traditional and those that identify as social enterprises), co-operatives, and others because of limited funding and more competitive markets. Co-ops with not-for-profit status are impacted by the funding constraints of traditional funding bodies in the same way as NFPs. Social enterprises and co-operatives are both affected by increasingly competitive marketplaces. These impacts have influenced and continue to influence the development of the overall social economy movement, and there are larger cross-sector conclusions that can be drawn from looking at these different forces.

○ Lack of Capacity for Strategic Thinking and Partnership Building

Funding and market condition pressures have important long-term and wide-ranging negative impacts on those organizations working toward building the social economy movement. Most important, without a stable base of funding from year to year and with a lack of dedicated and continual funding for senior staff, the development of long-term and strategic plans for an organization is extremely difficult. This has had impacts on the ability of the sector to build any kind of effective collaborative relationships, both within their own areas of interest and also in terms of effective public–private partnerships involving government or the corporate sector. More importantly, the unstable funding base limits the sector's ability to focus on building an effective movement and lobbying for policy changes that would improve the efficiency of the service delivery and lives of many Ontarians.

With so much time and effort devoted to securing funding, often on an ongoing basis, maintaining an outward focus that would facilitate partnerships on particular projects is difficult, especially if two or more potential partners are competing for the same funding. Because developing partnerships and collaborative relationships takes time and has to occur separate from the achievement of grant-based deliverables, it can be very difficult for organizations to justify spending time and energy on these types of initiatives. Using limited human resources on the time and effort required to build large-scale partnerships with other organizations can therefore be very taxing for these social economy organizations. This creates real limits on movement-building activity despite the fact that building a movement would help alleviate these limits and help program delivery. This is a central problem for the social economy.

○ Lack of Systemic Organizational Support for Work
    Developing the Social Economy

There are some real challenges with building an inclusive social economy movement, and perhaps the most challenging are the logistics involved with managing a vision-based discussion with a potentially very large group of organizations. It has also been challenging to define a scope of work that could attract or indicate value to this wide range of organizations that traditionally may not have a history of collaborating together. For many of these groups, the concept of social economy has no resonance. As mentioned above, although others would define their activities and mandate as belonging to the social economy, sometimes this language and definition is not enough to get a group to the table and thus embark on a collaborative relationship around building a movement. In other cases, organizations may not have the ability to consistently participate in such a large-scale and long-term process. It has also been difficult to define an effective working relationship and boundaries around effective collaboration due to different organizational cultures and capacity variances. One potential way around this challenge has been to build the movement based on finding key champions or advocates to participate. The ideal outcome in involving key champions is that they have the capacity to mobilize their organizations or a large group of individuals and get them involved in the process as a way to catalyze discussion around the creation of an organizational structure that would shepherd the movement. It puts enormous pressure on the individual champions to not only contribute their time and energy to the building but also to go back to their organization and spend time and effort convincing their own organization of the value of participation. The long-term challenge with this approach is that it is not easy to transition from a champion model that is heavily person dependent to a model where the support of the social economy movement is ingrained among the cultures and operations of all of the organizations involved with building the movement. It is also in contradiction to the social movement model outlined by Hawken and does not reflect the collaborative model of the social economy. But it may be the only way to move forward in this climate.

Both the lack of capacity and organizational support for the building of the social economy has consistently acted as a barrier to the core of the work that the practitioners are involved in: to get the social economy up and operating. Up and operating means that there is a jointly understood and accepted operational definition of social economy and that there is a strategic plan associated with the movement that consists of a clear policy and financial framework that can facilitate and sustain the development of organizations within that economy. This would lead to an ongoing relationship between the social economy movement and government that would be based on the achievement of mutually beneficial policy goals, rather than merely a one-time allocation of funding.

Ineffective Negotiation with Government

As explored in more detail in our reflection on the federal process, government, rightly or wrongly, has repeatedly demonstrated that they were not comfortable negotiating with multiple groups or a consortium. The ability of the group to identify one organization or leader that could take on the role of lead to negotiate with government on behalf of the network was hampered by the limited history that many of the partners had in working with each other, as we will examine in more detail below. This has also meant that the group did not have the ability to identify a unified policy position that they could discuss with government, and instead spent time and effort designing only the programs and tools they wished to have and that they felt would look best to government from a funding perspective.

Another contributing factor to the lack of definition and achievement in the Ontario social economy movement to date is related to our inability to negotiate effectively with the provincial government. Negotiation with government is key to the success of the movement because we require government to provide a policy and funding framework in order for the social economy to function most efficiently. The social economy provides excellent value to Ontario communities, and provides them more efficiently and effectively to boot. One ongoing challenge that exists is the inability of the primary organizations involved with the development of the social economy movement to recognize that they have not effectively been making the case for both their economic and social efficiency effectively with the Ontario government.

LIMITED HISTORY OF WORKING TOGETHER

One of the critical factors affecting the group's negotiation style with government is related to our limited history of working together in a broadly based group of strategically related organizations. This does not mean that there have not been examples of such collaboration. During the development of OSEC's response to the federal government's RFP, two key partnerships emerged around the development of the social economy in Ontario. Both partnerships represented different interests related to the social economy; the first was composed of grassroots collaborations (Ontario CED Collaborative, the original Social Economy Consortium) and the second a research centre based at University of Toronto (Southern Ontario Social Economy Research Node). These partnerships, however, did not involve a large number of organizations or agencies working on social economy issues, so they were only of limited use in developing the trust and understanding between partners that would have more effectively provided a base from which to build the social economy movement. As with the federal process, both of these collaborations were program-based and did not have a strategic focus to guide their activities or to dictate larger outcomes that could help develop the relationships between the partners or help to build the wider social economy movement. These early collaborations, however, are crucial to the possibility of developing a social economy movement in Ontario and deserve some attention.

○ Ontario CED Collaborative

In 2004, while the federal process was still in its infancy, a group of organizations were partnered under an Ontario Trillium Foundation grant to develop a series of social economy–related activities. The key partners were the Community Economic Development Technical Assistance Program (CEDTAP), the Ontario region of the Canadian CED Network (CCED-NET—Ontario Region), and the Ontario Co-operative Association (On Co-op). The three partners had originally made separate applications to the Trillium Foundation, but were asked to find a way to combine their individual applications into a single one in order to build on the mutual goals their applications all shared. The collaboration was termed OnCEDCo (Ontario Community Economic Development Collaborative) and was awarded $624,900 in June, 2005, the largest grant ever provided by the Ontario Trillium Foundation. The vision of OnCEDCo was "to build capacity of the community economic development and social economy sectors in Ontario" (Ontario Co-operative Association 2007c). This collaboration was intended to offer a comprehensive program to support the emergence, growth, and sustainability of co-operatives, social enterprises, and community economic development (CED) initiatives. The grant's focus was to build knowledge, networks, and products to support the social economy in Ontario in the following project areas:

• Corporate sector engagement: CEDTAP was the lead on the development of a series of business-to-business workshops that were meant to engage members of the corporate sector by involving them in investment in the CED sector, thus providing long-term systemic support that would go both directly to grassroots organizations and support the larger umbrella organizations that in turn support the grassroots.

• Technical assistance: Both CEDTAP and On Co-op provided grants to not-for-profits and co-operatives to allow them to hire the expertise they required to build capacity.

• Knowledge sharing: CEDNET developed a series of case studies and a policy framework related to CED in Ontario that will be used to educate and advocate for change.

• Education Centre for Excellence: On Co-op developed curriculum content for postsecondary audiences on the topic of co-operative development as well as a guide to co-operative legislation and a series of fact sheets.

• Storytelling and dissemination of innovation: All three partners are creating stories related to their work and the sector more broadly that will be used to educate and engage stakeholders and the general public.

Each of these areas involved a variety of grassroots support, capacity building, network development, and other activities that were supported by a combination of the three partner organizations. However, despite the fact that these groups were officially working together, very few of the outcomes were worked on and planned by all three partners in collaboration. Furthermore, there was little opportunity to develop a full strategy for all three partners to negotiate with government for effective policy and financial supports for the movement. So, although the program supports that were key to this collaboration were very important in supporting the growth of social economy organizations, there was a missed opportunity to jointly

identify and advocate for shifts in provincial policy that would more systematically support the growth of these organizations.

This collaboration resulted in a few key learnings—namely, the importance of allocating the appropriate amount of time and energy toward developing effective collaborations, and a good understanding of the types of
tools and mechanisms that are required to build the social economy at a
grassroots level. Although there was time spent on developing a big-picture
understanding of some of the policy issues affecting the development of
social economy organizations, this was not done jointly by the partners—it
was largely done individually by each partner in the collaborative. For the
partners, this was a missed opportunity to work together to develop an
understanding of policy issues that would facilitate all their work and thus
set the stage for larger social economy movement building as had happened
in Quebec.

○ Social Economy Centre (OISE, University of Toronto)

As the partners mentioned above were organizing practitioners, the academic community in southern Ontario was involved in its own initiative to
study the social economy and, in 2005, the Social Economy Centre was
founded under the leadership of Jack Quarter and Laurie Mook. The centre
was created as a unit of the Ontario Institute for Studies in Education (OISE)
with a mandate to promote and disseminate research and policy analysis of
issues facing the social economy. Although housed within the University of
Toronto, there were a number of other project partners of the Social Economy Centre, including On Co-op, the Business and Society program and the
Schulich School of Business Non-Profit Management program of York University, and Imagine Canada. The Social Economy Centre is also connected
to the larger Canadian Social Economy Hub (CSEHub) housed at the University of Victoria. Despite the continuing good intentions of this initiative,
tension between the academics and practitioners is evident here, with many
of the learning events focusing on the theoretical research behind the concepts and needed policy framework involved in the social economy. While
important, this focus is often of less relevance to those working directly with
the grassroots and struggling within a policy framework that is unfriendly
to the development of social economy organizations like co-operatives,
social enterprises, and not-for-profit organizations. As with the OnCEDCo,
this disconnect represents for a number of partners from different back-
grounds and having different approaches a missed opportunity to synthesize
a comprehensive policy framework that incorporates the research findings
of academics to meet the needs of practitioners.

BOX 8.6 The Canadian Social Economy Hub

The CSEHub acts as a facilitator and promotes collaboration among six regional research centres across Canada (Quebec, Southern Ontario, Prairies, Alberta, British Columbia, and the North) by creating opportunities and exchanges with international networks. This project is funded through a grant of $2.1 million from the Social Sciences and Humanities Research Council (SSHRC) of Canada. In Ontario, it represents 18 universities and 30 community organizations working on over 30 projects. The national hub brings Ian MacPherson, an elder in the co-operative sector, as well as the Canadian CED Network (CCEDNet) into a central role in the social economy network. CSEHub's vision is to "build collaboration between researchers and practitioners to better understand and encourage initiatives at the local, provincial, and national levels so that the Social Economy and its related approaches will be more widely known" (CSEHub n.d.).

GOVERNMENT UNWILLING TO WORK WITH MULTI-PARTNER GROUP

This disconnect between academics and practitioners returns us to a problem outlined above. Both the federal and provincial governments have indicated a high degree of discomfort in dealing with sectors where there is not one clear organization that can negotiate a policy framework with government officials. Consequently, the governments have begun to identify these organizations for the movement without consultation. This is a problem for the grassroots, as years of hard work can come to nothing because the bureaucratic logic of government does not understand the consensus model of the movement. For example, provincial premier Dalton McGuinty in the 2007 Liberal Party platform announced a "Venture Capital Fund for Social Financing" housed at the Social Innovation Generation@MaRS Centre (SiG@MaRS) (Liberal Party of Ontario 2007, 18). This fund was then confirmed in the 2008 budget. MaRS was an obvious choice for this funding from a government perspective because it is located in downtown Toronto, near the Bay Street financial district, the provincial legislature, and key government organizations, and its purpose is to connect and foster collaboration among the communities of science, business, and capital. Along these lines in 2007, MaRS began a serious movement into networking and collaborative activities related to social financing through a series of educational workshops and events designed to raise the profile of social financing and the bringing together of experts from abroad and of those involved in social financing activities in Ontario. Many of those involved in the sector were wondering how this fund would fit within the context of social financing that had been a part of the discussions related to the social economy "movement" that had already taken place. Some of the more grassroots organizations associated with the social economy even felt that the grassroots character of the movement was not adequately reflected in the activities of MaRS. There was concern among this group that the government had selected MaRS over their heads as their social enterprise development vehicle because funding had been provided to MaRS without having being requested, while their request for funding for a social enterprise trust had been denied. This created a potential schism in the early redevelopment of the social economy movement because, while these groups were not opposed to MaRS per se, MaRS was not connected or related to many of the grassroots organizations already working on social economy movement building. Further, as a social finance report published in 2008 demonstrated (Mulholland 2008, Appendix B), many in the government felt that they had fulfilled their duty to support CED and social enterprise development through their contributions to MaRS. This essentially closed the door to future funding to the groups involved in building the social economy at the grassroots. Further, the report indicated that government bureaucrats felt that MaRS was carrying out capacity-building activities in the social economy, a perception not shared by many grassroots organizations currently working on the development of the Ontario Social Economy Consortium. Rather than accept this as a defeat however, social economy movement actors in Ontario attempted to bring MaRS into their group. Representatives of MaRS were approached and asked to join in the building of a social economy movement—thereby ensuring that MaRS would hear the concerns of the grassroots organizations working on the social economy. It also ensured that the consortium group working on the social economy could take advantage of the established connections between MaRS and the provincial government.

MAKING THE CASE TO GOVERNMENT

All of the work that was done both in the response to the federal government RFP on the social economy and in the work on the new social economy consortium focused to a large extent on the development of tools and financial instruments that would support the development of the social economy. The current focus of the social economy work in Ontario is on the development of a social enterprise trust that would provide early-stage grant support and low-interest loans for social economy organizations in order to help them build the sector. Little work has been done, however, on identifying key policy priorities that the provincial government (as well as the federal government) could initiate to facilitate the long-term growth and support of social economy organizations. The tools and instruments that were identified during the federal process and outlined above are critically important for supporting the growth of the sector at a grassroots level, but there also needs to be a policy framework developed to "house" these tools. Without such a framework, the initiatives are just "gap-filling" measures, not sustainable practices. Consequently, the sector is left in the position of having to take these well-defined tools and instruments to each new minister or government and of trying to convince them that these policies meet the current priorities of that minister or government—which is not a position of strength from a negotiating perspective. The organizations involved in the development of the social economy movement need to be able to bring wide-spread organizational and public pressure to bear on government and so force them to negotiate with the sector for the development of mutually beneficial sustainable policy positions that would achieve the goals of both government and the social economy movement.

THE EFFECTIVE ROLE OF PRACTITIONERS

Alongside the organizations working to define and build the social economy movement, there is an important role for grassroots organizations and the practitioners that comprise them or support them directly. The original tools and instruments that were included in the process of the federal RFP were identified to a very large extent as a result of the work that had been done for years by practitioners in the field to assist them in their work on a day-to-day basis. However, the reality is that although tools like technical assistance funding, support for networks, and others would facilitate the ability of practitioners to more effectively develop and support social economy organizations, this is only one aspect of needed support structures. As mentioned in other sections throughout this chapter, these tools need to be included as part of larger and more strategic policy positions and a framework that can assist in developing these organizations and the entire movement over the long term. Practitioners need to focus not just on their individual conversations or projects, but on building a larger movement with other organizations in order to get the attention of government.

What would these steps look like? The next step for long-term and large-scale development of support of the movement are things such as more progressive tax regimes and investment support, financial incentives and supports, and government and private procurement policies that preferentially support social economy organizations. It is critical for practitioners to understand the importance of this longer-term policy development and how their front-line work with groups can help make the argument for these more systemic supports. It therefore becomes critically important for practitioners to be involved in and understand a larger strategy for the building of the social economy movement. This will ensure that the tools and assistance designed for implementation in the shorter term are useful to practitioners. It will also make it easier for there to be a concerted effort among practitioners, grassroots organizations, and the larger provincial and regional associations for using the same language and to effectively make the case to government for the support of the movement. With the the shorter-term supports that were identified during the federal process the base has been built, and now it becomes important for those organizations involved in building the movement to ensure that they involve practitioners as a stakeholder group and also adequately communicate these efforts back out to the sector.

Where Do We Go from Here?

Building a Definition

The success of this movement will be defined by how rapidly it comes to be recognized by all other sectors of society. If it remains isolated, it will fail. If the social economy is integrated into education, business, and government, there is a chance that it will be sustainable. The movement will require a definition that is encompassing and inclusive so as to achieve this. More importantly, this definition needs to be the basis for a movement. This definition will need to expand beyond the players involved and their organizational mandates. It also has to be a definition that organizations can fit their mandate into rather than a committee that individuals have to dedicate their time or skills to work on.

The movement will require a structure that is a loose network focusing on its strategy and key deliverables. The network should be mainly virtual, with regular face-to-face meetings only to determine next steps. The leadership of this work should be mostly voluntary and should only move forward if there is enough dedicated human and financial capacity to move it forward. The strategy would need to be a set of deliverables in a phased approach of short-term, medium-term, and long-term goals. This strategy should include policy development, tools like financial instruments, education/capacity-building activities, and the ability to identify and create longer-term policy shifts. These policy shifts will be required in order to sustainably maintain the sector in Ontario and help to build the provincial, national, and worldwide movement.

Changing the Funding Environment

In an era in which governments are shrinking and deficits are high, the key issue is to get capital into social enterprises. In the economic climate of Canada, governments and public policy will need to facilitate this. An intermediate organization at the federal level is required, one such as the Fiducie in Quebec, created by Le Chantier; the Fiducie is an organization which has the expertise to facilitate the bridge between the investment community and social enterprises. Tax incentives will be required, ones similar to those in Manitoba and Nova Scotia that support investments in social enterprises while yielding some financial return. For the social economy network to receive greater government investment, it will require key programmatic elements with clear outcomes that are connected to government policy.

Throughout 2008, Ontario's Ministry of Small Business and Consumer Services reviewed the *Corporations Act*. One of the key benefits from the practitioners' point of view is that this review might conclude that non-profit corporations should have greater leeway in creating more fee-for-services revenue. The not-for-profit sector has been lobbying during this process for a new regulatory framework that would support community interest companies, a structure based upon that already developed in the United Kingdom. Community interest companies would enhance the financing structure of non-profits while attracting investors. Unfortunately, the current McGuinty government in Ontario did not in the end recommend the implementation of these structures.

Negotiating with Government

The social economy network needs to be more effective at building stronger relationships with the provincial government. Rather than having a "hit-and-miss" approach to government relations, the overall tactics need to be embedded in a government relations strategy. This could be achieved through the efforts of a small working group that represents the concerns and aspirations of the larger network. They should exhibit a similar type of leadership and drive that the consortium had with the negotiations with the federal government. High-profile champions who represent the diversity and importance of the movement and who already have relationships with government would be instrumental in making the case to government.

The first objective of such a working group would be to educate the provincial government about the social economy—the landscape, the players, the strategy, and so on. This essential promotion and "branding" would facilitate for both elected officials and key bureaucrats a better understanding of what the social economy is in Ontario and what is occurring in other provinces and countries. Case studies could highlight the benefits and results associated with supporting the social economy. It would be crucial for the working group to develop some short-term actions that could demonstrate the social economy's value to government mandates—for example, an anti-poverty focus. This would create a "win–win" situation for both the movement as well as government. It is still important for those involved in building this movement to understand that this is only one short-term component that needs to be worked on, and the longer-term vision and the policy supports must transcend any individual and partisan policy agendas of the current government.

Building a Strategy

Overall, the key need going forward is for the development of a strategy for the development of the social economy movement that addresses all of the above points. This strategy must clearly define the social economy both theoretically and practically and also outline the roles and responsibilities of the different organizations and stakeholder groups in the development of the movement. This will ensure that a broad base of organizations can see how they can support and be involved in the social economy, and will help organizations that are already involved to recruit from sectors that are not currently represented.

This strategy must also reflect that those involved in the movement are dealing with real funding and capacity constraints that are limiting their ability to move forward. The strategy must also recognize that these funding constraints are not likely to ease anytime in the near future, and so the organizations involved in the social economy have to make the development of the movement a priority. This will also assist in developing broader-based support for the social economy by organizations, not just by certain individuals within certain organizations.

Ensuring that these issues are both adequately addressed in the definition of a strategy would assist the group in developing a policy position that can then be used to effectively make the case to government. Rather than being consistently in the position of having to take a series of tools and instruments and develop them into a strategic position that meets the policy position of the government currently in power, such a strategy would also enable the group to develop their own vision and idea of what is required for the support of the arenas in which they are working. This would allow them to mobilize wider support from organizations and the general public and pressure government to negotiate with the movement as a whole in order to determine mutually beneficial policy frameworks. It would also allow for the effective empowerment of a smaller group of dedicated negotiators to work with government because they will understand the larger strategy that they are tasked with implementing. They would therefore be able to both effectively represent the larger interests of the network and meet the government's desire for limiting the number of people or organizations that they need to work with.

From a practical perspective, it is important to understand that the development of a strategy and generating buy-in from a wide cross-section of organizations working in the social economy will take time. However, taking such time is critical in order to assist the group in building a strong foundation for the movement that will survive for years to come, through changeovers in staff and organizational support as well as changes in government structures that the movement is hoping to negotiate with.

Relative to the magnitude of the setbacks associated with the messy end of the federal RFP process and the long delay in coming back together to begin redevelopment of the social economy, the movement is well on its way to defining itself as well as the social economy and becoming a functional network of key organizations. Discussions are currently under way to begin a strategic planning process, and the consortium is seeking additional resources to facilitate the involvement of the key partners and ensure that building the social economy movement is a priority. After a period of struggle, the social economy movement in Ontario is building momentum by learning the lessons from its past.

Appendix: Ontario Financing Matrix

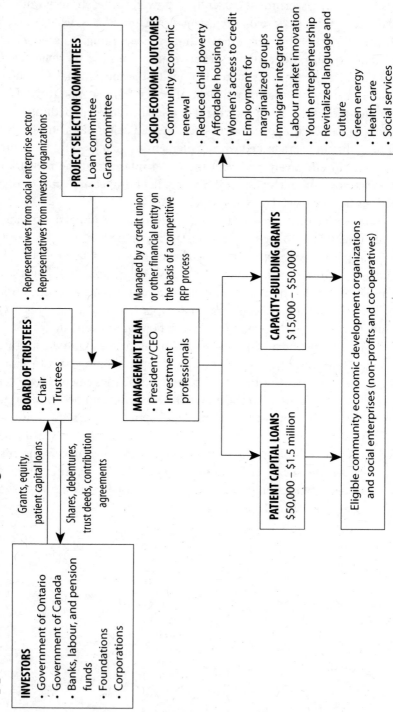

Ontario Financing Matrix: Summary Table

	Grant organization/ foundation	Credit union	Community Futures Development Corporation	Community loan fund	Micro-fund	Equity fund
Jurisdiction	Mainly regional, some provincial	Regional, member-based	Regional	Regional	Regional, member-based	Federal, provincial
Ownership, governance, and structure	Usually not-for-profit structure, advisory board or committee to oversee the funds	Community/ member ownership and governance	Community-based governance, local board of directors; non-profit structure	Community-based governance; non-profit structure	Community-based advisory group	Independent advisory board; not-for-profit or for-profit structure
Criteria to access funding	Criteria vary depending on the size of the grant organization; some require matching funds, financial statements, etc.	Multiple funding sources, strong financial and business plan, collateral required	Start-up, expansion, and stabilization funding for organizations that are community-based or may not have been able to obtain conventional financing	Only able to fund part of the total funding package that is required	Start-up operating subsidies required	Commitment from multiple funding sources, and collateral required; generally, do not fund start-ups; if venture capital, may require some ownership
Other services	Not offered	Front-end financial institution services	Some offer business advisory services	Some offer business advisory and technical assistance services	Financial literacy, peer support, and some business advisory services	Not offered

(The matrix is continued on the next page.)

Ontario Financing Matrix   Continued

	Grant organization/ foundation	Credit union	Community Futures Development Corporation	Community loan fund	Micro-fund	Equity fund
Grants	Eligibility for grants depends on the specific criteria set by each grantor— usually grants are specific to groups, sectors, and catchment areas	Some credit unions also have grant programs, such as Meridian's Good Neighbour Program[1] and Libro's Community Builder Program[2]	Not offered.	Sometimes grants are available.	Not offered.	Rare
Loans	Not offered	Consumer loans, lines of credit, company accounts, some mortgage and small business loans; borrowing interest rate comparable to market	Repayable financing of up to $150,000 on commercial terms through loans, loan guarantees, or equity investments	Likely to come second behind other lenders and/ or must be secured by other guarantees; rates and terms are flexible and vary in comparison to the market	Micro-loans for self-employment and small business (home-based business); borrowing interest rate ranges from below-market to credit card rates	Loans available for the growth of established social enterprises; interest rates vary but are typically lower than traditional financial institution rates

(The matrix is continued on the next page.)

Ontario Financing Matrix   Continued

	Grant organization/ foundation	Credit union	Community Futures Development Corporation	Community loan fund	Micro-fund	Equity fund
Leverage	Some grant funds can be leveraged with grant funds from other sources but this depends on the grantor	Offer loan syndication, small sub-debt lending; some will syndicate deals with community futures corporations	Help finance new or existing small businesses and social enterprises for start-up, expansion, or stabilization plans	Primary purpose is to leverage other capital; typically do not invest the total capital package	Not offered	Equity and subordinated debt from equity funds leverage additional financing from conventional sources
Examples	Ontario Trillium Foundation,[3] Laidlaw Foundation,[4] The Co-operators,[5] Ontario Arts Council,[6] Ontario Natural Food Co-op,[7] Ontario Credit Union Charitable Foundation,[8] Rural Economic Development Program (RED),[9] Toronto Community Foundation,[10] Toronto Enterprise Fund[11]	Check www.coopsontario.com or www.ontariocreditunions.com to identify a credit union in your community	Perth Community Futures, Nottawasaga Futures, Chatham Kent Community Futures, etc.	Tenacity Works,[12] Carrot Cache,[13] Ottawa Community Loan Fund[14]	Alterna Savings,[15] PARO[16]	Social Capital Partners,[17] Canadian Alternative Investment Co-operative (CAIC),[18] Investeco[19]

(The matrix is continued on the next page.)

Ontario Financing Matrix   Continued

Notes

* Indicates an organization that is part of the Funders' Forum Network.

1. Meridian Credit Union—Good Neighbour Program:* Funding requests of up to $3,000 submitted to a local Meridian branch manager, for initiatives involving newcomer settlement support programs, parks and green spaces, neighbourhood events and organizations. To be eligible must be in the operating area of a Meridian branch.

2. Libro Financial Group—Community Builders Grant:* Two levels of funding are available through this program to support projects that involve young people up to the age of 23, in communities located in southwestern Ontario. A branch grant funds to a maximum of $10,000 per year for up to three years. Corporate grants will fund a maximum of $25,000 per year for three years.

3. Ontario Trillium Foundation:* Offers grants to projects falling into one of four broad categories: arts and culture, environment, human and social services, and sports and recreation. Grant seekers can also apply for funding from one of three grant sources: operating grants, project grants, and capital grants. Operating and capital grants can be for multi-year funding (maximum five years) up to $75,000 per year. Capital grants are one year only, up to $150,000. Deadlines are March 1, July 1, and November 1.

4. Laidlaw Foundation: Funds youth-led initiatives in the arts, the environment, and the community through two different streams: catalyst grants, up to $5,000, and project grants, up to $50,000. There are no deadlines for catalyst grants; project grants can be submitted in the spring or in the fall of each year.

5. The Co-operators:* Offers two programs that provide financial assistance to community organizations. The Community Economic Development Fund offers multi-year grants of up to $20,000 per year. Applications are reviewed January 31 and August 30 each year. Through the Co-operative Development Program $100,000 is given out per year through investments (up to $25,000 per applicant) and another $100,000 is given out per year in grants ($5,000 to $20,000 per initiative). Proposals are reviewed three times each year—summer, winter, and spring.

6. Ontario Arts Council:* Offers grants to individual artists and arts organizations through three different granting programs: project grants, operating grants, and programming grants. Project grants are one-time grants only for specific projects. Operating grants cover the operating costs of established arts organizations and programming grants for activities that occur annually.

7. Ontario Natural Food Co-op (ONFC):* ONFC has created a Community Development Fund to support organizations that educate people about natural and organic foods and sustainable food systems. Projects receive up to $2,000. Applications are accepted throughout the year.

8. Ontario Credit Union Charitable Foundation:* Focusing on projects that support the environment and youth, the foundation matches funds of Ontario Credit Union charitable community programs.

9. Rural Economic Development Program (RED): Eligible projects must accrue benefits in rural Ontario. Matching funding is required through this program, with the provincial government investing up to 50 percent of the project's eligible costs. Under special circumstances funding may be provided for up to 90 percent of the total eligible project costs.

(The matrix is continued on the next page.)

Ontario Financing Matrix   Continued

10. Toronto Community Foundation: The Vital Idea grant is a capacity-building grant for programs that are currently in operation in Toronto. Vital Idea grants provide funding of up to $30,000 over one year for activities involving documentation, replication, or promotion.

11. Toronto Enterprise Fund (TEF): To receive a grant from TEF, groups must meet the eligibility criteria and apply for the annual business plan competition. Submissions are reviewed by a committee and six finalists are chosen. After revisions to the business plan and a presentation to the panel of judges, seed funding of up to $50,000 is awarded.

12. Canadian Worker Co-op Federation—Tenacity Works: This fund supports the development of the worker co-op sector by making investments and funding technical assistance. A development fund provides $1,500 for an initial assessment. Investment into a co-op is used primarily to leverage other capital. The minimum investment from the fund is $25,000 and the maximum investment is $200,000.

13. Carrot Cache:* Invests in small, beginning-stage projects by people who are working either in a worker co-op or for an organization promoting organic agriculture and/or community food strategies. The investment can take the form of a loan, the purchase of class A non-voting preferred shares, or simply a grant, with amounts ranging from $500 to $5,000.

14. Ottawa Community Loan Fund: Provides short-term loans of up to $15,000 to small business owners, aspiring entrepreneurs, social enterprises, co-operatives, and talented individuals with international training and community groups. This is a focus on the micro-credit needs of the Ottawa-area community.

15. Alterna Savings:* Two main programs support community and social initiatives. The Immigrant Employment Loan Program provides specialty loans for training or certification programs that allow immigrants or Convention refugees to successfully enter the Canadian job market. To be eligible for the micro-loan program, individuals must be a member of Alterna.

16. PARO Centre for Women's Enterprise: Community lending circles and loans for the development of small to medium-sized businesses on Northern Ontario, developed by and in support of women.

17. Social Capital Partners:* Provides financing to both for-profit and not-for-profit social enterprises. Loan financing is available generally in amounts of $30,000 to $200,000. Equity and near-equity financing, such as subordinated debt, mezzanine financing, and convertible or preferred debt. The funding is available from $100,000 to $250,000.

18. Canadian Alternative Investment Co-operative (CAIC):* Invests in groups working for positive social change and community economic development in Canada that lack access to traditional financing. CAIC focuses on lending in the following three areas: social enterprise financing, mortgages for community-based projects, and social and affordable housing initiatives. Interest rates are set on a case-by-case basis.

19. Investeco: Aims to invest in promising North American companies specializing in alternative power, water technologies, organic and natural foods, and environmental technologies. Its portfolio includes private and public equity funds as well as a separate portfolio for start-ups. Preference is given to private companies that have over $2 million in revenue and need expansion capital.

Source: Ontario Co-operative Association (2008).

Notes

1. For example, the social economy organizations that are part of Le Chantier in Quebec have a shared branding program called "Values Added" that showcases the common values that all organizations in the movement share as values-based, regardless of their structure or sector affiliations.
2. The Ontario Co-operative Association (On Co-op) has prepared a financing matrix that outlines the key areas of financing available to NFPs, social enterprises, and co-operatives based on a number of resources that have been developed in the area of social finance over the last 18 months. See the appendix for more information.
3. Credit Union Central of Canada includes a number of credit unions as part of their annual reporting (CUCC 2008, 16).

Glossary

Capacity building   Assistance provided to developing organizations in order to help them increase their internal skills and abilities and fulfill their mandate or contribute to the economic or social fabric of a community. Assistance can take the form of many different activities, including funding, coaching, education, or facilitation. Capacity building is historically provided by government or other large-scale or umbrella organizations but can be provided by any number of agencies, including government.

Community development (CD)   The process of facilitating the participation and capacity of local people to identify and work toward their own solutions to enhance the long-term social, economic, and environmental conditions of their community.

Federal Economic Development Initiative of Northern Ontario (FedNor)   A federal regional development organization in Ontario that works with a variety of partners, both as facilitator and as catalyst, to help create an environment in which communities and business can grow and thrive. It supports specific economic development goals and agencies in northern and eastern Ontario, as well as the Community Futures Development Corporation Network, which operates throughout Canada.

Movement   A group of people, formal or informal, who are working toward a particular political or social change or goal.

Policy   A framework of activity that governs a particular organization or institution. For example, the Ontario government has policies that govern the activities of co-operatives in Ontario.

Practitioner   A person who is actively engaged in an activity (such as a co-operative) as opposed to someone who studies this activity (academic) or regulates this activity (government agent).

Roundtable   A meeting that is structured to be non-hierarchical, consultative, and open; usually convened to determine the position of a variety of central stakeholders.

Social economy   "A bridging concept for organizations that have social objectives central to their mission and their practice, and either have explicit economic objectives or generate some economic value through the services they provide and purchases that they undertake" (Mook, Quarter, and Richmond 2007).

Social enterprise   A business that sells goods or provides services in the market for the purpose not of maximizing profits for shareholders but of creating a blended return on investment, both financial and social, and whose profits are returned to the business or to a social purpose. Social enterprises contribute to building healthy communities through direct participation in the market and by strengthening non-profit organizations (Loewen, Reimer, and LePage 2008).

Discussion Questions

1. What is distinct about the practitioner's viewpoint on the social economy? How are their concerns unique?
2. Why has it been so hard for the Ontario and federal governments to develop a position on the social economy?
3. Why is it necessary for the social economy to organize itself as a movement in Ontario specifically and Canada more generally?

Suggested Further Readings and Resources

Hawken, P. 2007. *Blessed unrest: How the largest movement in the world came into being and why no one saw it coming.* New York: Viking.

Imagine Canada. http://www.imaginecanada.ca.

Mook, L., J. Quarter, and B.J. Richmond. 2007. *What counts: Social accounting for nonprofits and cooperatives.* 2nd ed. London: Sigel.

Ontario Co-operative Association. http://www.ontario.coop.

Ontario Social Economy Research Node. http://socialeconomy.utoronto.ca.

References

Alex Laidlaw Housing Co-op. 2000. *Ontario Social Housing Reform Act at a glance: A guide for co-op members.* Ottawa: Alex Laidlaw Housing Co-op. http://alexlaidlawcoop.bizland.com/news_views_e.html.

Canadian Broadcasting Corporation (CBC). 2007. Unemployment rate among new immigrants 11.5%: StatsCan. September 10. http://www.cbc.ca/consumer/story/2007/09/10/immigrant-statcan.html.

Canadian CED Network (CCEDNet). n.d. Canadian social economy hub. http://www.ccednet-rcdec.ca/files/ccednet/W-178_CCEDNET.pdf.

Canadian Social Economy Hub (CSEHub). n.d. http://www.socialeconomyhub.ca/hub/.

Credit Union Central of Canada. 2008. *2008 annual report.* Toronto: Credit Union Central of Canada. http://www.cucentral.ca/AR2008.

Crowe, C. 2006. Homelessness is a national disaster. *Vote Toronto.* April. http://www.votetoronto.ca/test/htdocs/issue_crowe.html.

Department of Finance. 2004. *The budget plan 2004.* Ottawa: Department of Finance. http://www.fin.gc.ca/budget04/pdf/bp2004e.pdf.

Eakin, L. 2007. We can't afford to do business this way. Working paper. Toronto: Wellesley Institute of Urban Health.

Goldberg, M., and D.A. Green. 2009. *Understanding the link between welfare policy and the use of food banks.* Ottawa: Canadian Centre for Policy Alternatives. http://www.policyalternatives.ca/reports/2009/04/reportsstudies2208.

Hawken, P. 2007. *Blessed unrest: How the largest movement in the world came into being and why no one saw it coming.* New York: Viking.

Howatt, D. 2007. Evaluation of the OnCEDCO Collaborative. Project evaluation. Solutions Consulting Group.

Imagine Canada. 2005. Imagine Canada factsheet: The non-profit and voluntary sector in Ontario. Fact sheet. http://www.imaginecanada.ca.

Industry Canada. 2004. Invitation from Industry Canada to On Co-op. Ontario Social Economy roundtable. December 22. Ottawa: Industry Canada.

Industry Canada. 2005. Invitation from Industry Canada to On Co-op. Ontario Social Economy roundtable. January 26. Ottawa: Industry Canada.

Liberal Party of Ontario. 2007. *Moving forward together: The Ontario Liberal plan, 2007.* Toronto: Ontario Liberal Party. http://www.ontarioliberal.ca/pdf/platform/MovingForwardTogether.pdf.

Loewen, G., B. Reimer, and D. LePage. 2008. Social enterprise policy workshop. 2008 CCEDNET National Conference. Canadian CED Network/Le Réseau canadien de DÉC (CCEDNet/RCDÉC). PowerPoint. Victoria, BC: CCEDNet/RCDÉC.

McBain, E., and M. Thompson. 2008. *Profile of community economic development in Ontario: Results of a survey of community economic development across Ontario.* Toronto: CCEDNet.

Mook, L., J. Quarter, and B.J. Richmond. 2007. *What counts: Social accounting for nonprofits and cooperatives.* 2nd ed. London: Sigel.

Muggeridge, J. 1996. Ontario's new crop of co-ops. *Farm and Country: The Farm Business Resource.* May 28. http://www.agpub.on.ca/text/cov_my28.htm.

Mulholland Consulting. 2008. *Social enterprise: Ontario strategic inquiry.* Final report. July 29. Toronto: SiG@MaRS.

Ontario Association of Food Banks (OAFB). 2003. *Child poverty persists: Time to invest in children and families: 2003 report on child poverty in Ontario.* Toronto: Ontario Association of Food Banks. http://oafb.ca.

Ontario Co-operative Association (On Co-op). 2007a. *OnCEDco newsletter.* April. Guelph, ON: On Co-op.

Ontario Co-operative Association (On Co-op). 2007b. *OnCEDco newsletter.* September. Guelph, ON: On Co-op.

Ontario Co-operative Association (On Co-op). 2007c. Ontario CED Collaborative spring 2007 update. http://ontario.coop/upload/ONCEDCO-SPRING07.pdf.

Ontario Co-operative Association (On Co-op). 2008. List of funders and funding sources. http://www.ontario.coop/pages/index.php?main_id=12.

Ontario Social Economy Consortium. 2005. RFP from consortium, capacity building initiative of the Social Economy Program. September 15.

A proposal to empower the social economy movement in Ontario. 2005. Discussion paper. February 18.

Scott, K. 2003. Funding matters: The impact of Canada's new funding regime on nonprofit and voluntary organizations. Working paper. Ottawa: Canadian Council on Social Development.

Siegel, D. 2006. Recent changes in provincial–municipal relations in Ontario: A new era or a missed opportunity? In *Municipal–Federal–Provincial Relations in Canada,* ed. R. Young and C. Leuprecht, 181–197. Montreal: McGill-Queen's University Press.

Struthers, M. 2003. *Getting down to the details: Conceptualizing organizational sustainability in a changing economy.* May 30. Toronto: Ontario Trillium Foundation.

Tuckman, B.W. 1965. Developmental sequence in small groups. *Psychological Bulletin* 63: 384–399.

World Commission on Environment and Development (WCED). 1987. *Our common future* [the Brundtland report]. Oxford: Oxford University Press.

Index